WESTERN PASSAGES

DECADES

AN EXPANDED CONTEXT FOR WESTERN AMERICAN ART, 1900–1940

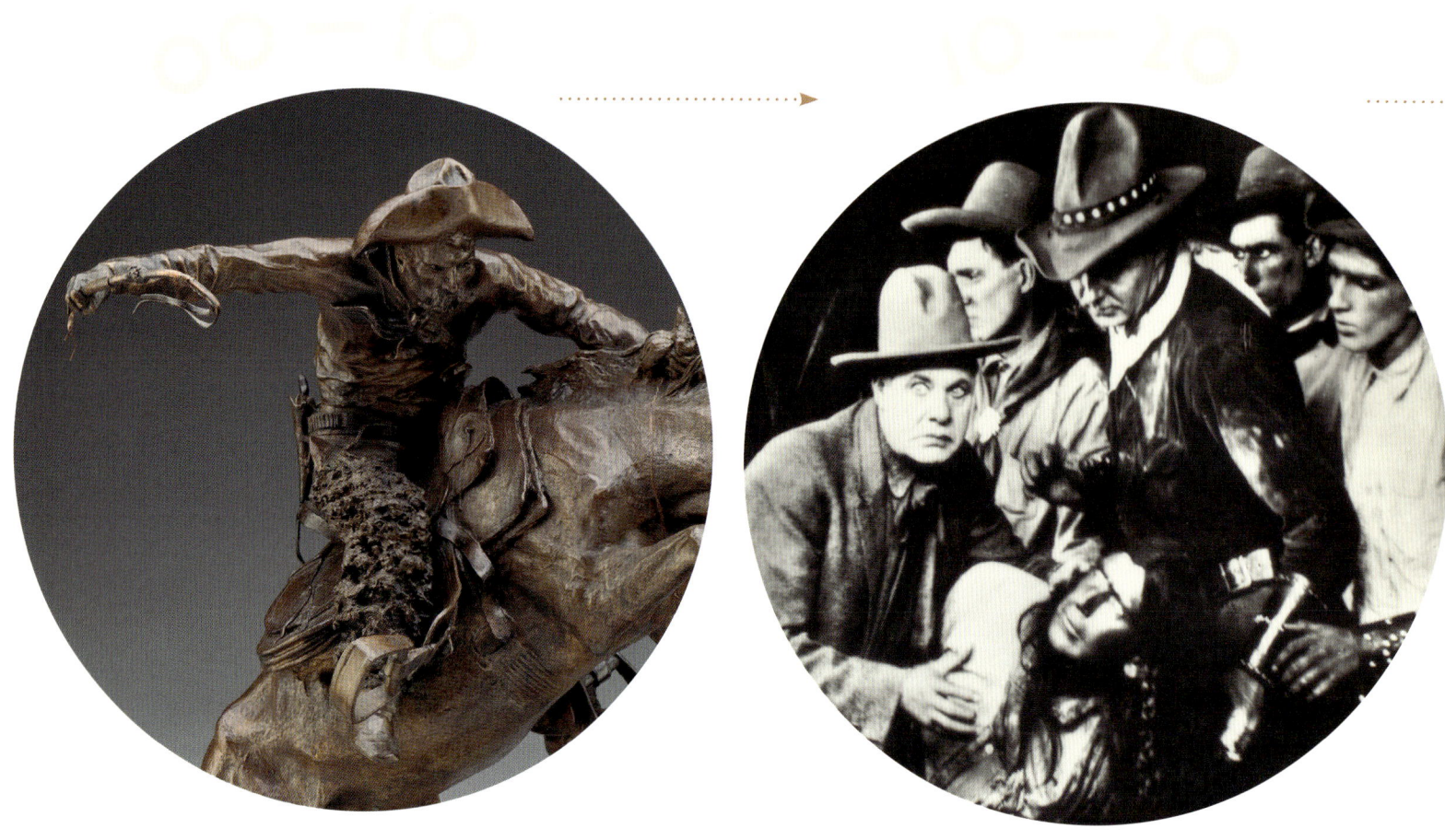

PETRIE INSTITUTE OF WESTERN
AMERICAN ART, DENVER ART MUSEUM
100 WEST 14TH AVENUE PARKWAY
DENVER, COLORADO 80204-2788

Western Passages is an ongoing series published by the Petrie Institute of Western American Art, Denver Art Museum.
©2013 by the Denver Art Museum. All rights reserved.
ISBN 978-0914738893
Library of Congress Control Number: 2013937063
Printed in Korea

EDITING Laura Caruso, Senior Editor and Manager of Museum Publications, Denver Art Museum
DESIGN AND PRODUCTION Carol Haralson, Carol Haralson Books, Sedona, Arizona

Dimensions of images are in inches, height preceding width.
Distributed by University of Oklahoma Press
2800 Venture Drive, Norman, OK 73069-8218
1-800-627-7377 www.oupress.com

COVER:
Raymond Jonson, *Pueblo Series, Acoma,* 1927
Oil on canvas, 36½ x 43½. Denver Art Museum, William Sr. and Dorothy Harmsen Collection, 2001.44

ABOVE, LEFT TO RIGHT, DETAILS:
See full images and captions on pages 22, 34, 61, 74.

PAGES 4–5:
Thomas Hart Benton, *The Arts of Life in America: Arts of the West,* 1932. Tempera with oil glaze on linen mounted on panel, 96 x 156. New Britain Museum of American Art, Harriet Russell Stanley Fund (1953.21). Art ©T. H. Benton and R. P. Benton Testamentary Trusts / UMB Bank Trustee / Licensed by VAGA, New York, NY

CONTENTS SPREAD:
William Gropper, *Construction of the Dam,* 1938.
See image and caption on page 78.

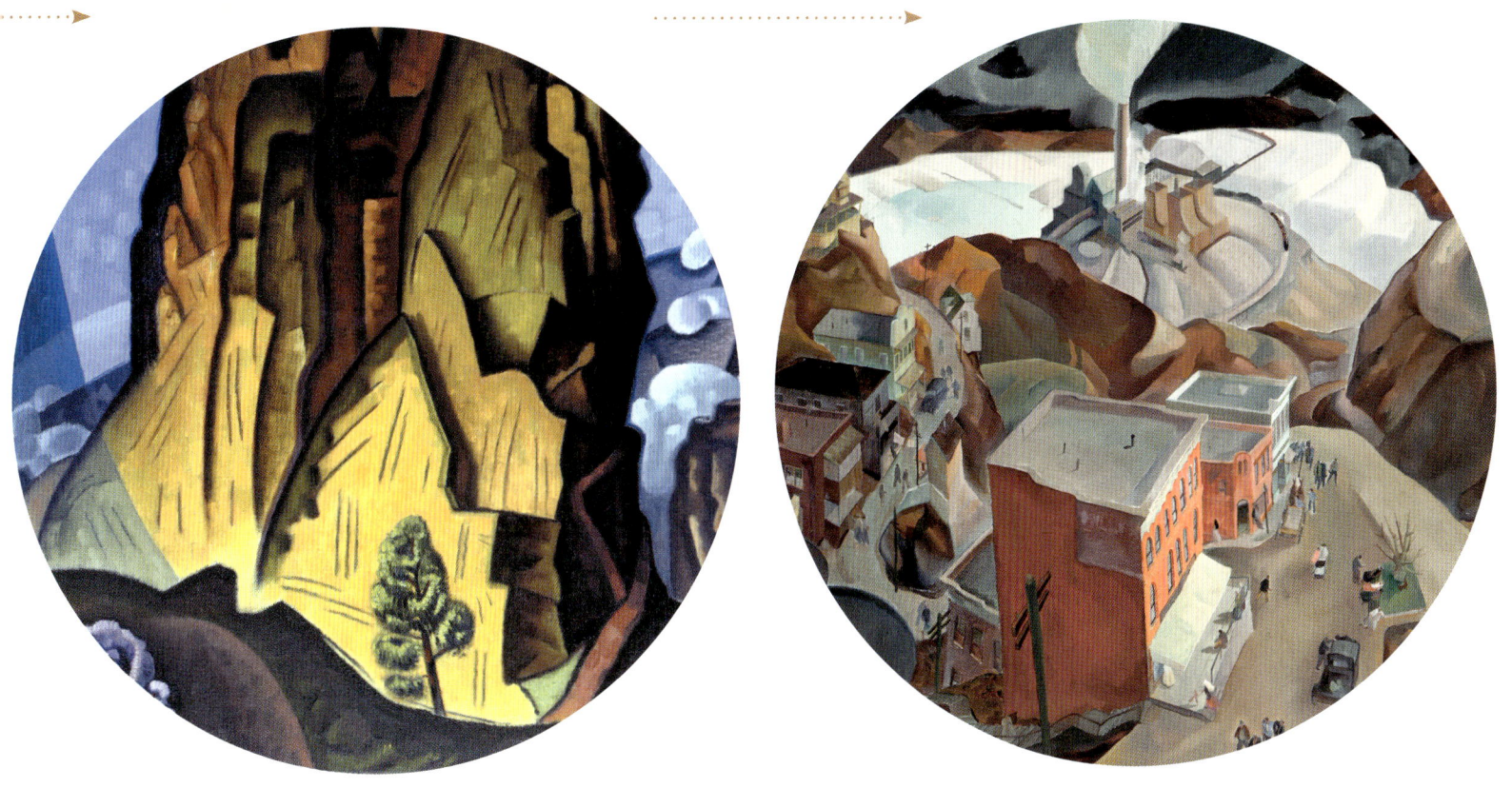

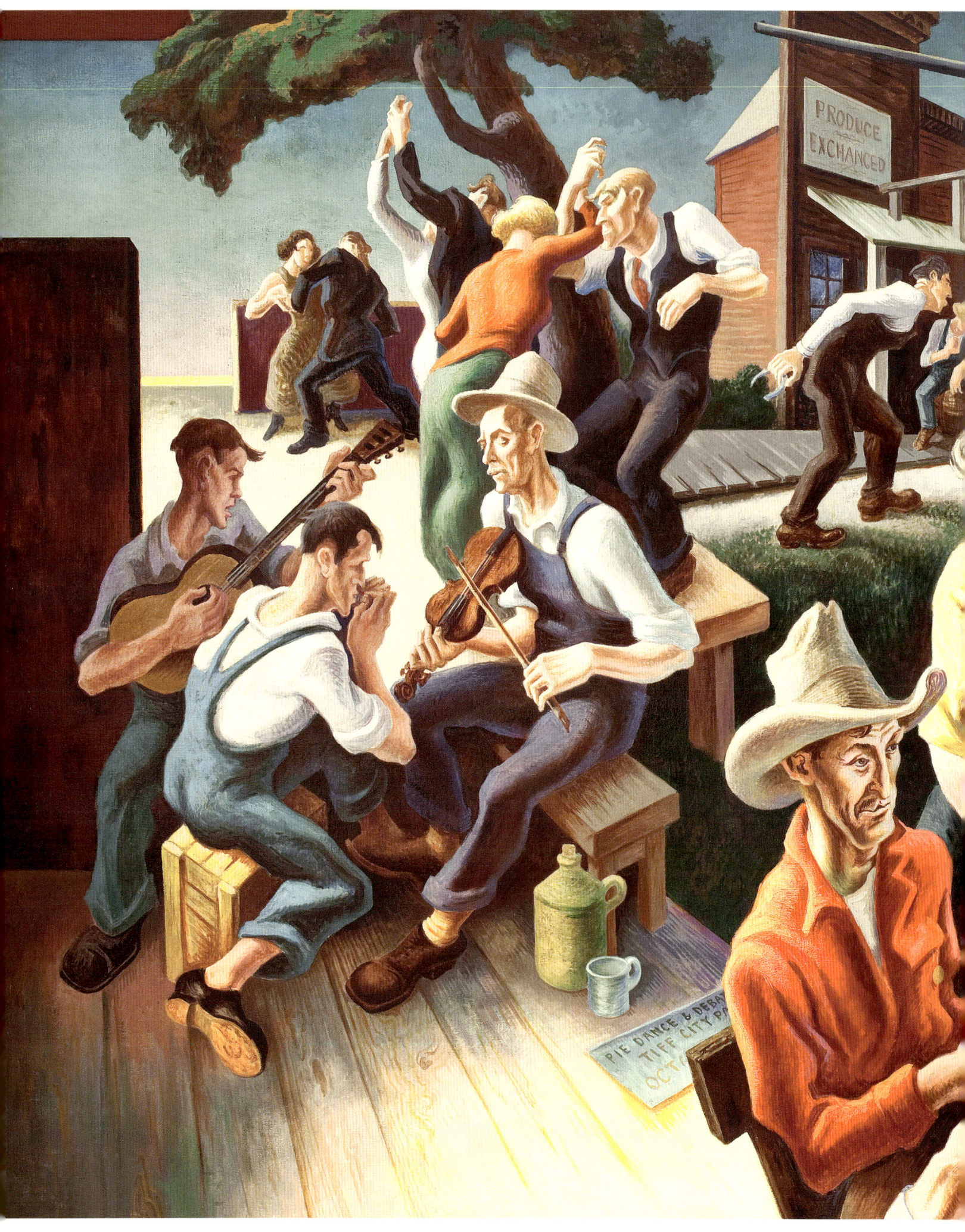

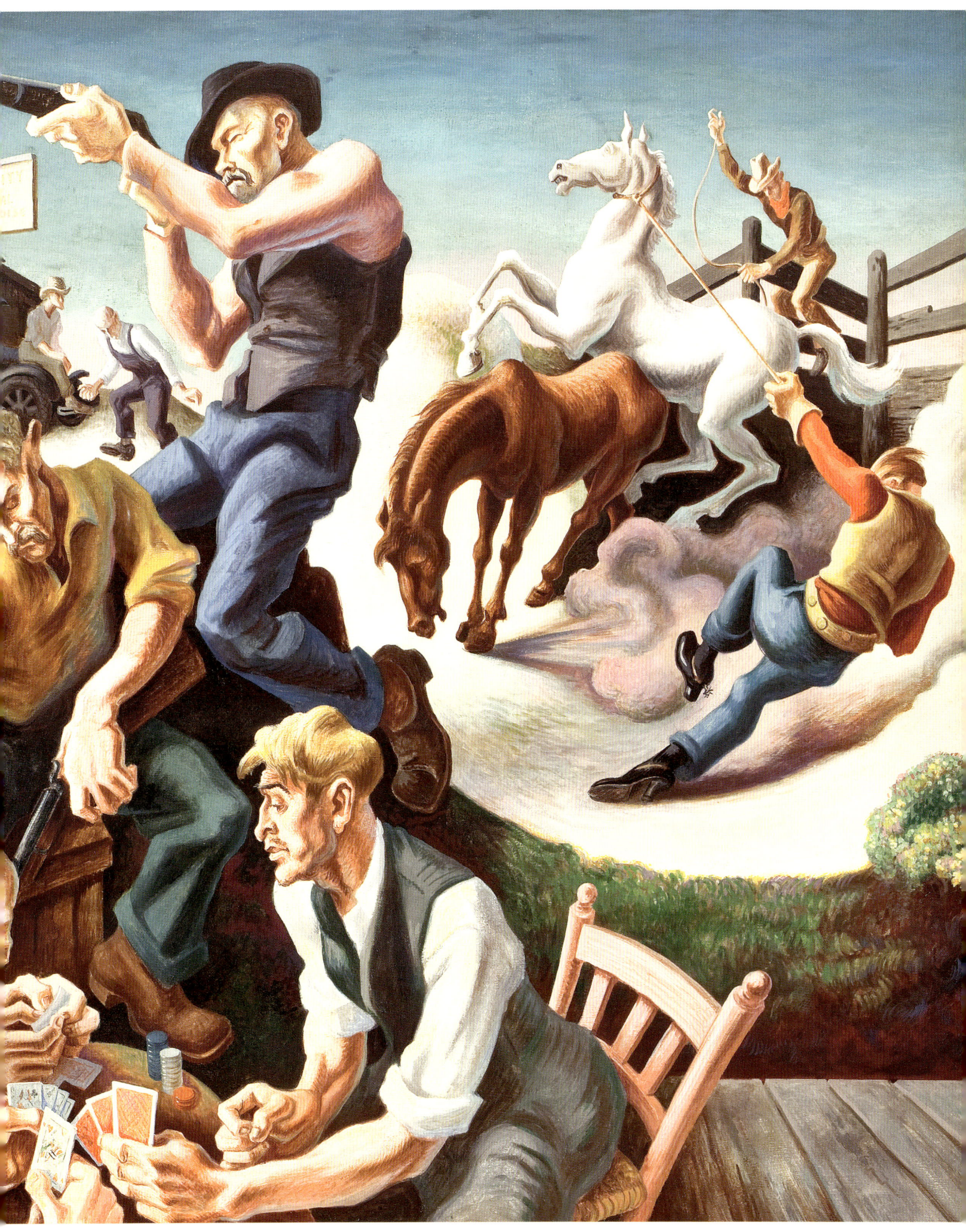

FOREWORD AND ACKNOWLEDGMENTS

THE MOST RECENT VOLUME OF *Western Passages*, titled *Elevating Western American Art: Developing an Institute in the Cultural Capital of the Rockies* (2011), was published to celebrate the Petrie Institute of Western American Art's tenth anniversary. We marked this milestone—the establishment and maturation of a new department within the Denver Art Museum devoted to the study of western American art—with a 300-page-plus volume that looked at the art of this region across the museum's collections and surveyed the Institute's achievements in exhibitions, publications, and collecting in its first decade. The Institute now stands as the national leader in programming and scholarship within the field of western American art. In the decade ahead the Institute looks to further its programming and collecting for the benefit of our field of study, the Denver Art Museum, and the public.

Publishing *Elevating Western American Art* was a multiyear project. All the while, the Institute continued to plan a busy exhibition schedule for the years ahead. In 2012, the Institute presented two exhibitions featuring contemporary artists. The first was devoted to California artist Ed Ruscha. *Ed Ruscha: On the Road* was followed by *Theodore Waddell's Abstract Angus,* which focused on a series of paintings by the contemporary Montana artist. In 2013, the Institute followed up with *Georgia O'Keeffe in New Mexico: Architecture, Katsinam, and the Land,* which was the Denver Art Museum's first exhibition of important paintings by the iconic artist. *Rocky Mountain Majesty: The Paintings of Charles Partridge Adams* was the first major art museum exhibition of Colorado's foremost painter at the turn of the twentieth century. The year ended with *Thomas Moran's Yellowstone: A Project for the Nation,* which highlighted the collaborative chromolithography portfolio created by Thomas Moran and Louis Prang to celebrate America's centennial in 1876.

In January 2013, the Institute held its seventh annual symposium, for which this is the eponymous publication. With this, the ninth volume of *Western Passages,* we begin our second decade with the appropriately titled *Decades: An Expanded Context for Western American Art,* which explores western American art during the first four decades of the twentieth century. It is common practice to organize western American art chronologically by single artists, but by investigating vertically within single decades it is possible to compare what multiple artists were producing at a given time. This approach reveals, for example, the interesting fact that artists Thomas Moran and Charles M. Russell (*and* Claude Monet) all died in 1926.

Decades divides the period from 1900 to 1940 into ten-year increments to investigate major artistic movements and important figures in western American art across mediums, styles, and subjects. In many ways, the turn of the twentieth century marked the closing of the frontier, or—as it was more widely and romantically considered—the end of the Old West. The notion that the West "as it was" had passed into history had a profound effect on artists. No longer was art of the American West centered on exploration or ethnology; rather, artists of the new century shifted their focus toward art movements, aesthetics, and art for art's sake. However, artists in the West quickly found themselves promoting tourism and, later, when faced with major financial and environmental obstacles, their art would again reflect the concerns of a region.

In wide-ranging essays, four art historians examine western American art alongside concurrent events in American art and history. These essays reveal intriguing—and often surprising—intersections among American history, western American art, and the larger canon of American art.

I thank the authors of this volume, Charles Eldredge, Betsy Fahlman, Randall Griffey, and, Ron Tyler, not only for their insightful and well-considered contributions to the publication but also for their exceptional lectures at the annual symposium. Each author welcomed the challenge and pushed the boundaries of this exercise to collectively present an unconventional view of western American art in the first four decades of the twentieth century.

This publication has been greatly enhanced by Carol Haralson's effective and beautiful design and production and Laura Caruso's thorough and sensitive edits. I wish to thank Nicole Parks, curatorial assistant, and Karen Brooks, department assistant, for their dedication to the Institute and for their efforts in organizing our annual symposium and publication.

Major support for this publication was provided by the endowment of the Petrie Institute of Western American Art, to which dozens of individuals in the Denver community have generously donated. We wish to thank Thomas Petrie, Cortlandt Dietler, George and Beth Wood, Al and Gerri Cohen, Joe and Judy Wagner, Intrepid Potash, Inc., the LARRK Foundation, the Anschutz Foundation, Don and Susie Law, Robert Boswell, Pat Grant, the Logan family, the Moran family, Frederic Hamilton, Jim Volker, William and Louise Barrett, Patrick Broe, Nancy Petry, Mick Merelli, Paul Zecchi, Robert and Joan Troccoli, Patricia and Ralph Nagel, Chuck and Barb Griffith, Don Wolf, Tim Travis, Jon Hughes, Stephen Good, Neal and Marie Stanley, Janeen Hogan and Henry Fisk, Peter and Philae Dominick, David Kirk, Kyle Miller, Centennial Holdings, Gerald Middleton, Nick Muller, and a number of anonymous donors, who all helped to make this project possible.

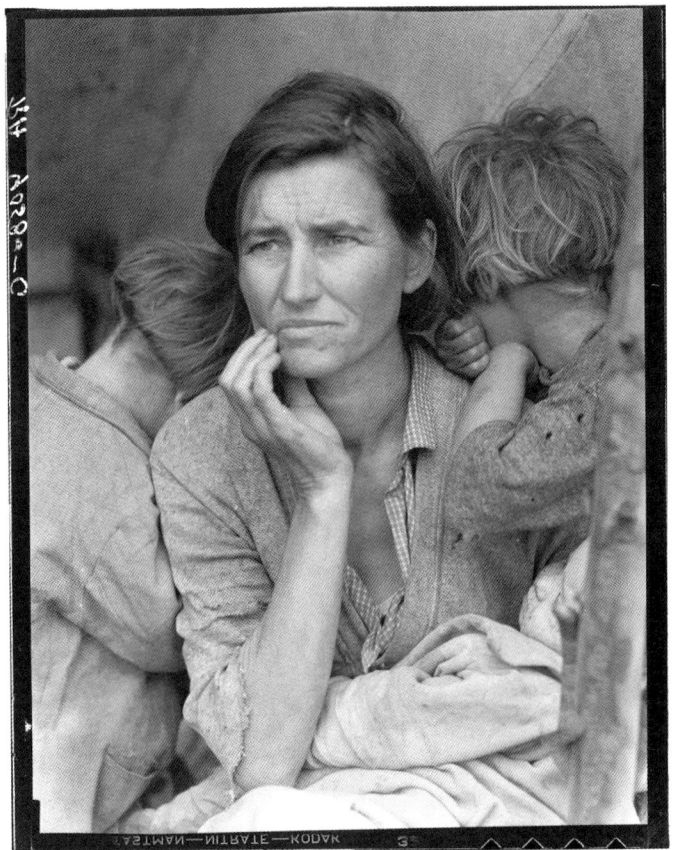

Dorothea Lange
Migrant Mother, 1936
Library of Congress, Prints & Photographs Division, FSA/OWI Collection
[LC-USF34-9058-C]

THOMAS BRENT SMITH
Director, Petrie Institute of Western American Art

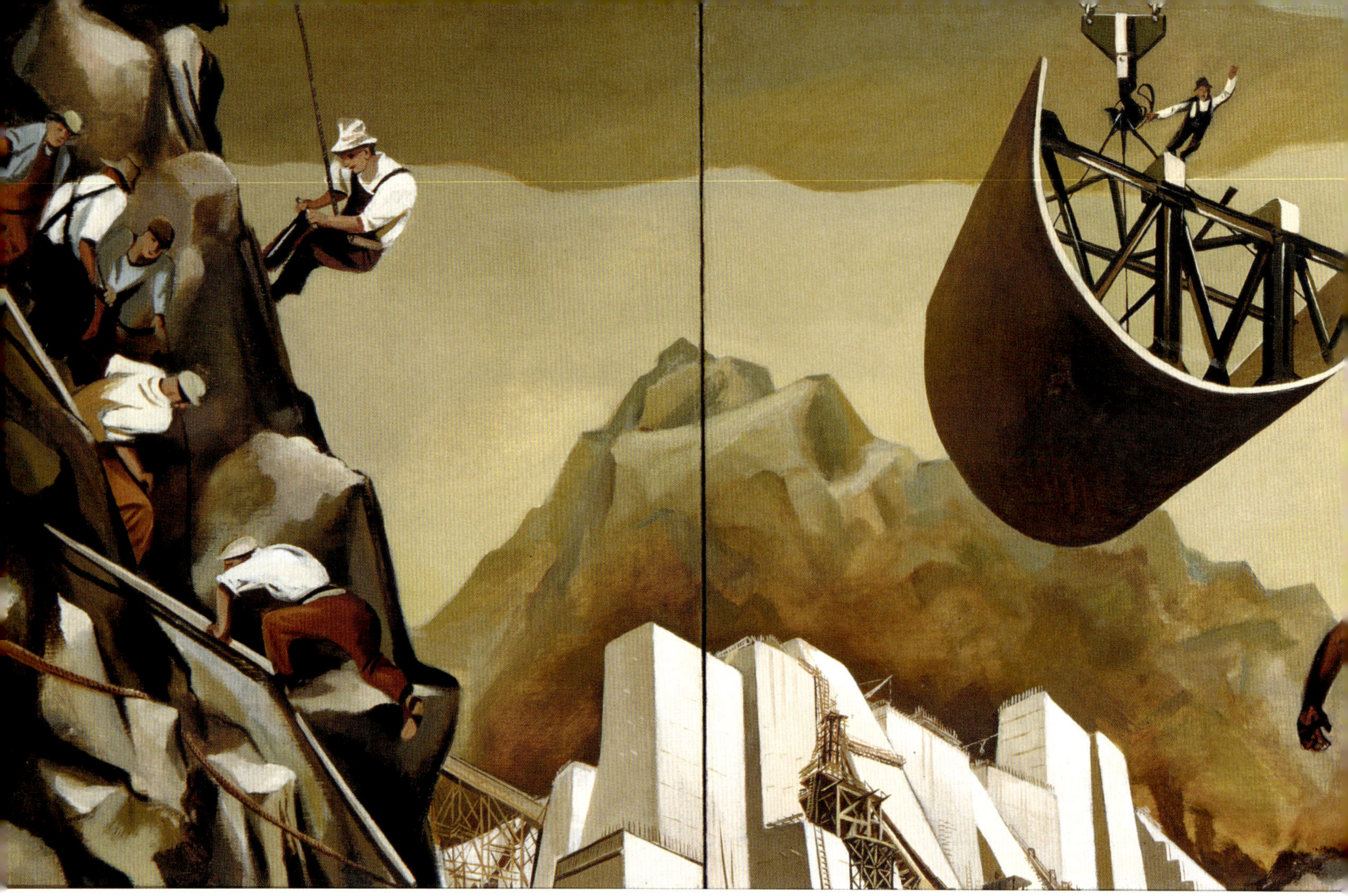

nineteen 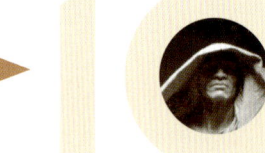 ·········▶ 20

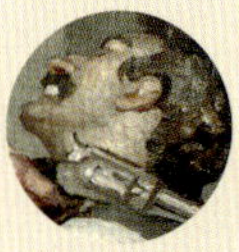

The Frontier Has Closed
Western American Art
during the First Decade
of the 20th Century

RON TYLER 10

"Racy of the Soil"
Cowboys, Indians, and
Western Landscapes
1910–1920

CHARLES C. ELDREDGE 26

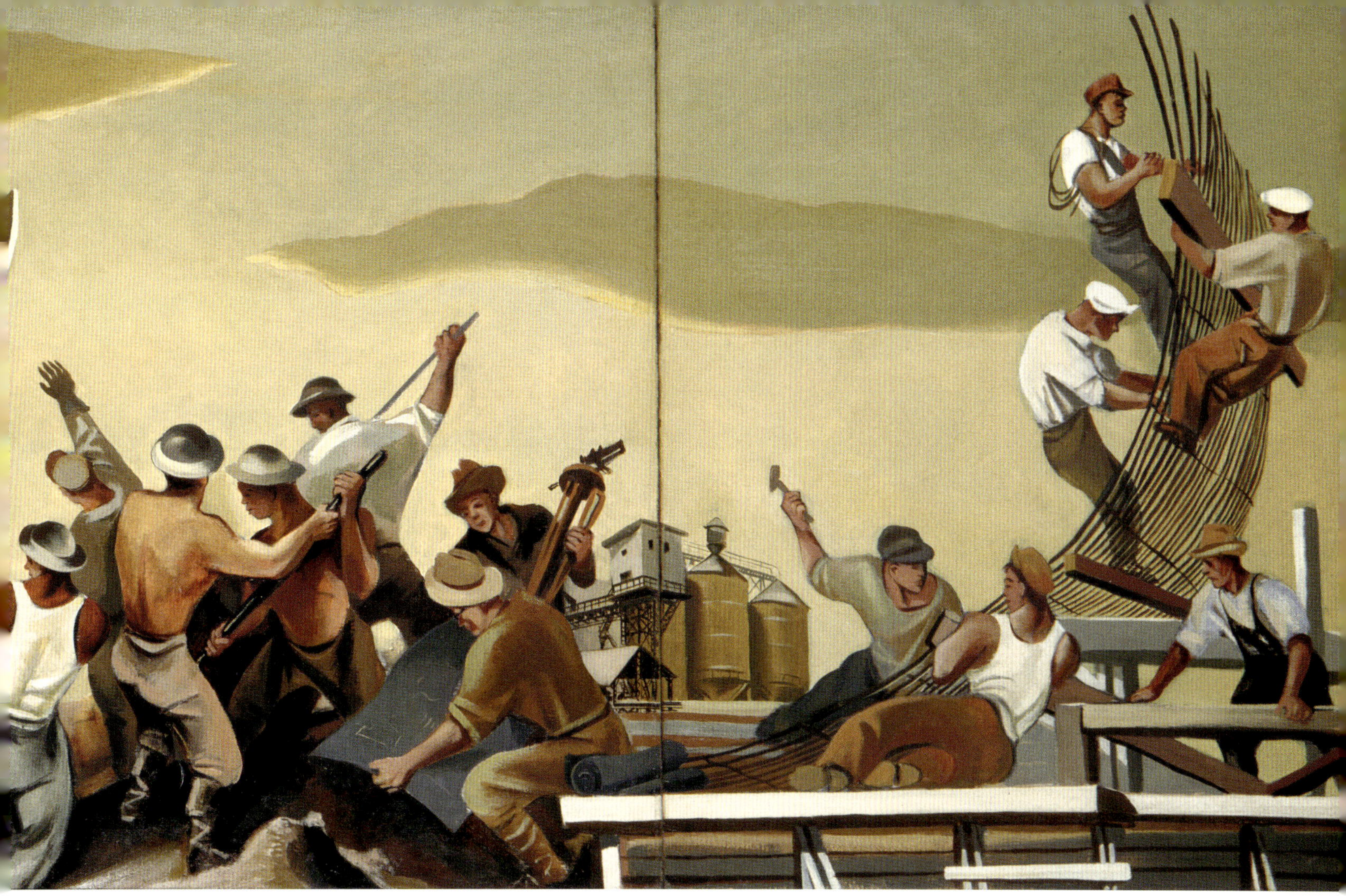

••••••▶ 3○ 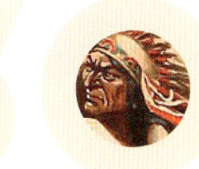••••••▶ 4○

You Ain't ~~Heard~~ *Seen*
Nothin' Yet
American Art in the 1920s

Tumult and Triumph
Taking the Pulse of
Western American Art
in the 1930s

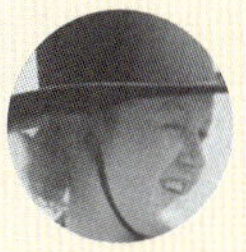

RANDALL R. GRIFFEY 44

BETSY FAHLMAN 64

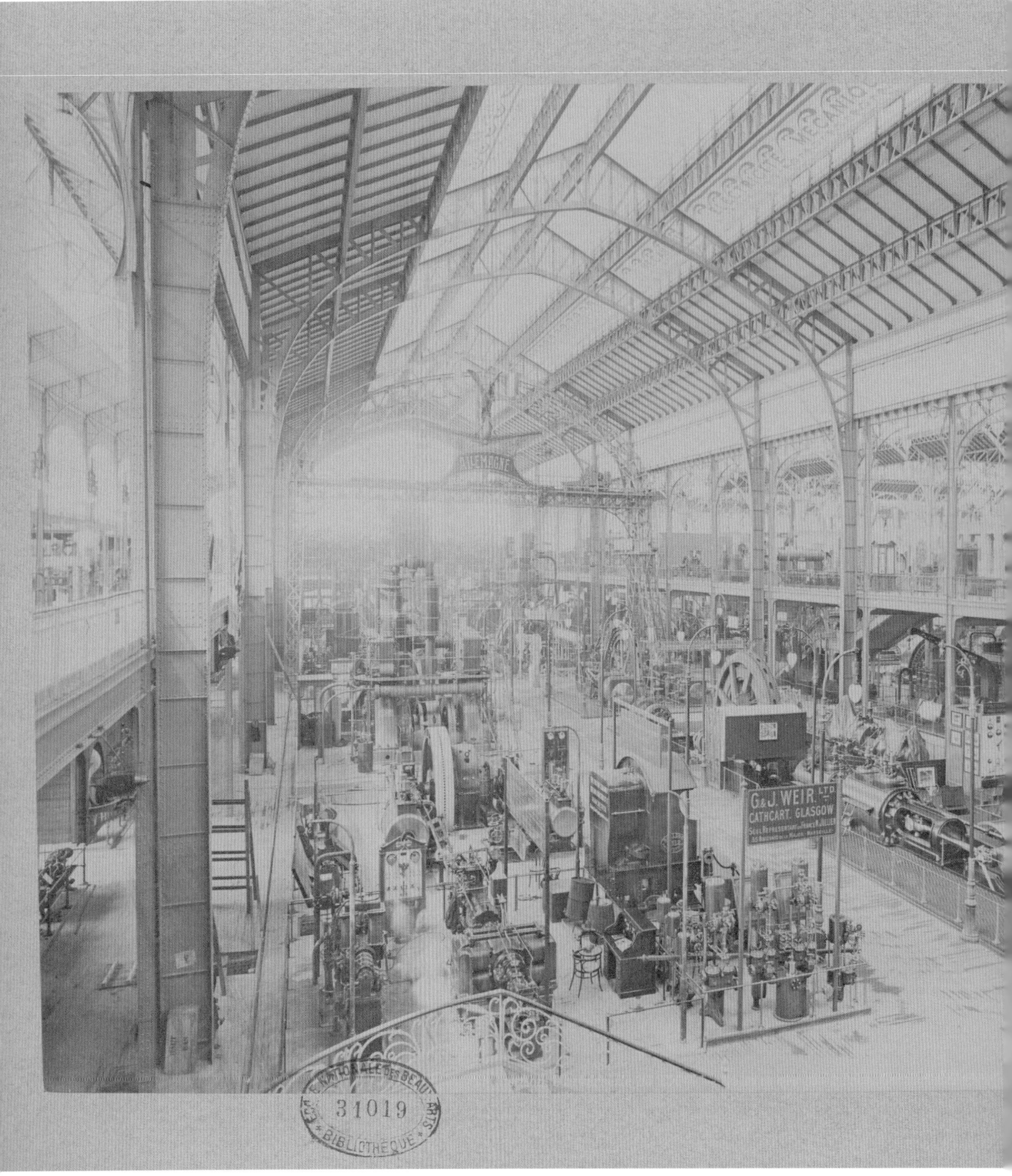

Neurdein Brothers, *Universal Exhibition of 1900, Gallery of Machines, Foreign Section*. Albumen print on paper, 8½ x 10⅘

Ecole de Beaux-Arts, Paris, France. ©RMN-Grand Palais / Art Resource, NY

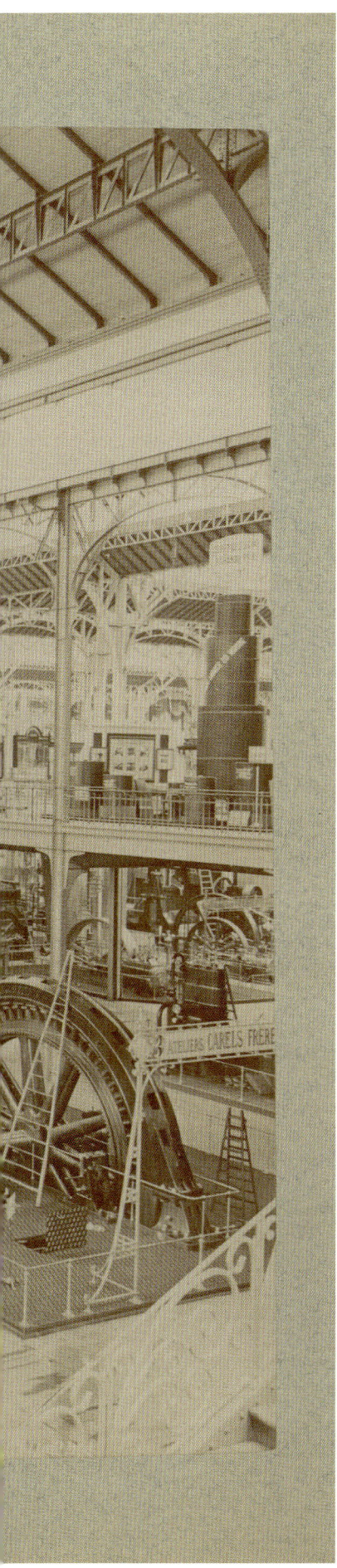

The Frontier Has Closed
Western American Art during the First Decade of the 20th Century

RON TYLER

Historian Frederick Jackson Turner and artist Frederic Remington came to the same conclusion within a few years of each other—the frontier had closed, and the Old West was no more. Turner read his now-famous paper before the American Historical Association meeting at the World's Columbian Exposition in Chicago in 1893—"The superintendent of the census for 1890 reports . . . that the settlements of the West lie so scattered over the region that there can no longer be said to be a frontier line"[1]—and seven years later Remington agreed. "Shall never come west again," he wrote his wife from Santa Fe in 1900. "It is all brick buildings—derby hats and blue overhauls [sic]—it spoils my early illusions—and they are my capital."[2]

But it was not just the American West. The Western world was changing. It was a *new* century, a *new* beginning, and the byword was *modernism*. H. G. Wells's fictional Time Machine, which challenged both time and conventional space, seemed a fitting symbol for the age. New scientific discoveries, shown in the successive world's fairs in Chicago in 1893 and in Paris in 1889 and 1900, dazzled the intellectuals. Sigmund Freud's *Interpretation of Dreams* (1899) introduced a new world, the unconscious, while Wilhelm Wundt and William James proposed other concepts such as stream of consciousness through psychoanalysis. Lord Kelvin's Second Law of Thermodynamics (entropy) fundamentally contradicted Charles Darwin's still fairly new theory of positive evolution (as interpreted by Herbert Spencer). Non-Euclidean geometry, stemming from discoveries by Georg Friedrich Bernhard Riemann in Germany and George B. Halsted in Texas, laid the groundwork for Einstein's theories of relativity (1905, 1916), and this new mathematics inspired Bertrand Russell to rethink Newton's mathematical universe in his *Principia Mathematica* (3 vols., 1910, 1912, 1913). Physicist turned anthropologist Franz Boas pioneered the rise of cultural relativism in anthropology, which sent legions of proto-anthropologists into the American West and other remote areas to study native peoples. Excited by the new discoveries, historian James Harvey Robinson at Columbia University proclaimed a "new history" that would produce a "usable past," a new tool for social reform.[3] No wonder author Henry Adams, "maundering among the magnets" at the Exposition Universelle in Paris in 1900, found his "historical neck broken by the sudden irruption of forces totally new."[4] "Life in the United States," wrote English historian Frederic Harrison in 1900, "is one perpetual whirl of telephones, telegrams, phonographs, electric bells, motors,

> The Western world was changing. It was a *new* century, a *new* beginning, and the byword was *modernism*.

lifts, and automatic instruments."⁵ And a little-known statistic clearly documented progress: dealers in ready-made clothing began to stock larger sizes, in both width and length, to accommodate a generation of larger and taller people, who enjoyed better food and shelter, a more balanced diet, more leisure time, and better health than their forebears.⁶

But whatever "modernism" was, it had not come to American art by the turn of the century. Elsewhere in society, changes were afoot: muckraking journalists like Lincoln Steffens (*The Shame of the Cities*, 1904), Ida Tarbell (*The History of the Standard Oil Company*, 1904), and Upton Sinclair (*The Jungle*, 1906) called attention to egregious abuses in municipal government and child labor, John D. Rockefeller's illegal domination of the oil industry, and the exploitation of immigrant workers and shocking conditions in the meat-packing industry (which led to the passage of the Pure Food and Drug Act in 1906). But in art, the conservative values of the nineteenth century prevailed into the twentieth, supported by schools, educational programs, and the relatively new museums such as those in New York, Boston, and Philadelphia. A group of artists led by Robert Henri had begun a modest protest—not yet a revolution, but recognition of the fact that significant change had brought new challenges, especially in the cities. They became known as "The Eight," or the "Ashcan School," and had their first important exhibition in 1908 at the Macbeth Gallery in New York. Their "revolt" consisted of including urban scenes and working people in their paintings, rather than copying nature as so many of the nineteenth-century artists had done. They painted street scenes and portraits of common life.⁷

> But whatever "modernism" was, it had not come to American art by the turn of the century.

Many western artists reacted to the new social order of the industrial world by taking refuge in the image of a past western wilderness.⁸ Already fallen from critical grace, Albert Bierstadt painted one of his last major compositions in 1900, *The Golden Gate,* a florid view with a sunset and rainbow and sailing ships, not long before he died in 1902. Thomas Moran produced the last of his majestic wilderness landscapes, *Shoshone Falls on the Snake River*, in 1900, a 71-x-144½-inch machine that seems to burst with the energy of cascading water as it sweeps over the jutting rocks and foams into the precipice below. Moran pictured the site as if it were still pristine, but it had already been tamed into a tourist destination, and within a few years a massive irrigation project would rob it of its sublimity as well. The critical reception for what is now regarded as one of Moran's masterpieces was "respectful rather than enthusiastic."⁹

One of the more successful illustrators of the day, Henry F. Farny, an Alsace-born and European-trained Cincinnati artist, made a specialty of Indian and western images and sold dozens of them to illustrated journals such as *Harper's Weekly*. He seemed particularly adept at portraying small groups or solitary Indians in wide vistas, but with a jarring modern note: in *Song of the Talking Wire* (1904), he depicts the bewilderment of an Indian man with his ear to a telegraph pole, apparently mystified by the noises it is transmitting. In *Morning of a New Day* (1907) he successfully evokes the melancholy that he no doubt felt for the Native Americans' new life on government reservations by contrasting a group of Indians pulling their travois along a snow-covered mountainside with a speeding train across the canyon.¹⁰ Charles Schreyvogel, a New York City-born artist who like Farny had studied in Europe, gained instant fame when his *My Bunkie* (1899) won one of the principal awards at the National Academy of Design exhibition and became a part of the Metropolitan Museum of Art collection. Perhaps inspired by Remington's well-known sculpture *The Wounded Bunkie, My Bunkie* shows a cavalryman rescuing his "bunkie," i.e., barracks bunkmate, who has lost his horse. But in 1903 Schreyvogel retreated into history to depict *Custer's Demand,* an 1869 parley between Custer and his staff and several Kiowa tribal leaders.

---

1 Frederick Jackson Turner, "The Significance of the Frontier in American History," in *Annual Report of the American Historical Association for the Year 1893* (Washington, DC: Government Printing Office, 1894), 199.

2 Frederic Remington to Eva Remington, Santa Fe, NM, 6 November 1900, in *Frederic Remington: Selected Letters,* ed. Allen P. Splete and Marilyn D. Splete (New York: Abbeville Press, 1988), 318.

3 I am indebted to my late colleague, William H. Goetzmann of the University of Texas at Austin, for many of these ideas that he presented in a paper, "The Paradox of Modernism: Romantic Continuity or Scientific Fault Line?" in the fall of 1999, sponsored by The Phillips Collection in Washington, DC.

4 Henry Adams, *The Education of Henry Adams: An Autobiography* (Boston and New York: Houghton Mifflin, 1918), 382, 398.

5 Quoted in George E. Mowry, *The Era of Theodore Roosevelt, 1900–1912* (New York: Harper & Bros., Publishers, 1958), 1–2.

6 Arthur Meier Schlesinger, *The Rise of the City, 1878–1898* (New York: Macmillan Company, 1933), 432–33.

7 Joshua C. Taylor, *The Fine Arts in America* (Chicago: University of Chicago Press, 1979), 155–56.

8 G. Edward White, *The Eastern Establishment and the Western Experience: The West of Frederic Remington, Theodore Roosevelt, and Owen Wister* (New Haven: Yale University Press, 1968), 50.

9 Nancy K. Anderson et al., *Thomas Moran* (Washington, DC, and New Haven: National Gallery of Art and Yale University Press, 1997), 162–63. Also see Stephen May, "Changing Times, Unchanging Visions: Western American Art—1900–1910," *Southwest Art* 28 (February 1999): 75–81.

10 Denny Carter, *Henry Farny* (New York: Watson-Guptill Publications in cooperation with the Cincinnati Art Museum, 1978), and Emily Ballew Neff, *The Modern West: American Landscapes, 1890–1950* (New Haven and Houston: Yale University Press and Houston Museum of Fine Arts, 2006), 64–65.

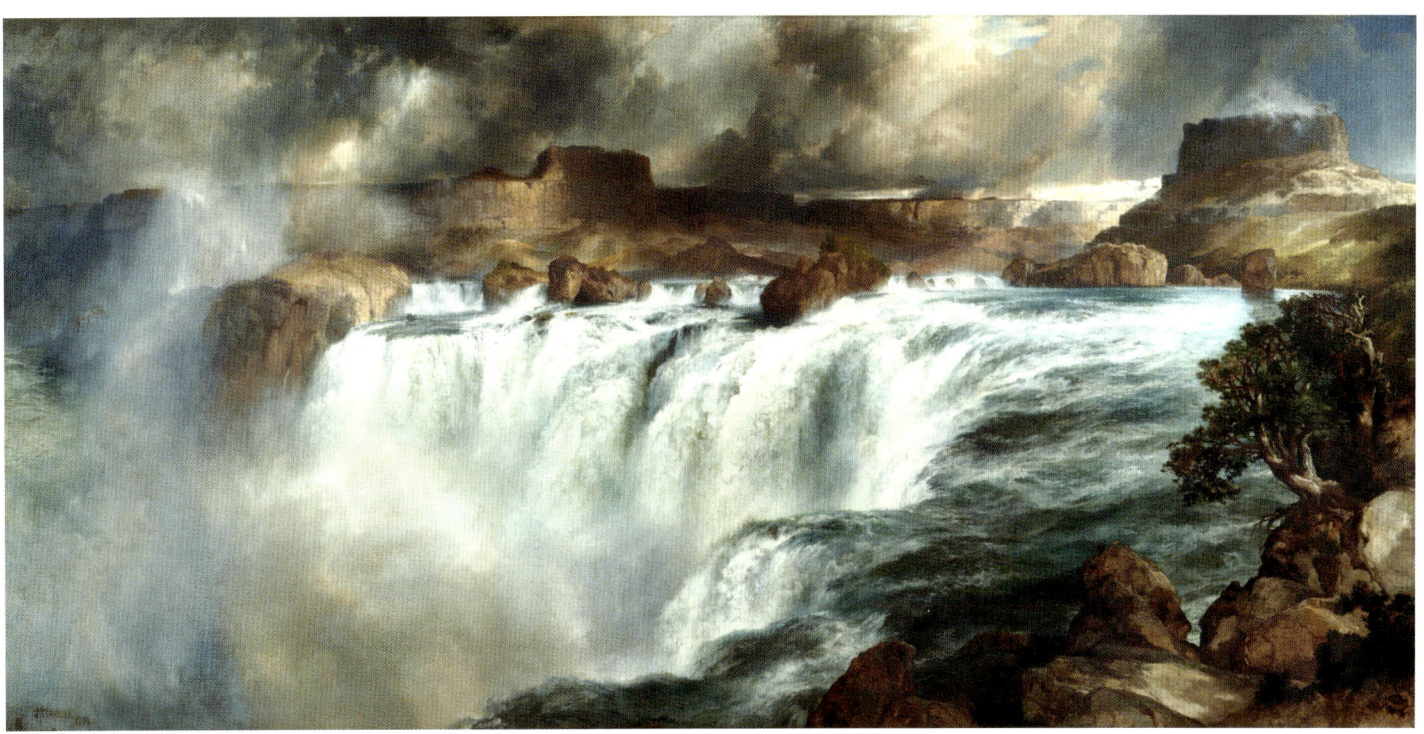

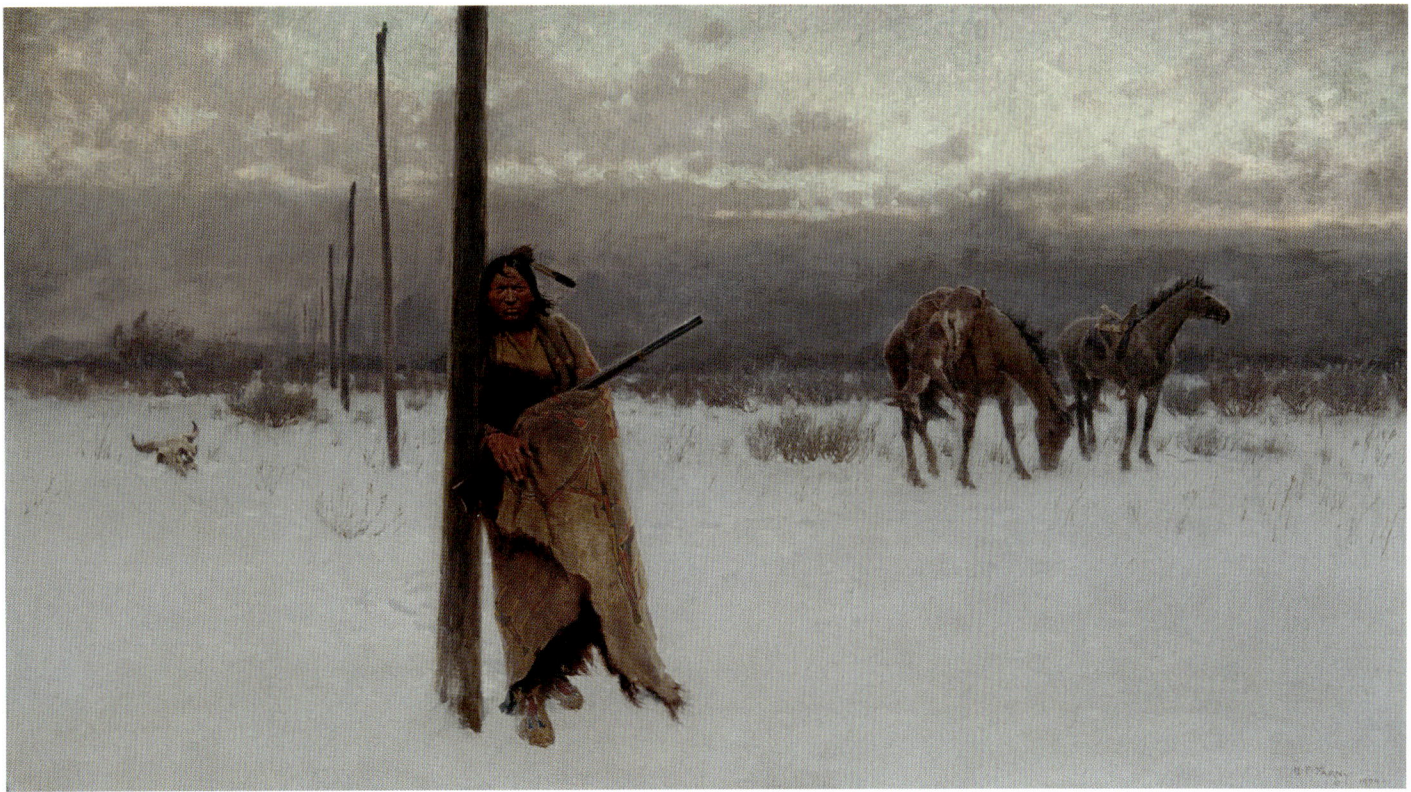

TOP: Thomas Moran
Shoshone Falls on the Snake River, 1900
Oil on canvas, 71 x 144½
Gilcrease Museum, Tulsa, Oklahoma, 0126.2339

ABOVE: Henry Farny
Song of the Talking Wire, 1904
Oil on canvas, 21½ x 39½
Bequest of Charles Phelps Taft and Anna Sinton Taft, Taft Museum of Art, Cincinnati, Ohio, 1931.466
Photo by Tony Walsh, Cincinnati, Ohio

One of the fresher faces in western art that year was Charles M. Russell, a thirty-six-year-old, self-taught Montana painter who excelled at images of cowboys and Indians and had developed his own watercolor technique before he visited New York City in 1903. But he, too, shunned the modernisms creeping into his life—"you wouldent know the town or the country eather its all grass side down now," he wrote a friend in his eclectic style in 1913—and admitted to a newspaper reporter in 1919 that "I live back there in those days all the time."[11]

Remington also recognized, of course, that the country had changed dramatically by the end of the century. Settlement had continued unabated with western states steadily entering the Union: North Dakota, South Dakota, Montana, and Washington in 1889; Idaho and Wyoming in 1890; Utah in 1896; and Oklahoma in 1907. Of the contiguous states, only New Mexico and Arizona remained as territories. He felt fortunate to have seen what he called the "living, breathing end" of the Old West during his first trip to Montana in 1881.[12] Two decades later, immigration, mainly from southern and eastern Europe, continued, and cities grew at the expense of the countryside as rural youths left farms for brighter opportunities in the cities. Others set out for Alaska to try to strike it rich in the latest gold rush, while some joined the army as the United States went to war with Spain in 1898. But, as with Russell, Remington's creative context was the previous century, where his "men with the bark on" lived. In 1900 he published an anthology of previously written articles under that title.[13]

Remington was already one of the most popular artists in the country by the time citizens of St. Louis began to plan the 1904 Louisiana Purchase Exposition to commemorate the centennial of the acquisition of Louisiana Territory from France and to celebrate the fact that the United States had fulfilled its "manifest destiny" to spread across the continent to the Pacific Ocean.[14] He had been illustrating for a number of popular magazines for

11 Quoted in Rick Stewart, *Romance Maker: The Watercolors of Charles M. Russell* (Fort Worth, TX: Amon Carter Museum of American Art, 2011), 23.

12 Frederic Remington, "A Few Words from Mr. Remington," *Collier's* 34 (March 18, 1905): 16.

13 Remington's 1900 anthology, *Men with the Bark On*, consisted of articles that he had previously published in *Harper's* magazines and depicted "a grim, harsh land" where "a man must take care of himself." Quotation in White, *The Eastern Establishment and the Western Experience*, 184. Remington had used the phrase earlier, in a letter to Poultney Bigelow, 29 January 1893. See Brian W. Dippie, *The Frederic Remington Art Museum Collection* (Ogdensburg, NY: Frederic Remington Art Museum, 2001), 148, note 1.

14 "Manifest destiny" was a term popularized in the 1840s when it was first used in an article in the *Democratic Review*, a journal edited by John O'Sullivan, who is commonly credited with coining the phrase. See Thomas R. Hietala, *Manifest Design: American Exceptionalism and Empire*, rev. ed. (Ithaca, NY: Cornell University Press, 2003), 255, for example. However, Linda S. Hudson makes a good argument for Jane McManus Storm Cazneau as the author of the term in *Mistress of Manifest Destiny: Jane McManus Storm Cazneau, 1807–1878* (Austin: Texas State Historical Association, 2001). Cazneau was a writer for the *Democratic Review* at the time and apparently often ghost-wrote for the alcoholic O'Sullivan.

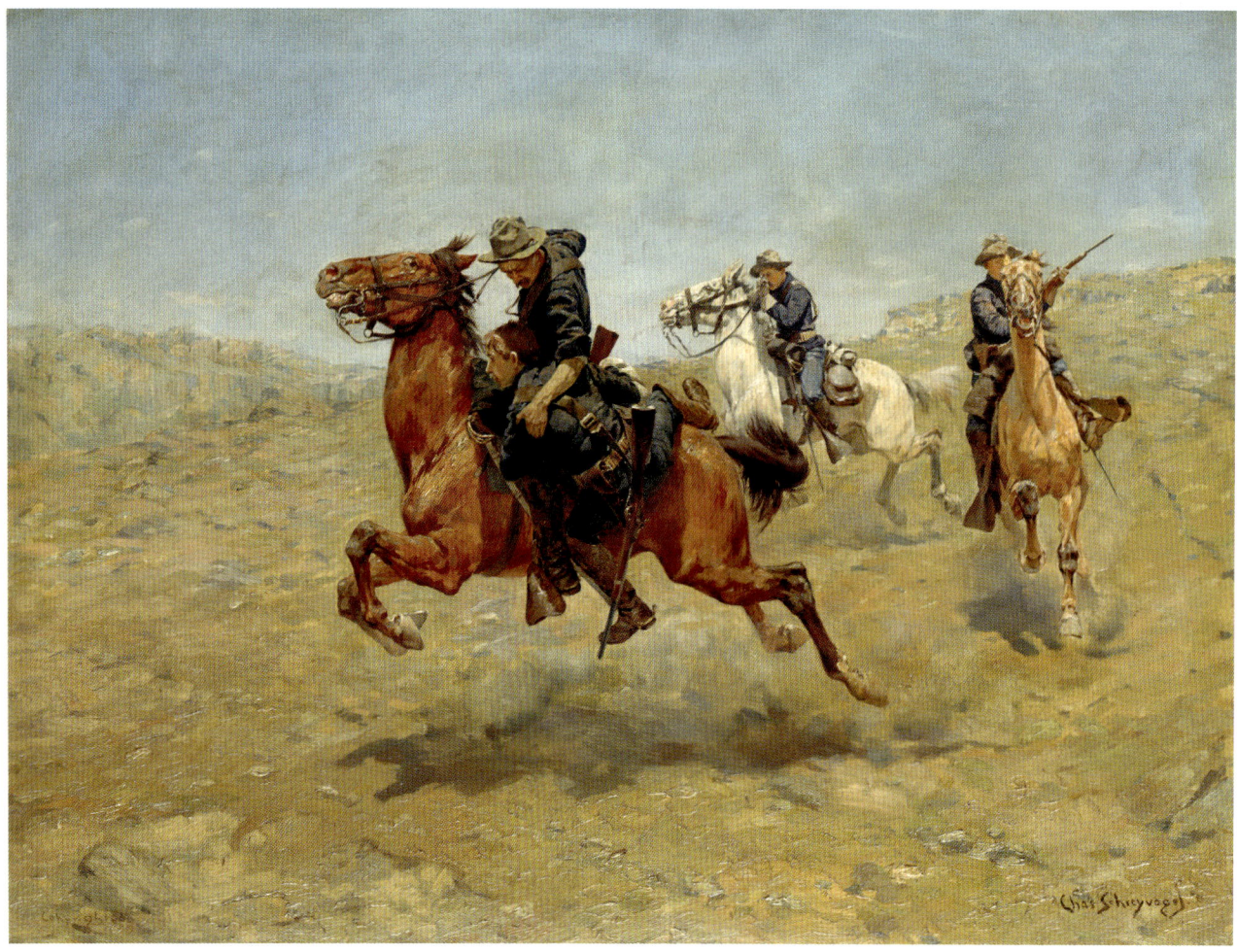

FACING: Charles Schreyvogel *My Bunkie*, finished 1899 Oil on canvas, 25³⁄₁₆ x 34 The Metropolitan Museum of Art, gift of the friends of the artist, by subscription, 1912 (12.227). Image ©The Metropolitan Museum of Art

Cowboys off the Trail, sculpture after painting by Frederic Remington at the east entrance to the Louisiana Purchase Exposition, St. Louis, Mo., 1904. Stereograph by C. L. Wasson, International View Co. Library of Congress, Prints & Photographs Division [LC-USZ62-57682]

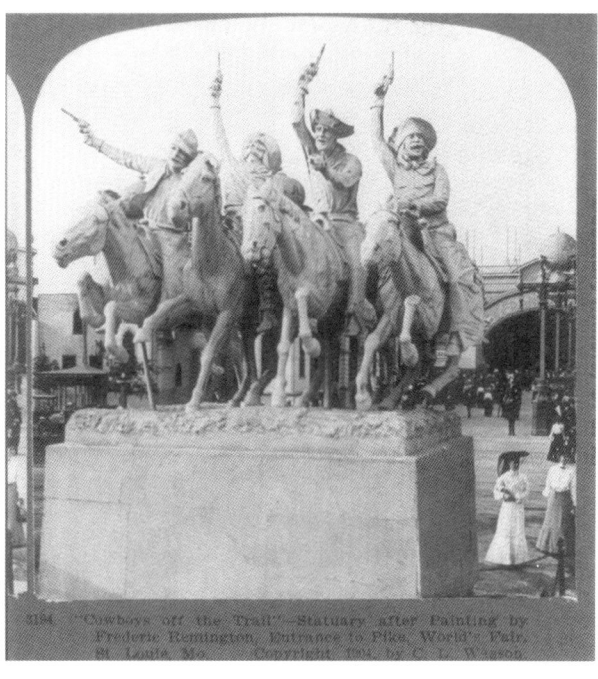

15 *Harper's Weekly* 33 (December 21, 1889): 1,016–17. See Lonn Taylor and Ingrid Maar, *The American Cowboy* (Washington, DC: Library of Congress, 1983), 98–99, for a discussion of the similarity between Rufus F. Zogbaum's *Painting the Town Red*, done for *Harper's Weekly* 30 (October 16, 1886): 668–69, and Remington's *Cow-Boys Coming to Town for Christmas*.

16 Founders in France and Italy had begun to revive this ancient method of bronze casting, not used since the 1600s, in the first half of the 1800s. The first known American foundry to use the process was Gorham Manufacturing Company in Providence, Rhode Island, but it did not immediately catch on. Bertelli made it popular with American sculptors. See Michael Edward Shapiro, *Cast and Recast: The Sculpture of Frederic Remington* (Washington, DC: Smithsonian Institution Press for the National Museum of American Art, 1981), 33–34.

17 Remington did four sculptures with Henry-Bonnard: *Broncho Buster* (1895), *The Wounded Bunkie* (1896), *The Wicked Pony* (1898), and *The Scalp* (1898). See Shapiro, *Cast and Recast*, 37–46.

18 Ibid., 50–51.

19 Michael Edward Shapiro, Peter Hassrick, et al., *Frederic Remington: The Masterworks* (New York: Harry N. Abrams, Inc. [St. Louis Art Museum in conjunction with the Buffalo Bill Historical Center, Cody, WY], 1988), 207.

20 Owen Wister, "The Evolution of the Cow-Puncher," *Harper's New Monthly Magazine* 91 (September 1895): 661.

21 Remington quoted in Perriton Maxwell, "Frederic Remington—Most Typical of American Artists," *Pearson's Magazine* 18 (October 1907): 396–97; see also Brian W. Dippie, *Remington & Russell: The Sid Richardson Collection*, rev. ed. (Austin: University of Texas Press, 1994), 4.

well over a decade and, in 1895, had produced one of the icons of the West, the *Broncho Buster*, in his first effort as a sculptor. He had sculpted what may well be his masterpiece in 1902. *Coming Through the Rye* depicts four horsemen galloping at full stride while waving their pistols in the air, a slightly different take on his 1889 illustration for *Harper's Weekly* of *Cow-Boys Coming to Town for Christmas*.[15] It was a technical feat of lost-wax bronze casting, an ancient method of bronze casting that Italian immigrant Riccardo Bertelli had brought to New York City in 1897.[16] Remington initially did his sculptures with the Henry-Bonnard Bronze Company in New York City by the sand-casting method, but he began working with Bertelli in 1900, after Bertelli had founded Roman Bronze Works.[17] Remington sculpted both *The Cheyenne* and *The Norther* for the new process and seemed to grow more enthusiastic about Bertelli's work with each sculpture, appreciating the increased detail and action that he could incorporate into the bronzes. He redid the *Broncho Buster* in 1902 and, in that same year, the freedom of the process encouraged him to began his most ambitious work to date, *Coming Through the Rye*. Remington excitedly explained to Bertelli, "now I have six horse[']s feet on the ground and 10 in the air." Ultimately, only five horse's feet touch the base of the sculpture, with eleven in the air.[18]

No wonder the St. Louis fair organizers approached Remington to create a monumental version of *Coming Through the Rye* for the exposition. The huge sculpture, called *Cowboys off the Trail* or *Cowboys on a Tear*, was made of staff, a mixture of plaster and straw, which was not substantial enough to support the weight of the outside horse as bronze could, and it had to be supported by a metal rod. Remington called the result "pretty rotten," but the work was positioned at the east entrance of the fair and was popular enough that the organizers of the Lewis & Clark Exposition in Portland, Oregon, in 1905 asked that it be exhibited there as well.[19]

Remington's paintings were the equal of his sculptures. In addition to the 1889 tour de force, *A Dash for the Timber*, he painted *The Fall of the Cowboy* (1895; see page 33), a melancholy exercise in pictorial restraint, as an illustration for Owen Wister's "The Evolution of the Cow-Puncher";[20] *The Old Stage-Coach of the Plains* (1901), one of his early nocturnes, as a color cover for *The Century Magazine* (January 1902); and *His First Lesson* (1903), his first picture published in color in *Collier's* (September 26, 1903), as he accepted his critics' challenge to move from illustrator to painter. "Romance and adventure have been beaten down in the rush of civilization," Remington said a few years later; "the country west of the Mississippi has become hopelessly commercialized, shackled in chains of business to its uttermost limits. The cowboy—the real thing, mark you . . . disappeared with the advent of the wire fence, and as for the Indian, there are so few of him he doesn't count . . . "[21] He was doing his bit to bring some of the drama of the Old West back, and he had a national audience.

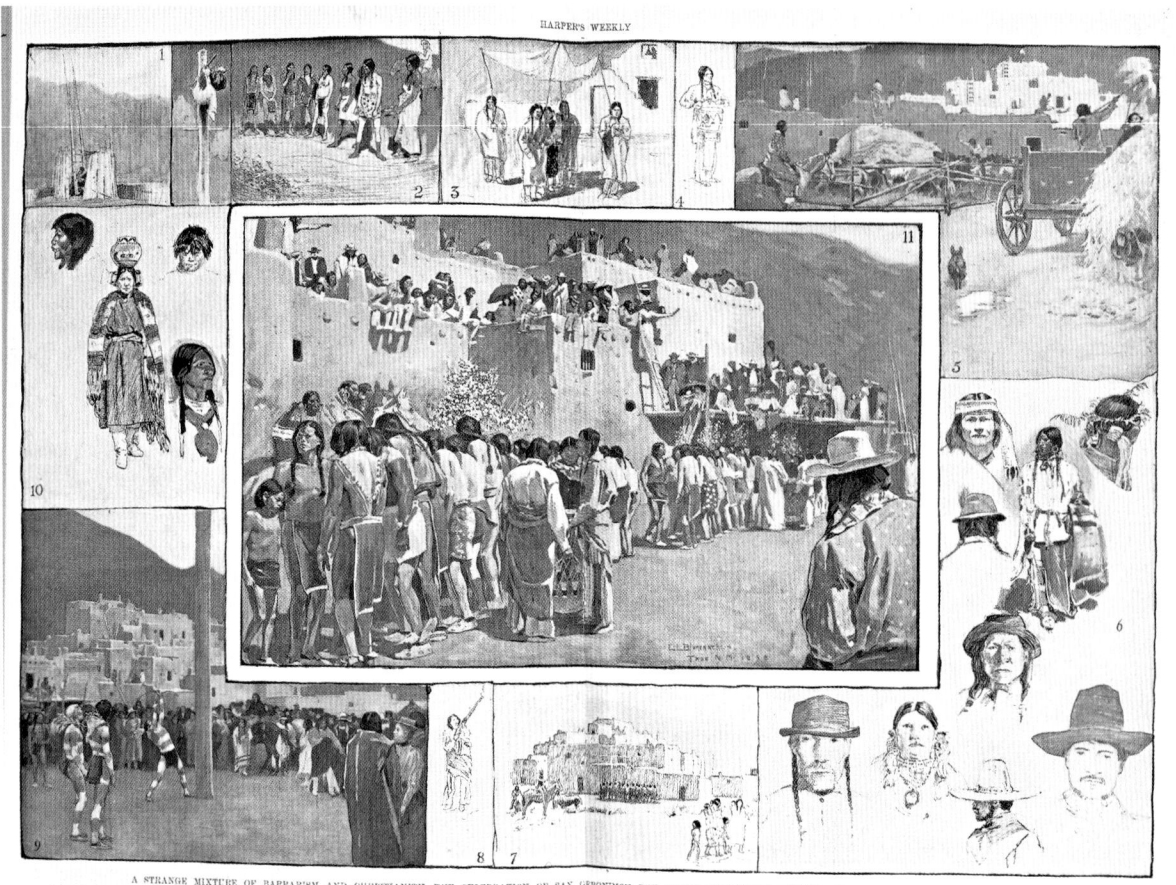

TOP: Ernest L. Blumenschein, *A Strange Mixture of Barbarism and Christianity – The Celebration of San Geronimo's Day Among the Pueblo Indians*, 1898. Halftone engraving, 13¼ x 19. From Ernest L. Blumenschein, "San Geronimo: The Pueblo Indian's Holiday," *Harper's Weekly,* December 10, 1898, pp. 1,205-6. Collection of the New Mexico Museum of Art Archives

ABOVE: Solon H. Borglum, *Cowboy Resting [Cowboy at Rest]*, 1905. Reproduced in Mark Bennett, *History of the Louisiana Purchase Exposition* (St. Louis: Universal Exposition Publishing Co., 1905), p. 138. Photo courtesy of General Research Division, The New York Public Library, Astor, Lenox and Tilden Foundations

In 1898, two years before Remington wrote to his wife of his disappointment in Santa Fe, Ernest L. Blumenschein and Bert Geer Phillips had accidentally stumbled upon Taos, New Mexico, a small village in the Sangre de Cristo Mountains.[22] The two artists were headed from the Colorado Rockies to Mexico when their wagon broke down near this sparkling high desert outpost. On the way into town to get the wheel repaired, Blumenschein was smitten with the scenery: "The sky was a clear, clean blue with sharp moving clouds," he recalled. "The color, the effective character of the landscape, the drama of the vast spaces, the superb beauty and serenity of the hills, stirred me deeply."[23] They never made it to Mexico. They rented a house in Taos for the summer and soon discovered Taos Pueblo's celebration of San Geronimo Day. Blumenschein sold several of his sketches to *Harper's Weekly*, and when he went back East that fall, he took several of Phillips's paintings with him and quickly sold them to a Chicago dealer who promised future purchases.[24]

22 Cincinnati artist Joseph Henry Sharp had told them of the village and suggested its artistic potential several years before, when they met in Paris. He had been there on a sketching trip in 1893. See Dean A. Porter, Teresa Hayes Ebie, and Suzan Campbell, *Taos Artists and Their Patrons, 1898–1950* (Notre Dame, IN: University of Notre Dame Snite Museum of Art, 1999), 21.

23 Quoted in Laura M. Bickerstaff, *Pioneer Artists of Taos*, rev. and exp. ed. (Denver: Old West Publishing Co., 1983), 30–31.

24 Porter, Ebie, and Campbell, *Taos Artists and Their Patrons*, 20.

25 Porter, Ebie, and Campbell, *Taos Artists and Their Patrons*, 21, 23–24. See also Sherry Clayton Taggett and Ted Schwarz, *Paintbrushes and Pistols: How the Taos Artists Sold the West* (Santa Fe: John Muir Publications, 1990).

26 *Official Catalogue of Exhibitors: Universal Exposition of St. Louis, USA, 1904; Division of Exhibits; Department B—Art*, rev. ed. (St. Louis, MO: Published for the Committee, 1904); see also Diane Rademacher, *Still Shining! Discovering Lost Treasures from the 1904 St. Louis World's Fair* (St. Louis, MO: Virginia Publishing Co., 2003).

27 Peter H. Hassrick, "Solon Borglum, Poet Sculptor of the West," in *Shaping the West: American Sculptors of the 19th Century* (Denver: Petrie Institute of Western American Art, Denver Art Museum [*Western Passages*], 2010), 41–45. The Goodrich quote appears on page 44.

Blumenschein and Phillips spread the word that Taos offered a unique aesthetic environment, and other artists followed. Oscar E. Berninghaus of St. Louis visited for a week in 1899 while on commission to paint scenery along the route of the Denver and Rio Grande Railroad and was so impressed that he began spending part of each year in the village. Joseph Henry Sharp, who had been to Taos in 1893, returned in 1902 for a summer visit and continued to spend summers there until 1909, when he bought a former Penitente chapel for use as a studio. E. Irving Couse also visited in 1902 as a part of his effort to paint the myth of the American Indians. W. Herbert "Buck" Dunton did not arrive until 1912 to complete the roster of artists who became known as the founders of the Taos art colony. After completing its spur line to the South Rim of the Grand Canyon in 1901, the Atchison, Topeka and Santa Fe Railway began using southwestern art to promote its destinations, and in 1907 began producing its famous calendar, which provided the Taos artists with a popular and well-paying outlet for their art.[25]

The artists of the Taos art colony were well on their way to establishing themselves by the time of the St. Louis World's Fair in 1904. The St. Louis fair was but one of a number of world's fairs held during the first decade of the twentieth century. The Paris exposition in 1900 and the 1901 Pan-American Exposition in Buffalo, New York (where President William McKinley was assassinated), were only the most recent in a long line of expositions that showcased eye-popping modernisms of the new century. But the St. Louis fair was one of the largest, attracting more than eighteen million people during the course of its run. Portland, Oregon, subsequently hosted the Lewis & Clark Centennial Exposition in 1905, and Seattle welcomed the Alaska-Yukon-Pacific Exposition in 1909. These fairs provided opportunities for American artists to show their work to literally millions of people who might never have gone to an art gallery. The St. Louis fair selected "The Winning of the West" as its theme, and the fair organizers accepted a number of paintings and sculptures by western artists for exhibition as well as western subjects by artists not normally associated with the West.[26] In keeping with the theme, the Fine Arts Committee even borrowed Richard Caton Woodville's seminal painting *War News From Mexico* (1848), which shows a group of townspeople gathered on the steps of a local hotel to hear news of the war as it is read from a newspaper. One of the pivotal pictures associated with Manifest Destiny, the painting suggests the interest with which Americans read about the American conquest of Mexico and expansion into the Southwest in 1848, and with which it was remembered in 1904.

One of the most prominent sculptors at the St. Louis fair was Solon H. Borglum, a former Nebraska cowboy whose remembered experiences of the West provided him with numerous subjects and themes. He had recently returned from studying and exhibiting in Paris and had shown some of his pieces at the Pan-American Exposition in Buffalo, where he won a silver medal. The St. Louis fair commissioned him to do four monumental groups in plaster staff for the grounds: *Pioneer in a Storm*, *Sioux Indian Buffalo Dance*, *An Old Chief Urging His Child to Seek Civilization*, and *Cowboy at Rest*. This last piece seemed to be autobiographical, fitting the critic Arthur Goodrich's description of Borglum in 1902:

> Many a time he would urge or lead his pony up some undiscovered ridge of country and, reaching the top, he would sprawl on the sand hill and watch the wind mow paths in the bunch grass below or, looking over the stretch of silent plain and hill to the illimitable blue beyond, he would unwittingly know himself a part of a great inexplicable Something that he could not understand or express.[27]

It was quite a contrast to Remington's cowboys roaring through a cattle town with guns blazing.

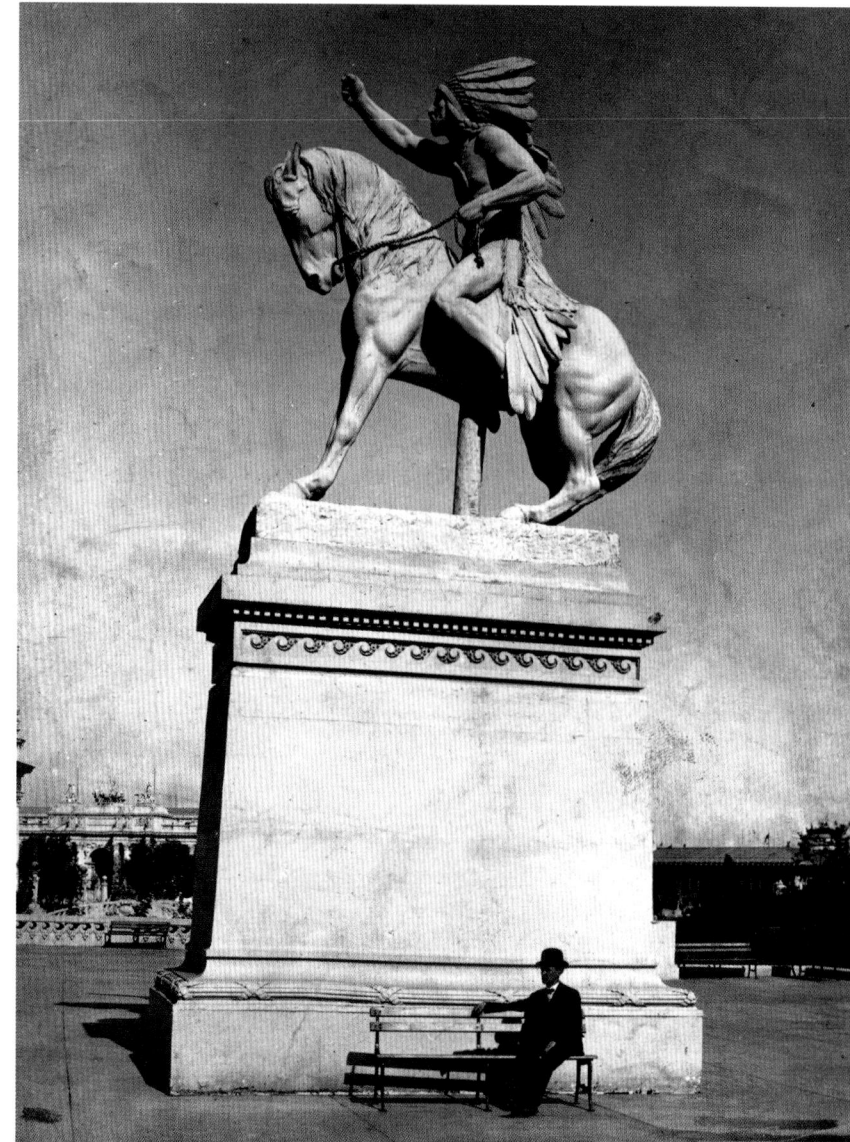

Cyrus Dallin, *Protest of the Sioux* [*The Sioux Chief*]
Exhibited at the Louisiana Purchase Exposition, St. Louis, Mo.,
1904. Missouri History Museum, St. Louis

Western artists at the 1904 fair, for the most part, offered monumental paeans to the past—huge plaster sculptures memorializing that recent but heroic era, smaller bronze pieces, and dozens of paintings, drawings, and prints: Cyrus Dallin, *Protest of the Sioux*, a monumental sculpture, and the smaller *Medicine Man* (1899); sculptor A. Phimister Proctor, *Indian Warrior* (1895–97); Frederic Remington, *Your Soldier—He Say* (1901), a picture that he destroyed in 1908; Texas artist Frank Reaugh, *In the Rain* (1904), a pastel of cowboys watching a herd of cattle in a rainstorm. St. Louis native Charles M. Russell submitted four pictures, but the judges accepted only *Pirates of the Plains* (1904); the others he showed in the Montana pavilion. George de Forest Brush had moved beyond his Indian pictures to other subjects by the time of the fair, but he submitted an 1889 composition, *The Weaver*, for exhibition. E. Irving Couse's *Indian Drinking* (1903) and Thomas Moran's *Solitude* (1897) were more products of the romantic nineteenth century than the new century, and William Wendt represented the relatively new school of California impressionists. Other large-scale staff sculptures included *Physical Liberty* (1904) by Hermon Atkins MacNeil and *Destiny of the Red Man* (1903) by Adolph A. Weinman, two sculptors better known for designing American coins later in their careers.

Rufus F. Zogbaum represented western illustrators at the fair. As publishers were entering what is now seen as the golden age of magazine illustration, artists found increased opportunities to publish their work. Magazines and newspapers were growing rapidly between 1900 and 1905. *Collier's* was the advertising leader in 1905 with over thirteen quarto pages a week, but *The Saturday Evening Post* was closing rapidly. Frederic Remington sold pictures to a number of magazines including *Collier's* (one of the early leaders in color illustration), *Cosmopolitan*, *Scribner's*, and *Outing*. N. C. Wyeth illustrated for the *Post* as well as *Outing* and others. Maynard Dixon's work appeared on a number of covers of the leading journals in the West, including *Overland Monthly*, *Sunset*, and *Out West*, with Charles F. Lummis as editor.[28] But more contemporary references began to seep into the illustrations as the public and the artists both became more at home with societal changes: the automobile in J. H. Smith's caricature *Pride Goeth* (about 1910), in which a cowboy tries to impress eastern women with riding stunts; and the Cream of Wheat box used as a mailbox in N. C. Wyeth's painting, *Where the Mail Goes, Cream of Wheat Goes* (1907).

28 Frank Luther Mott, *A History of American Magazines, 1885–1905*, 5 vols. (Cambridge, MA: Harvard University Press, 1957), 4:20, 102–8, 151, 484, 496, 635, 637, 692, 726. Census reports during these years did not distinguish between magazine and newspaper advertising.

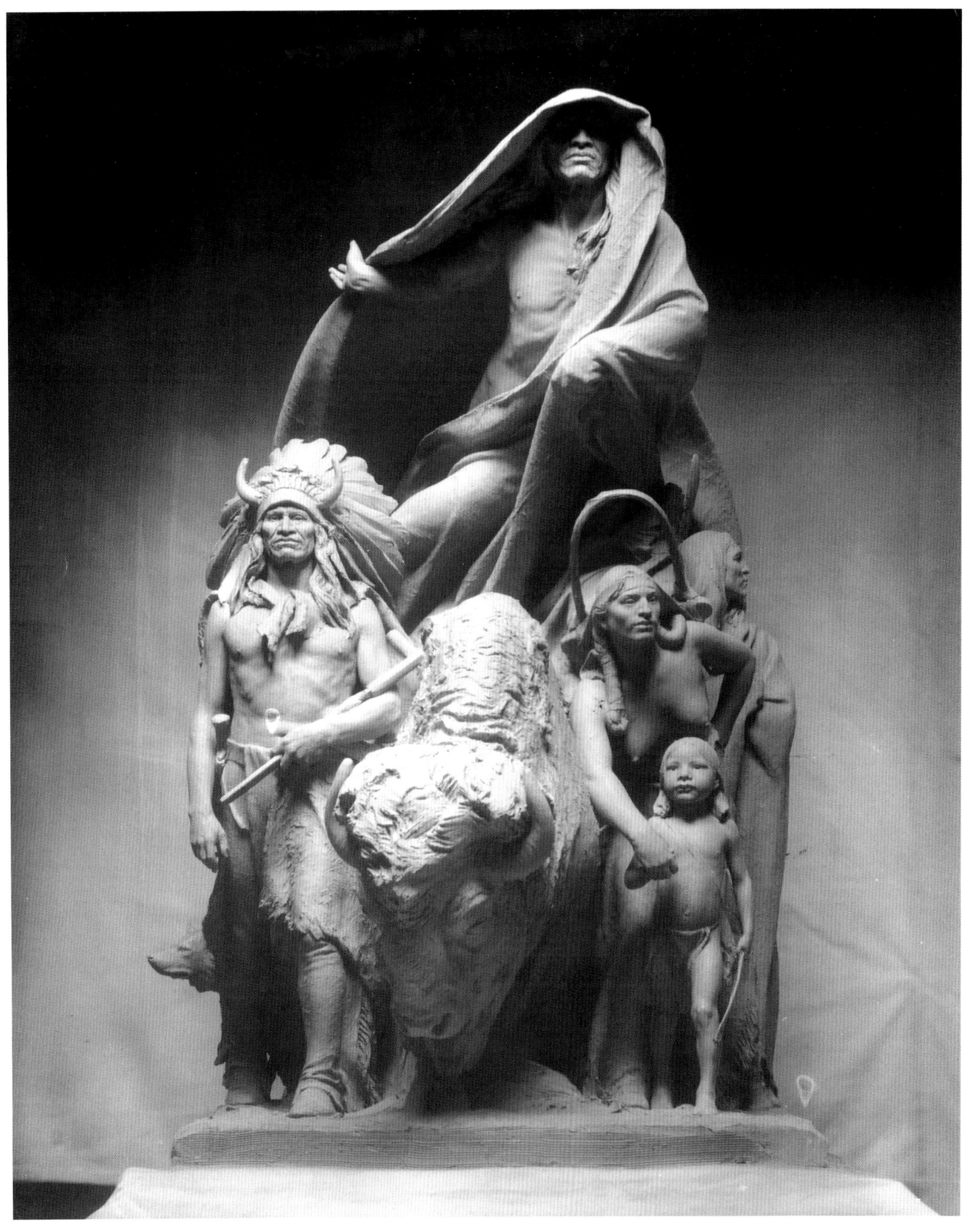

Adolph A. Weinman
Destiny of the Red Man, 1903
Exhibited at the Louisiana Purchase Exposition, St. Louis, Mo., 1904
Missouri History Museum, St. Louis

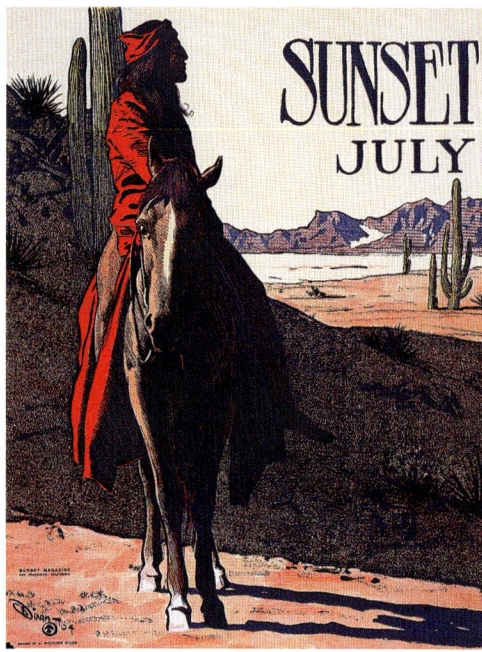
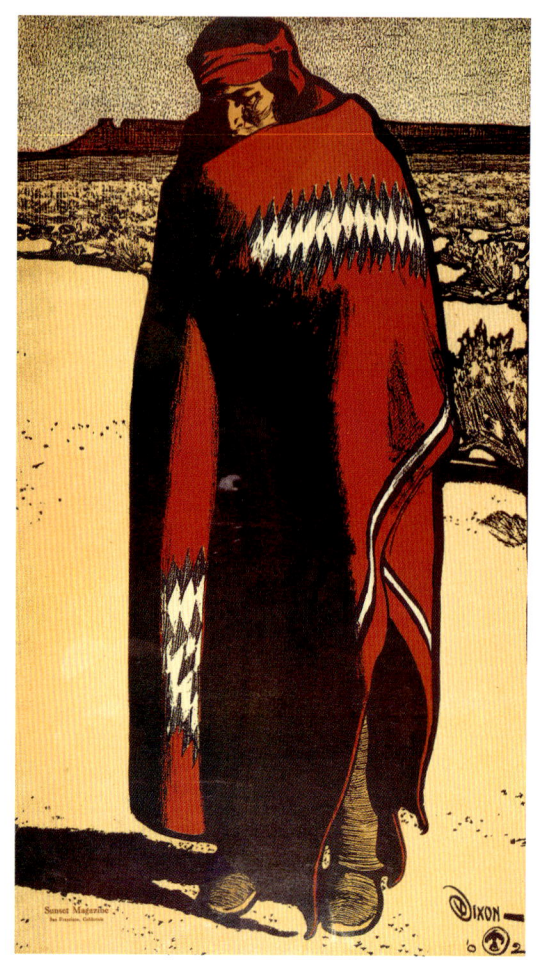

Maynard Dixon, *Sunset* magazine cover, 1904 (above); Dixon, *Blanket-wrapped Navajo Indian*, *Sunset* magazine cover, 1903 (right). Courtesy of the California State Library, Sacramento, California

The years 1903–4 were a turning point for Charles M. Russell. He had his first one-man show at Noonan-Kocian Company's galleries while he was in St. Louis to submit his work for the world's fair and had become reacquainted with a couple of artist friends, John N. Marchand and Will Crawford, who encouraged him to visit New York in December 1903. The trip was a great success, with Russell meeting other artists and writers who shared his interests and making contacts with publishers who commissioned him to produce illustrations as well as some of his own stories. Russell had been modeling wax figures for years, but had not had any of them cast in bronze until this trip. He modeled a cowboy on a bucking horse while there, which, according to a *New York Press* reporter, shows "a convivial cowboy, which he calls 'Smoking Up.' The cowboy is on his return to camp, he is full of 'bottled happiness,' and wishes the entire community to know of it." One of the casts was given to President Theodore Roosevelt. That fall Russell visited the St. Louis fair before it closed and probably gained a new appreciation for small bronze sculptures after viewing work by Dallin, Proctor, Borglum, Paul Wayland Bartlett, Frederick G. R. Roth, Edward Kemeys, and many others. At the same time, Nancy, Russell's wife and business manager, had become bolder in touting her husband's work and in the prices that she asked. "Charles' work was as good, if not better than Remington's, he ought and must be paid Remington's prices," a friend recalled her saying.[29]

As the fair ended, President Roosevelt, who had succeeded to office when President McKinley was assassinated in 1901, was elected to serve in his own right. He had gained a measure of fame as a cowboy and had written extensively about it in an 1888 book, *Ranch Life and the Hunting Trail*, which Remington had illustrated. That might have been the beginning of a "cult of westernizing," as historian G. Edward White put it.[30] The reputation of cowboys up to that point was as ruffians. As recently as 1881, President Chester A. Arthur had denounced a group of Arizona cowboys as "armed desperadoes"[31] in a message to

29 Rick Stewart, *Charles M. Russell, Sculptor* (Fort Worth, TX: Amon Carter Museum, 1994), 34–37. Russell apparently sold the model to a third party who had the work cast at Roman Bronze Works. See also John Taliaferro, *Charles M. Russell: The Life and Legend of America's Cowboy Artist* (Boston: Little, Brown and Company, 1996), 141–52.

30 White, *The Eastern Establishment and the Western Experience*, 50–51.

31 Chester A. Arthur, "First Annual Message, December 6, 1881," in James D. Richardson, ed., *A Compilation of the Messages and Papers of the Presidents, 1789–1897: 1881–1889* (Washington, DC: Government Printing Office, 1898), 8:53–54.

32 Roosevelt quoted in *Bismarck Tribune*, August 8, 1884, page 8, column 4.

33 Remington to Wister, 1 September 1899, quoted in Hassrick et al., *Frederic Remington*, 39.

Charles M. Russell
Smoking Up, 1904
Bronze, 13 x 7½ x 5
The Petrie Collection

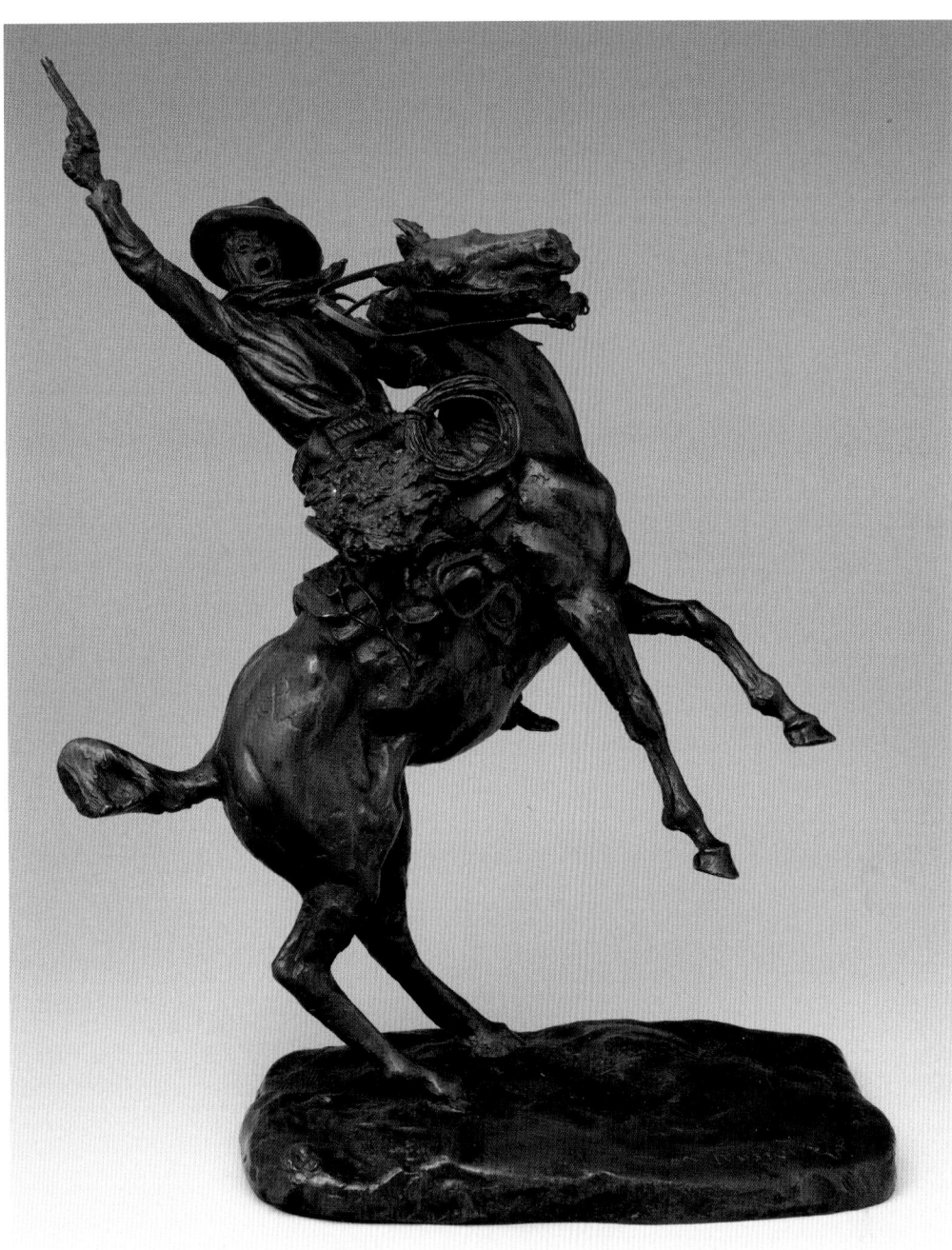

34 Frederic Remington, *Men with the Bark On* (London: Harper & Bros., 1900). See also Peggy Samuels and Harold Samuels, *Frederic Remington: A Biography* (Garden City, NY: Doubleday & Company, Inc., 1982), 269–97; and Ben Merchant Vorpahl, *Frederic Remington and the West: With the Eye of the Mind* (Austin: University of Texas Press, 1978), 268.

Congress, but Roosevelt protested that "cowboys are a much misrepresented set of people . . . there are many places in our cities where I should feel less safe than I would among the wildest cowboys in the West."[32] By 1902, President Roosevelt's persona, along with Remington's paintings and sculptures and Owen Wister's best-selling novel, *The Virginian*, had pushed the "westernizing" process along and prepared the country for an Old West that provided a spiritual foil for the industrialized and urbanized East.

Remington had found no setting—either in Europe or the East Coast—that energized his work like the West. He returned there after his trips to both Europe and Cuba, hoping to regain that inspiration. "This is the war I am going to put in the rest of my time at," he had written Wister in 1899.[33] He had found his subjects in the heroic past of the West—not the events of the Gold Rush, Custer's defeat, the cattle drives, or even the pursuit of Geronimo, but the freedom and space that permitted the characters that he had come to call his "men

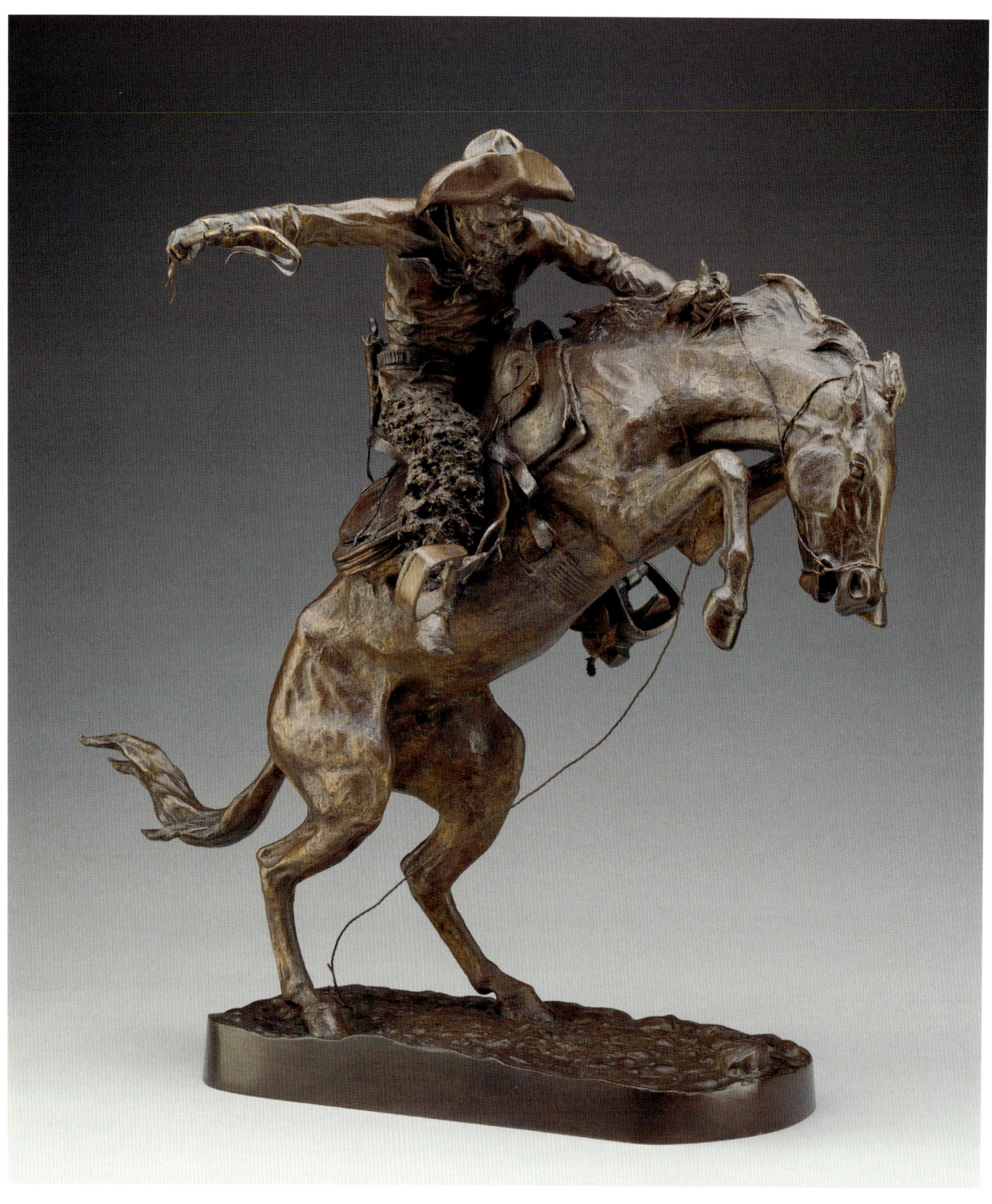

Frederic Remington
Broncho Buster No. 44 (Wooly Chaps),
modeled 1895, cast 1906
Bronze, 24 inches tall
The Roath Collection

35 Quoted in Ben Merchant Vorpahl, *My Dear Wister: The Frederic Remington-Owen Wister Letters* (Palo Alto, CA: American West Publishing Company, 1973), 158, 165.

36 Alexander Nemerov, *Frederic Remington & Turn-of-the-Century America* (New Haven: Yale University Press, 1995), 48–49. Peter H. Hassrick and Melissa J. Webster, *Frederic Remington: A Catalogue Raisonné of Paintings, Watercolors and Drawings,* 2 vols. (Cody, WY: Buffalo Bill Historical Center in association with the University of Washington Press, Seattle and London, 1996), 1:57, discuss how one critic badly misinterpreted this painting.

Frederic Remington
His First Lesson, 1903
Oil on canvas, 27¼ × 40
Amon Carter Museum of American Art, Fort Worth, Texas, 1961.231

with the bark on" to survive and excel. The changes that had occurred had enabled Remington to recognize that their West—their war—no longer existed, and that the West of the imagination was their last refuge.³⁴ It had been evident in his mature paintings for years.

One of Remington's early efforts to express this intellectual dilemma was his resort to a medium free of time and geography: bronze. His dynamic *Broncho Buster,* copyrighted in 1895, embodies his message without the compromising baggage of a western landscape or an accompanying story. In his paintings the landscapes in the backgrounds had become increasingly sketchy; in the bronze there was no background at all. The rider is a cowboy, one of the "men with the bark on," but he could be any man struggling to handle a difficult situation. He stands alone, reminiscent of an era but not dependent on it. He is a man that "every man sees with his own eyes," wrote Remington, attempting to explain his excitement over the accomplishment. The critics also were pleased. One wrote that Remington had "struck his gait." Remington was even happier: "All paper is pulp now. My oils will all get old wasting . . . my watercolors will fade—but I am to endure in bronze . . . I am going to rattle down through all the ages," he wrote to Wister. "I am d___ near eternal."³⁵ His bronzes would not even rust, he claimed. His statement would endure.

Now that Remington had discovered the combination that would nourish his genius, he produced some of his most appealing and significant pictures in which a seemingly historical scene is imbued with symbolic and moral themes. Many are genre scenes so trivial in nature that one might not look beyond to the story. *His First Lesson*, painted in 1903, is a good example. The picture brings a chuckle even to novice horsemen: the man in the center is about to jump in the saddle, and bedlam will break loose. The mounted rider on

> The rider is a cowboy, one of the "men with the bark on," but he could be any man struggling to handle a difficult situation. He stands alone, reminiscent of an era but not dependent on it.

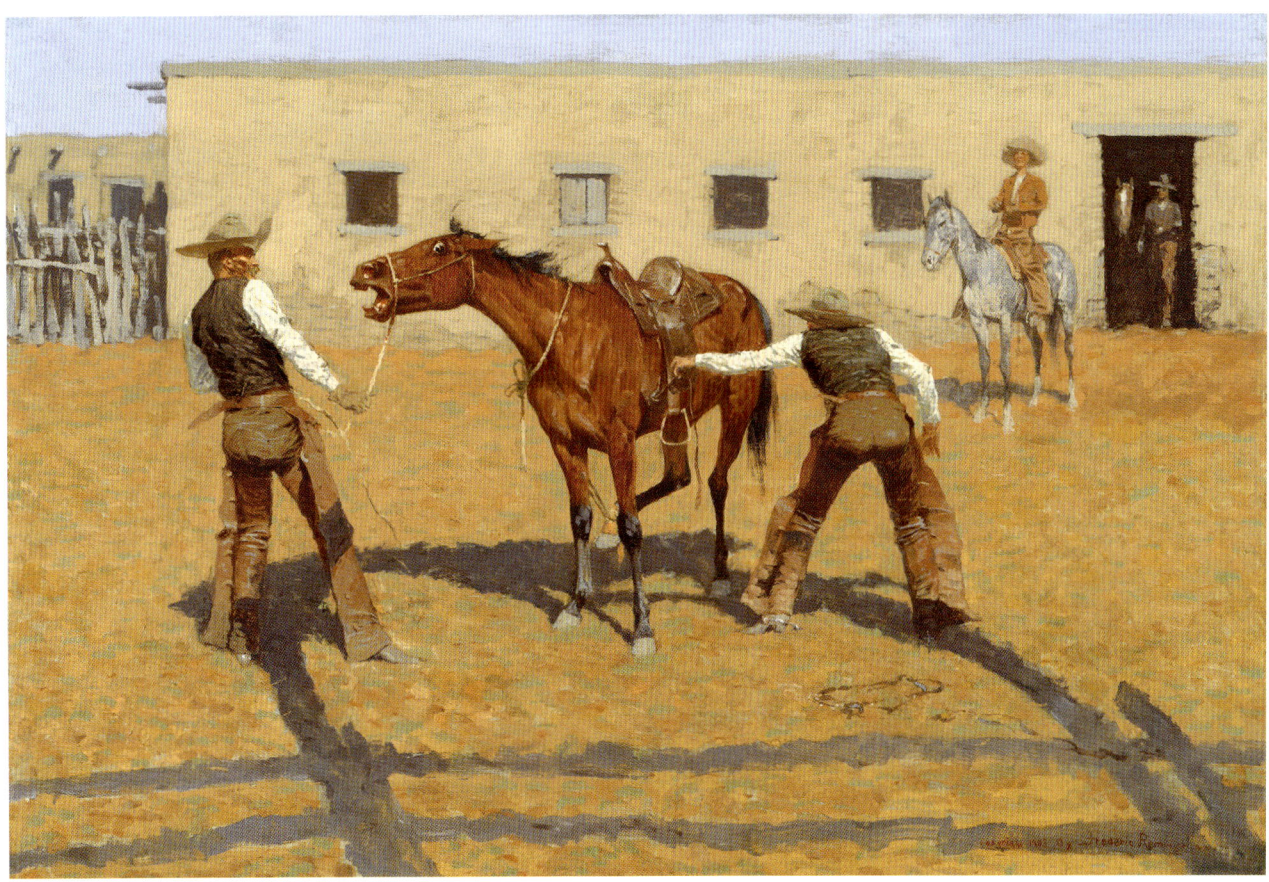

the right is already leaning back in his saddle, laughing, anticipating the fun to come. But a closer look at the picture changes the mood of the picture from humorous to one deeply sympathetic with nature's wild creatures. The pony is trapped in a corral (the confining shadow of the gate towers over him), has his hoof tied up, and has been saddled and bridled. He is about to be *broken*, *tamed*, and *civilized*. Remington was not complaining about cruelty to animals as much as he wanted the viewer to understand that this is what had been done, metaphorically, to his Old West.[36]

The publication of *His First Lesson* in color in *Collier's* led to an important commission from Robert Collier, the editor, which propelled Remington's career to new heights. In May 1903, Collier contracted with Remington for one picture a month for four years, which gave the artist a chance to further explore color, which had troubled him for some time. "For ten years I've been trying to get color in my things and I still don't get it," he confided to friend and illustrator Charles S. Chapman.[37] Just a few years before, he had begun to paint nocturnes, first as illustrations for his second novel, *The Way of an Indian,* which was published serially in *Cosmopolitan* in 1905 and in book form the following year, then as images not necessarily associated with stories.[38] In 1902 he painted *Indian Scouts in the Moonlight*, one of his most successful early nocturnes. It illustrated the artist's intent to "cut down and out—do your hardest work outside the picture and let your audience take away something to think about—to imagine."[39] These night pictures pose questions rather than answer them. What is going on in the picture? What danger are they facing? He is once again dealing with the universal situation of man and nature, and it was with obvious pleasure that he read the encouraging responses to his work.[40] Critic Royal Cortissoz observed the change in his work, "beginning with his exhibition of night scenes, where a painter took the place of the illustrator's brittle pen drawings and blaring reds and yellows."[41] The reviewer for the *New York Times* concluded that in "the painting of night" Remington "has made great progress, revealing genuine painter-like qualities."[42]

In the search for deeper meaning, Remington had moved away from narrative action pictures such as *A Dash for the Timber* to concentrate on the universal elements of western life.[43] *Ridden Down* (1905–6) is one of the best examples. A Crow warrior has been "ridden down" by a bunch of Sioux warriors who are obviously intent upon his extermination. The Crow stoically stands at the edge of a bluff, face blackened and war club in hand.[44] His pony stands uselessly by, exhausted, ridden to the point of death. The warrior is one of Remington's "men with the bark on." Metaphorically, he is every brave man preparing to meet his inevitable end, and the war party the agent of that doom, regardless of its nominal identity. The barren land is any place. Remington used the western setting and Indian warriors because they were a part of the West that he understood and that inspired him. It was his theater of expression, just as artist Winslow Homer used the Maine seacoast and sailors and the hunters of the Adirondacks for his depiction of man against the elements.

Remington found his place in the evolving cultural context of his time. He thought of himself as an artist, just as Homer and poet Walt Whitman did, and searched in the style of the romantic—because the search itself was noble. The solutions were individual: subject matter, style, personality. It is an artistic approach still honored. But for those who might still not comprehend, Remington produced two novels, *John Ermine of the Yellowstone* (1902) and *The Way of an Indian* (1907), which he said were written "to introduce people to the subjects I was trying to draw, paint, and sculpt . . . with the deliberate view of educating men and women, who knew not the West, up to a certain standard of appreciation for its beauties, its fascinations, its intrinsic worth."[45] To be sure that they did not miss the "intrinsic worth," Remington chose pictures for *The Way of an Indian* that would illustrate the various stages of the hero's life rather than pictures that one might be able to relate to an incident in the book and thus view as an illustration. Like his paintings, the two novels deal with heroic characters who lived and died in Remington's historic and idealized West. But the setting could have been any place, any time; Remington intended a universal message. He set them in the West because he had created a vision of the Old West that he understood and loved.

---

37 Quoted in Samuels and Samuels, *Frederic Remington*, 363.

38 Samuels and Samuels, *Frederic Remington*, 297, 361. See also Nancy K. Anderson, *Frederic Remington: The Color of Night* (Washington, DC: National Gallery of Art, 2003).

39 Quoted in William C. Sharpe, "What's Out There? Frederic Remington's Art of Darkness," in Anderson, *Frederic Remington: The Color of Night,* 18.

40 Quoted in Nancy K. Anderson, "Dark Disquiet: Remington's Late Nocturnes," in Anderson, *Frederic Remington: The Color of Night,* 69.

41 Quoted in Samuels and Samuels, *Frederic Remington,* 340.

42 *New York Times,* December 5, 1907.

43 It is true, of course, that Remington continued to do large, narrative pictures on commission, such as *The Charge,* also known as *A Cavalry Scrap* (1906, Blanton Museum of Art, University of Texas at Austin), which was hung in the grill room of the Knickerbocker Hotel in New York City.

44 Peter Hassrick, *Frederic Remington: Paintings, Drawings, and Sculpture in the Amon Carter Museum and the Sid W. Richardson Foundation Collections* (New York: Harry N. Abrams, Inc., in association with the Amon Carter Museum of Western Art, 1973), 151.

45 Maxwell, "Frederic Remington— Most Typical of American Artists," 405.

46 Samuels and Samuels, *Frederic Remington,* 424; Remington, *Men with the Bark On,* 191.

47 Newspaper quote in Remington's diary, December 11, 1909, quoted in James K. Ballinger, *Frederic Remington* (New York: Harry N. Abrams, Inc., Publishers, in association with the National Museum of American Art, Smithsonian Institution, 1989), 142.

48 Remington's diary, entry for December 9, 1909, quoted in Dippie, *Remington & Russell,* 4–5.

49 Royal Cortissoz, "Frederic Remington: A Painter of American Life," *Scribner's Magazine* 47 (February 1910): 192, quoted in Dippie, *Remington & Russell,* 60.

50 William A. Coffin, "American Illustration of To-Day," *Scribner's Magazine* 11 (March 1892): 348.

51 Doreen Bolger Burke, "Remington in the Context of His Artistic Generation," in Shapiro and Hassrick, *Frederic Remington,* 67; Edmund Morris, *Colonel Roosevelt* (New York: Random House, 2010), 267–72; and quote in Taliaferro, *Charles M. Russell,* 192.

That he was never accepted into the National Academy bothered Remington, for it meant that his fellow artists did not understand or appreciate the nature of his expression, or rejected it entirely. He could take solace in his popularity and prosperity, of course, and he forged on. "My art requires me to go down . . . the road where the human beings are . . . in the landscape which to me is overpowered by their presence," he wrote in *Men with the Bark On*.[46]

One critic finally provided a measure of the understanding that Remington craved, and the artist gloated in the recognition. The reviewer for the *New York Evening Mail* observed of Remington's 1909 exhibition that "no American artist interests the people more than Remington does, and none is really better worth going to see."[47] In his diary Remington reveled, "The art critics have all 'come down'—I have received splendid notices from all the papers. They ungrudgingly give me a high place as a 'mere painter.'"[48] Remington was right. After his premature death in December 1909, Royal Cortissoz, writing in *Scribner's Magazine,* agreed that Remington had "worked out an impressionism of his own."[49]

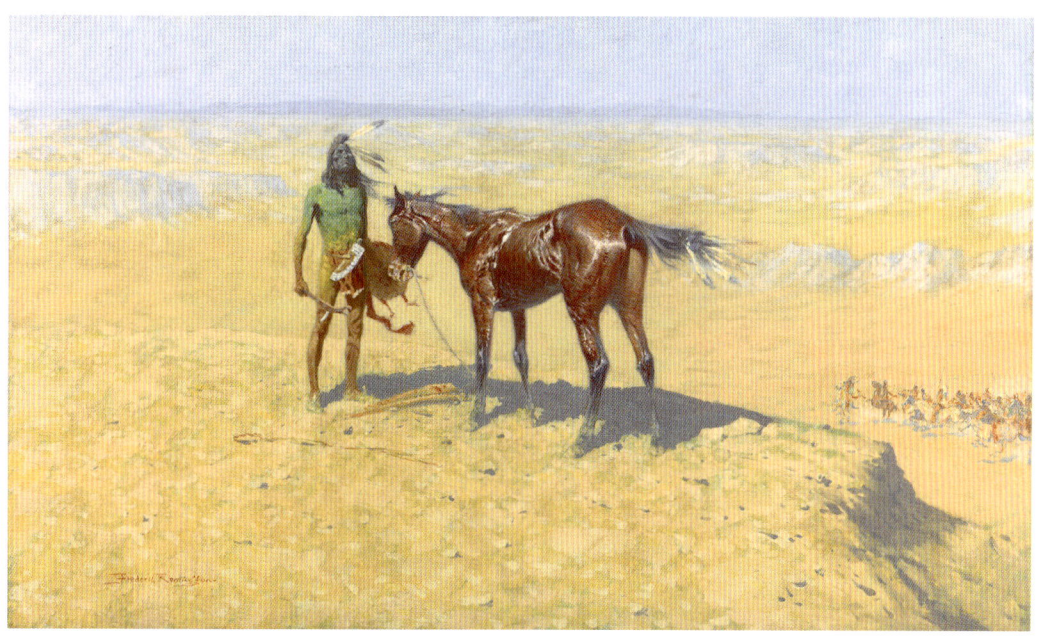

Frederic Remington
Ridden Down, 1905–6
Oil on canvas, 30¼ x 51¼
Amon Carter Museum of American Art, Fort Worth, Texas, 1961.224

In analyzing Remington's complex and brilliant career, many biographers have relied on an 1892 statement that William A. Coffin made in a series of articles on American illustrators: "The cavalryman, the Indian, the scout, the miner and the ranchman have furnished Frederic Remington with subjects that he illustrates with much vigor of line and striking effect . . . It is a fact that admits of no question that Eastern people have formed their conceptions of what the Far-Western life is like, more from what they have seen in Mr. Remington's pictures than from any other source."[50] While this statement is reasonably true, it was written early in Remington's career and does not take into consideration that he had evolved toward a higher goal. His subject was a legitimate and universal one for artists: the brave life. He believed that what we have come to know as the Old West—before the end of the frontier, before the invasion of eastern civilization and mechanization—was a laboratory, or a setting, in which his "men with the bark on" could grow and flourish. Like the Romantic Jean-Jacques Rousseau, Remington had found his "noble savage" in these frontier types. Using the West as an incubator for this kind of nobility made him the epitome of the western American painter. Remington would have appreciated the irony in the fact that we cannot really understand the point of much of his great body of work until we cease to see him as that western painter and instead see him in the universal context of artists as truth-seekers.

In that sense—as a searcher for truth—Remington might have been tolerant of the 1913 Armory show and many of the generation of modernists who were about to eclipse nineteenth-century styles and values, but, like President Roosevelt, who actually wrote a review of the exhibition, temperamentally and stylistically he would have been bewildered in their company. He probably would have been harsher than Charles M. Russell, who, after viewing the Armory show, told a reporter that, "Most people can't savvy all this dreamy stuff."[51]

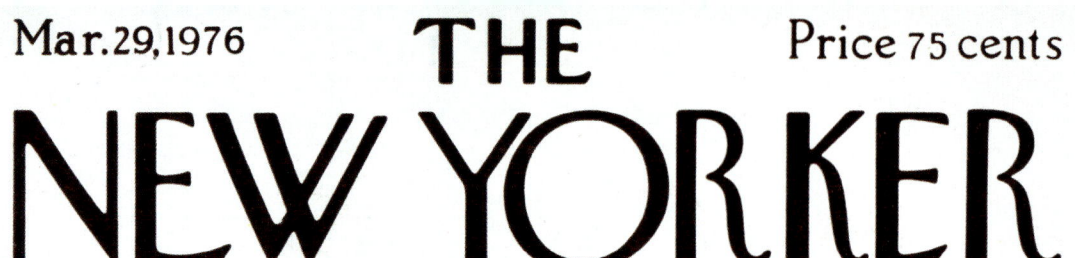

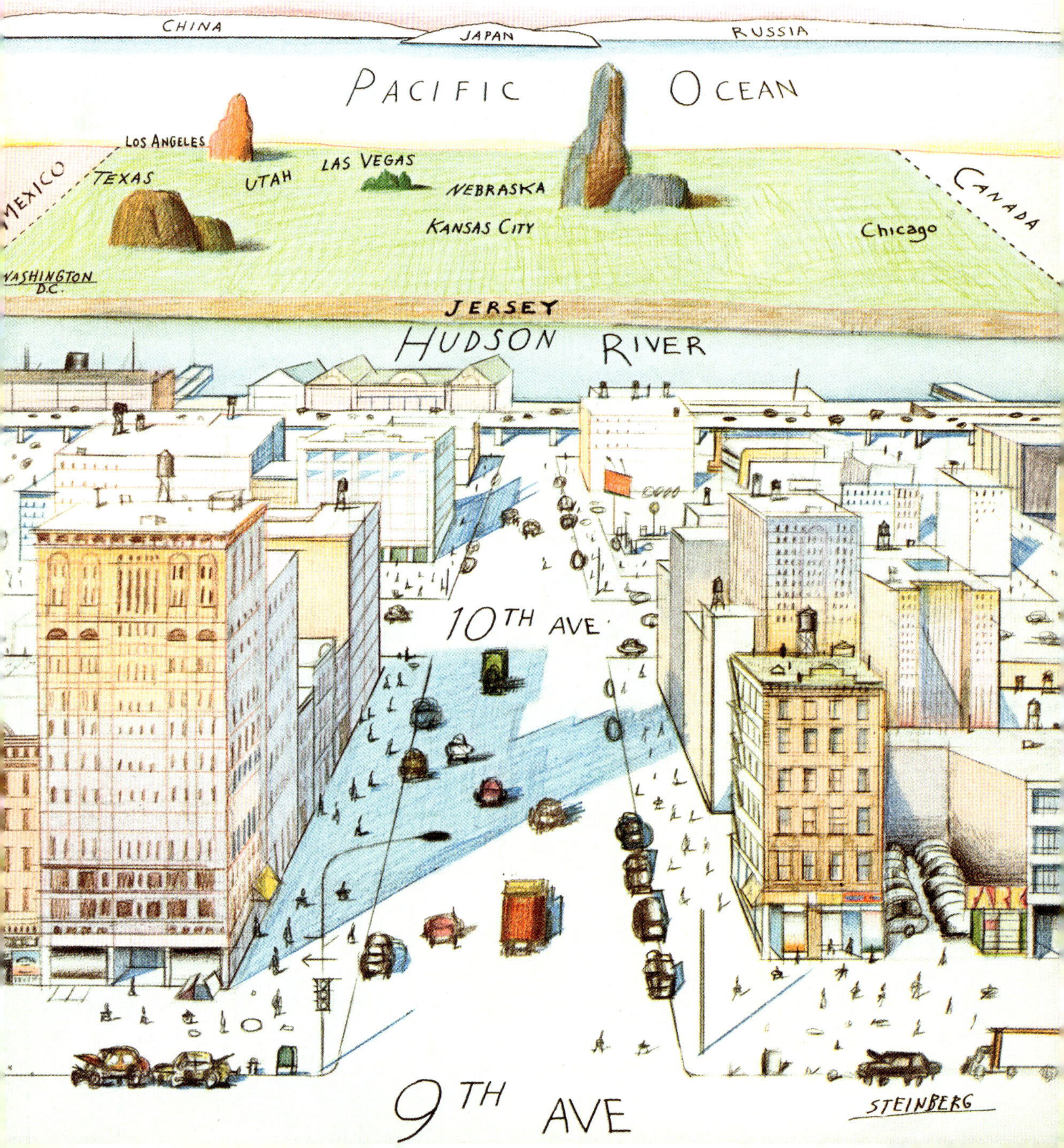

"Racy of the Soil"
Cowboys, Indians, and Western Landscapes 1910–20

CHARLES C. ELDREDGE

ANY PARENT CAN ATTEST that the teens may be challenging years. As with children, so too with centuries. For the United States, the centennial teens have been fraught with conflict, up to and including the present day. In the eighteenth century, the colonies were roiled by intracolonial competition before Queen Anne's War ended with the Treaty of Utrecht in 1713. A century later, the three-year War of 1812 continued the record of conflict, as did the First World War from 1914 to 1918. In each case, the turmoil affected and often overshadowed other pursuits, including the arts, complicating appraisal of the creative record of a society unsettled by war.

Evaluation of a region's record during a given time span, such as a decade, is further complicated by geography. Absent clearly defined boundaries, there is little consensus on the definition of the American West. Where you hail from, or where you now stand, or where you are heading—each affects the understanding of region. In Saul Steinberg's hilariously foreshortened view of the country that decorated *The New Yorker*'s cover on March 29, 1976, the great trans-Hudson West began at Manhattan's Ninth Avenue and elided the flat, fly-over country with (as playwright William Inge used to say of his native Kansas) "no mountains in the way" to arrive at the Pacific, with Japan on its far shore.

One hundred years earlier, when Colorado was admitted to the Union as the Centennial State, the Rocky Mountains were still very much in the way and on the minds of builders who had only recently linked the nation with transcontinental rails. They also confronted mobile Americans at the dawn of a new tourist era, among them numerous creative artists. In the West, poets rhapsodized over "purple mountain majesties." Writers recorded—or invented—stories of the region that persist in the American imagination to this day. Painters similarly captured the drama of the western scene and its colorful inhabitants in iconic and enduring images of the grand landscape and its inhabitants, particularly cowboys and Indians.

NATIVE AMERICANS AS SUBJECTS

The romanticized Indian provided a subject "with just the right note of sentiment" to evoke nostalgia for a lost past or, contrarily, to whet appetites for modern business.[1] A sense of change, and generally of loss, was a recurrent theme in many early twentieth-century depictions of Native Americans. In 1904 Edward Curtis photographed a band of Navajos on horseback riding into a darkened distance. His title, *The Vanishing Race*, represented the broadly held perception of Native Americans' future. Frederic Remington's late painting, *With the Eye of the Mind* (1908), conveyed a similar message. A trio of Indian warriors on horseback halts in an empty landscape, transfixed by ghostly images in the clouds. The

FACING: Saul Steinberg, cover of *The New Yorker* (March 29, 1976). ©The Saul Steinberg Foundation / Artists Rights Society (ARS), New York. Cover reprinted with permission of *The New Yorker* magazine. All rights reserved. Image courtesy of Condé Nast

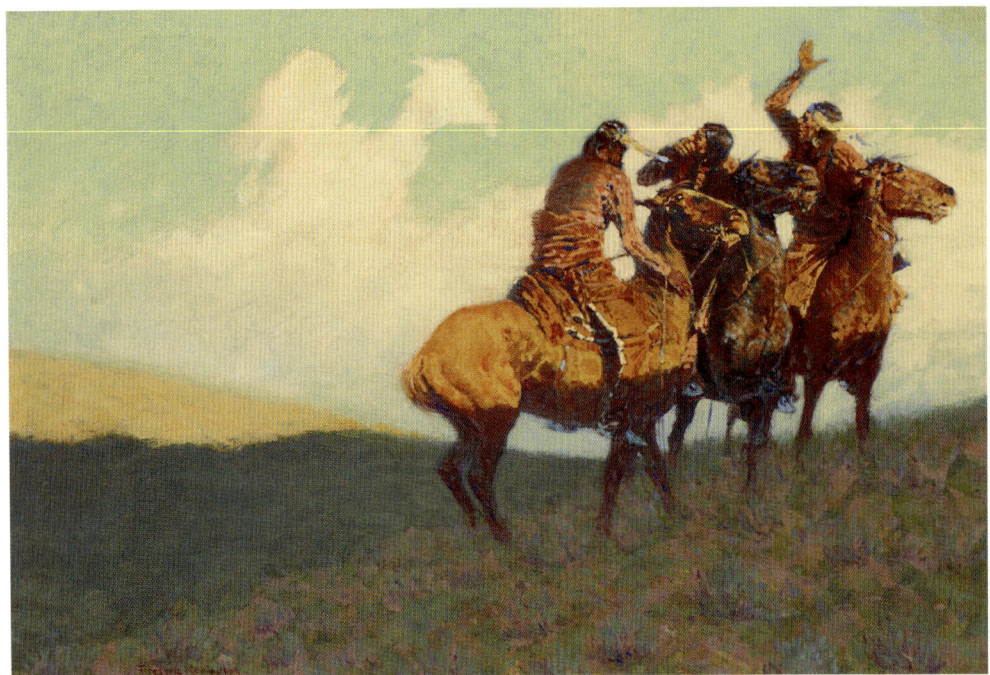

LEFT: Frederic Remington
With the Eye of the Mind, 1908
Oil on canvas, 33½ x 46⅜
Gilcrease Museum, Tulsa, Oklahoma,
0127.2332

BELOW: Rodman Wanamaker
Drawing of the proposed national memorial to the North American Indian, Staten Island, New York, 1913. Photographic print with ink and gouache, 12¼ x 8⅞. Image courtesy of the Mathers Museum of World Cultures, Indiana University

forms that coalesce overhead are vaguely defined, but their portent seems dire, leading one historian to describe the painting as "another evolutionary image of civilization replacing doomed savagery."² A few years later E. Irving Couse appropriated the motif in his painting *A Vision of the Past* (1913). Seated on the ground at the feet of three standing warriors, a young boy looks back into the distance where clouds again form a ghostly image; like a faded petroglyph, a band of mounted warriors races across the sky, another evocation of past native glory.

By the early 1900s, the "Indian problem" had in the eyes of most in white society been solved by the government's program of assimilation and the tribes' relocation to reservations. Perhaps only then could the nostalgic note flourish and the "vanishing race" be celebrated in art. In 1913 sculptor James Earle Fraser designed one of the most famous coins ever struck by the U.S. government. His Buffalo Nickel paired the vanishing North American bison with a Native American. It seems telling that an Indian was featured on the government's coin of next-to-smallest value, one in which the animal claimed both the obverse and the coin's popular name.

Elsewhere in art, however, the Indian was not so belittled. Once deemed defeated, he could be lamented and honored, nowhere more grandiosely than in Rodman Wanamaker's scheme for a national memorial to the North American Indian. A project of the Philadelphia merchant and philanthropist who had a long interest in the native populations, the design featured an elaborate confection of statuary, classical colonnades, and vast plazas. It was intended for a hilltop on Staten Island, from which perch a colossal figure of an Indian chief would look out toward the Statue of Liberty. In one of his last presidential acts, William Howard Taft broke ground for the memorial in February 1913, an event that provided the occasion for the initial distribution of Fraser's coin. The groundbreaking drew considerable press attention; however, nothing further was heard of the scheme and—whether due to

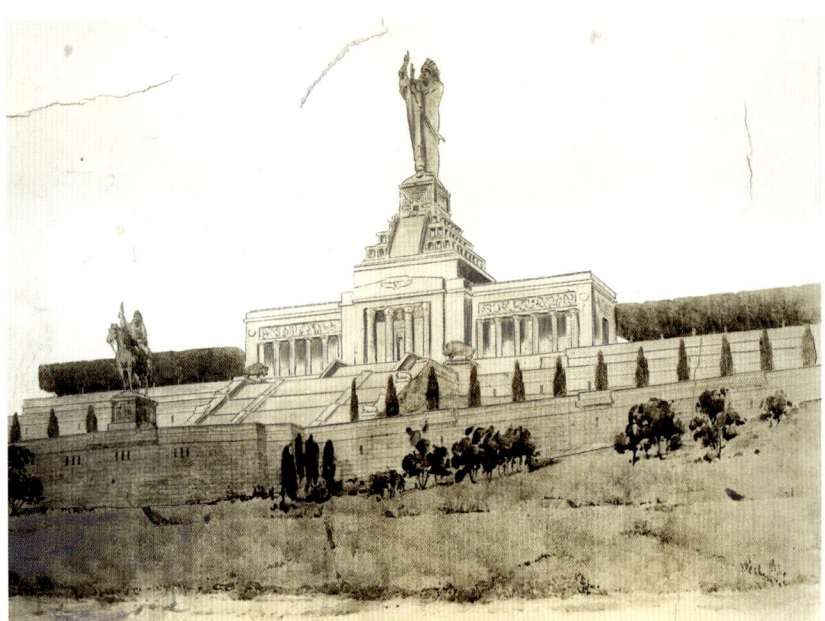

1 A. Stirling Calder used this phrase to describe James Earle Fraser's *End of the Trail.* Introduction, *The Sculpture and Mural Decorations of the Exposition* (San Francisco: Paul Elder and Co., 1915), 10. An expanded version of the quotation appears later in this essay.

2 Alexander Nemerov, *Frederic Remington and Turn-of-the-Century America* (New Haven: Yale University Press, 1995), 152.

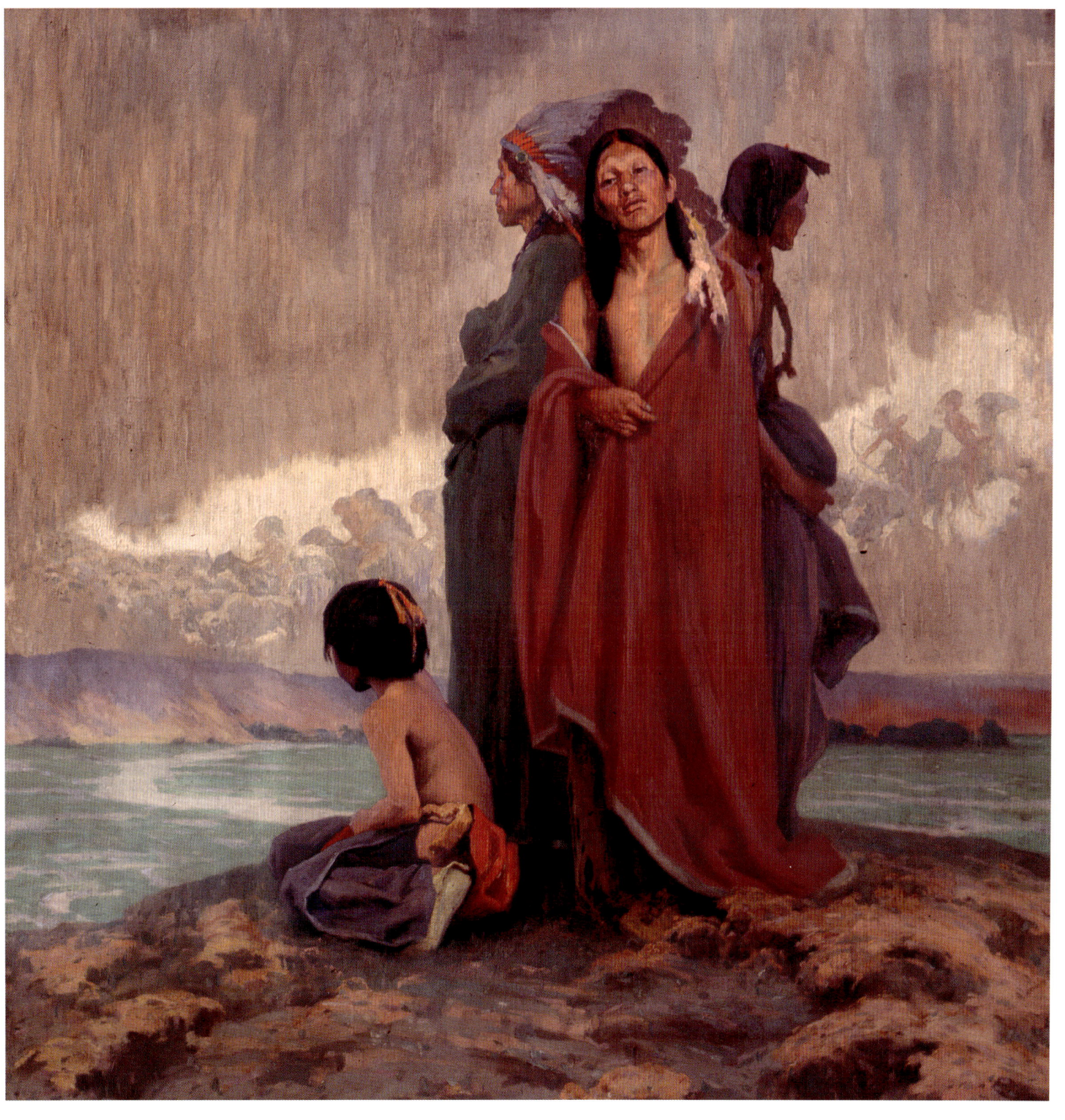

E. Irving Couse
A Vision of the Past, 1913
Oil on canvas, 59 x 59
Collection of The Butler Institute of American Art,
Youngstown, Ohio

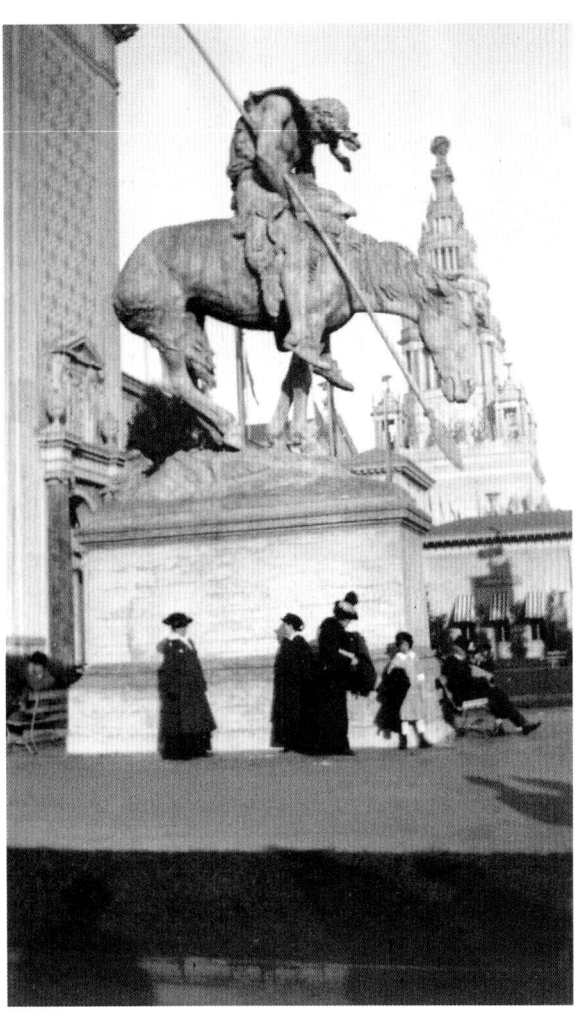

James Earle Fraser, *End of the Trail*, 1915 Photographed at the Panama-Pacific International Exposition. Photographic Study Collection, Dickinson Research Center, National Cowboy & Western Heritage Museum

costs or the outbreak of war the following year or simply changing tastes in monuments and in Indian subjects—Wanamaker's planned memorial was never realized.

In 1915 Fraser returned to the Indian motif with his monumental *End of the Trail*, which decorated the grounds at San Francisco's Panama-Pacific International Exposition. Eugen Neuhaus, prominent San Francisco artist, critic, and chair of the exposition's art advisory committee, wrote about Fraser's sculpture in conjunction with *The American Pioneer* by Solon Borglum, which was positioned nearby. Neuhaus thought the symbolism of these paired equestrian statues provided "a very fine expression of the destinies of two great races so important in our historical development." The pioneer, "erect, energetic, powerful . . . is very typical of the white man and the victorious march of his civilization," while Fraser's Indian offered "the overwhelming expression of physical fatigue," both man and beast "ready to give up the task they are not equal to meet."[3] It was this expression of fatigue—of a single rider, but also of his race—that won the interest of visitors. According to Alexander Stirling Calder, the exposition's chief of sculpture, *End of the Trail* was "the most popular work on the grounds—the symbolism is simple and reaches many, with just the right note of sentiment."[4]

If Indians depicted in art at the Panama-Pacific Exposition were but nostalgic emblems of a vanquished, if not fully vanished, race, in other ways and other contexts the subject was put to new use in the new century. Their image proved useful in promoting sales of many products and services, for instance, tourism in the American West. A campaign to "See America First" originated in 1906 with a group of the region's boosters who convened in Salt Lake City. These businessmen and government officials were united by their concern over the annual diversion of tourist dollars to Europe, and by a belief that "we [westerners] possess scenic attractions surpassing those of any other portion of the world, . . . assets capable of conversion into dollars and cents [through tourism]."[5] Native Americans were among those "assets," and they soon appeared in publications enticing well-heeled travelers westward.

Louis Hill, who in 1907 succeeded his father James J. Hill as president of the Great Northern Railway, was one of the most ardent champions of the burgeoning business. His line conducted passengers from the East through Montana's vast grasslands and rugged peaks toward cities in the Pacific Northwest. Hill was fascinated by the Blackfeet Indians of the northern Rockies and plains and eventually became an honorary member of the tribe. He used the image of Blackfeet to advertise travel to the region that in 1910 became Glacier National Park. More than any other national park, Glacier became synonymous with the Indian image; there travelers could debark the Great Northern's comfortable coaches, meet

3 Eugen Neuhaus, *The Art of the Exposition* (San Francisco: Paul Elder and Co., 1915), 31–32.

4 Calder, *The Sculpture and Mural Decorations of the Exposition*, 10.

5 The "See America First" Conference, Salt Lake City, Utah, January 25–26, 1906 (Salt Lake City, 1906); quoted in Marguerite S. Shaffer, "'See America First': Re-Envisioning Nation and Region through Western Tourism," *Pacific Historical Review* 65, no. 4 (November 1996): 571.

6 Marsden Hartley, Berlin, to Alfred Stieglitz, 12 November 1914; quoted by Wanda Corn, "Marsden Hartley's Native Amerika," in Elizabeth Mankin Kornhauser, ed., *Marsden Hartley* (New Haven: Yale University Press, 2002), 69.

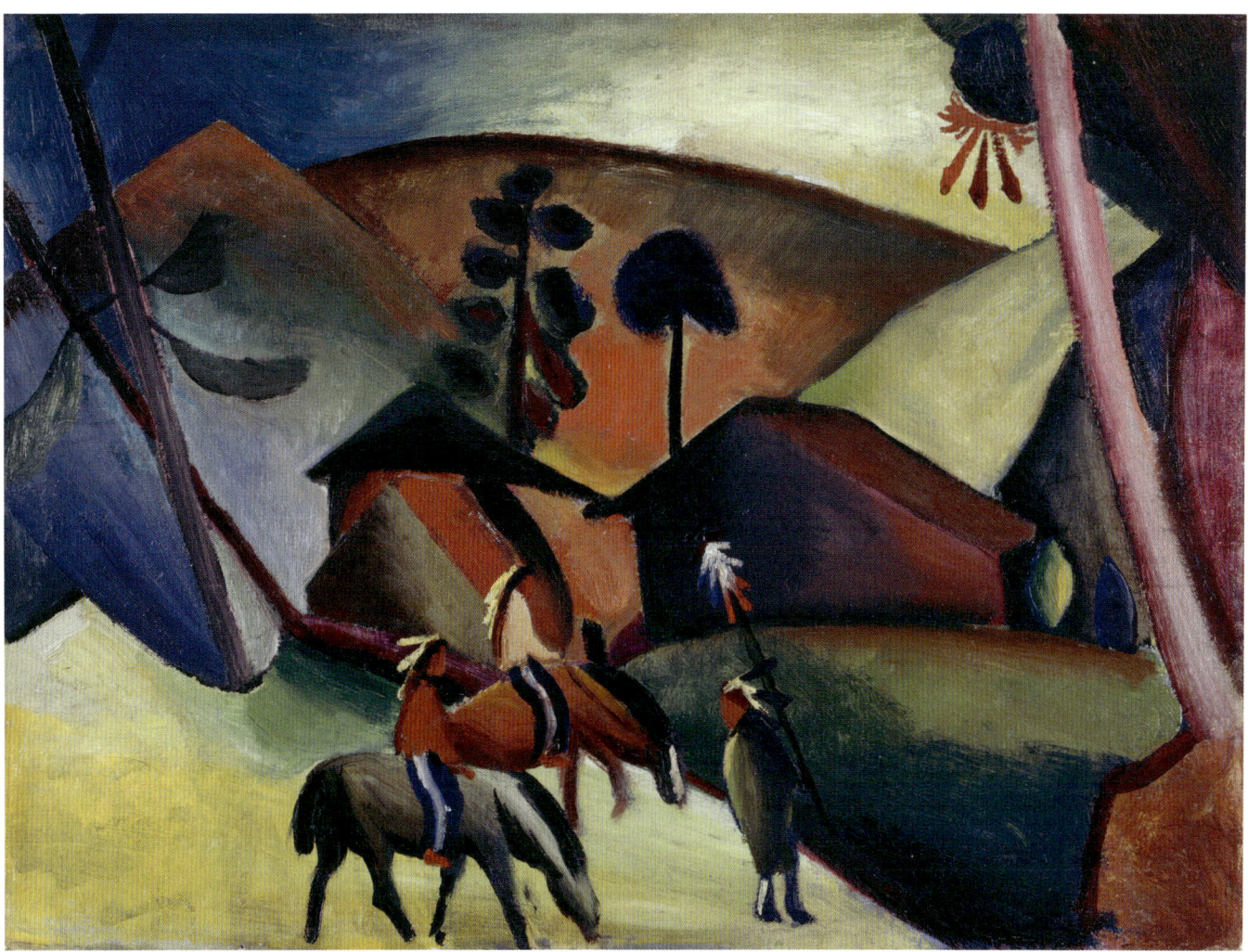

August Macke

Indians on Horseback

(Indianer auf Pferden), 1911

Oil on canvas, 17³⁄₁₀ x 23³⁄₅

Städtische Galerie im Lenbachhaus, Munich

the Blackfeet, and observe their tribal dances and ceremonials, as promised in the railroad's advertisements.

The Great Northern was not alone in using the local population; in the Southwest, too, travelers were lured by railroad promotions using Indian images and the prospect of encounters with Native America. In 1914 the Atchison, Topeka and Santa Fe Railway began reproducing paintings by E. Irving Couse on its annual corporate calendars, patronage that Couse enjoyed for more than twenty years. Couse's Santa Fe calendars, like the Great Northern's advertisements and other western promotions, used Indians to draw business as part of the flourishing "See America First" campaign. To judge from John Sloan's etching *The Indian Detour* (1927; see page 57), a witty design of a pueblo congested with tourist traffic, they succeeded brilliantly. The campaign slogan became so familiar that a decade later Norman Rockwell lampooned it in a cover design for *The Saturday Evening Post* (April 23, 1938) depicting an elderly Indian puzzled to discover in his U.S. mail an invitation to "See America First."

Another Indian image appeared in the decade of the 1910s, one modern in form but no less potent in romance. From Berlin in 1914, the expatriate American Marsden Hartley wrote to Alfred Stieglitz, his New York dealer, telling of his homesickness. "I find myself wanting to be an Indian," the artist wrote, "—to paint my face with the symbols of that race I adore[,] to go to the West and face the sun forever—that would seem the true expression of human dignity."[6] Hartley's series of "Amerika" paintings expresses his yearning pictorially with stylized Indian motifs. Even among his German hosts, the Indian image was a familiar one; it was, however, treated in decidedly modern style, for instance, in August Macke's paintings of Native Americans from around 1911.

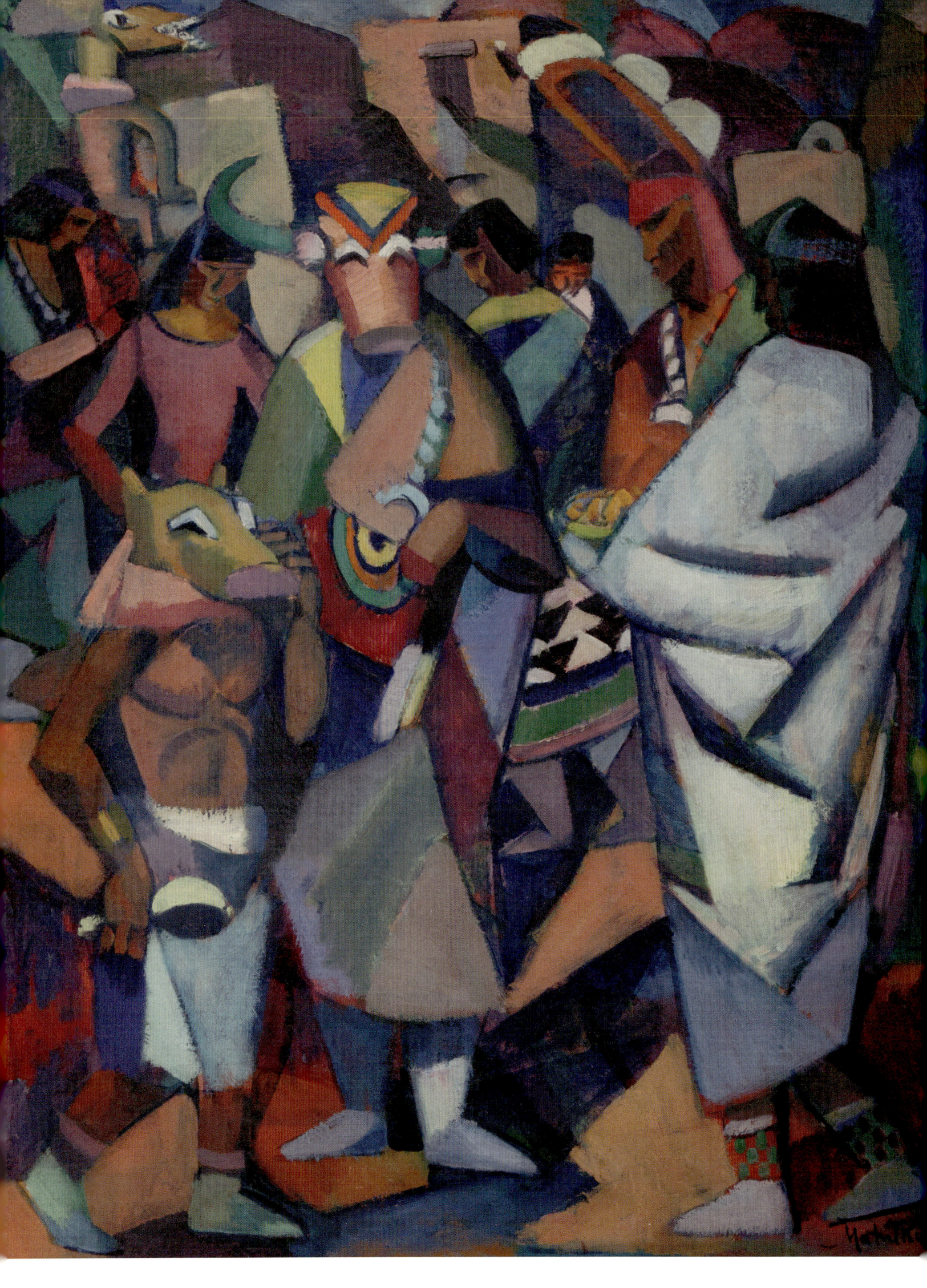

FACING: Jan Matulka
Indian Dancers with Masks, 1918
Oil on canvas, 50 x 41¾
James R. Parks Collection
Image courtesy of the Autry National Center of the American West

European artists immigrating to this country might bring with them preconceptions of Native Americans and the American West that upon actual acquaintance with the region and its indigenous people produced distinctive work of unfamiliar type. Such was the case with Czech-born Jan Matulka, who traveled to the American Southwest in 1917–18, a decade following his arrival in New York. The experience inspired a group of nearly abstract designs in prismatic color, expressive works that capture the bright colors and kinetic activity of the native dancers. Rendered in a quasi-cubist manner, like some Picasso at the pueblo, the young Matulka's paintings are very different from anything Remington or any other earlier western specialist might have imagined.

Cowboys as Subjects

Linked with the Indian image in American culture is that of the cowboy, the essential other half of a familiar western binary. Frederic Remington in 1895 forever immortalized the type in his first sculpture, the famous *Broncho Buster* (see page 22). Many artists paid homage to the cowboy, the embodiment of western horsemanship and manliness. Sometimes he was treated in documentary fashion; more often romanticized. In 1976, two Kentucky sisters made a Bicentennial gift of Remington's famous bronze to the White House, where they thought its presence might "inspire a feeling of strength and determination of the American spirit."[7] Ever since, the *Broncho Buster* has kept presidential company in the Oval Office, close by his desk and strategically aligned with the image of Lady Liberty's torch that hangs above it, providing strength and determination. Remington's cowboy, in addition to his role as western hero—or as advertisement for denims, salsa, Marlboros, and the like—now bears added responsibilities as a symbol of the American character, a national icon.

Even as Remington was modeling and painting the cowboy, he realized that the West his subject symbolized was vanishing. "The West is all played out in its romantic aspects," he lamented in 1894.[8] A year later, when Remington modeled the *Broncho Buster*, he also mourned the change in paint. His canvas *The Fall of the Cowboy* (1895) illustrates the transformation of the West, as barriers and barbed wire block the freedoms of an earlier day.

7 William Kloss, *Art in the White House: A Nation's Pride*, 2nd ed. (Washington, DC: White House Historical Association, 2008), 20–23.

8 "Remington's Fame Was Won Quickly," *New York Herald*, January 14, 1894; quoted in Michael Edward Shapiro and Peter H. Hassrick, *Frederic Remington: The Masterworks* (New York: Harry N. Abrams, 1988), 118.

Frederic Remington
The Fall of the Cowboy, 1895
Oil on canvas, 25 x 35⅛
Amon Carter Museum of American Art, Fort Worth, Texas, 1961.230

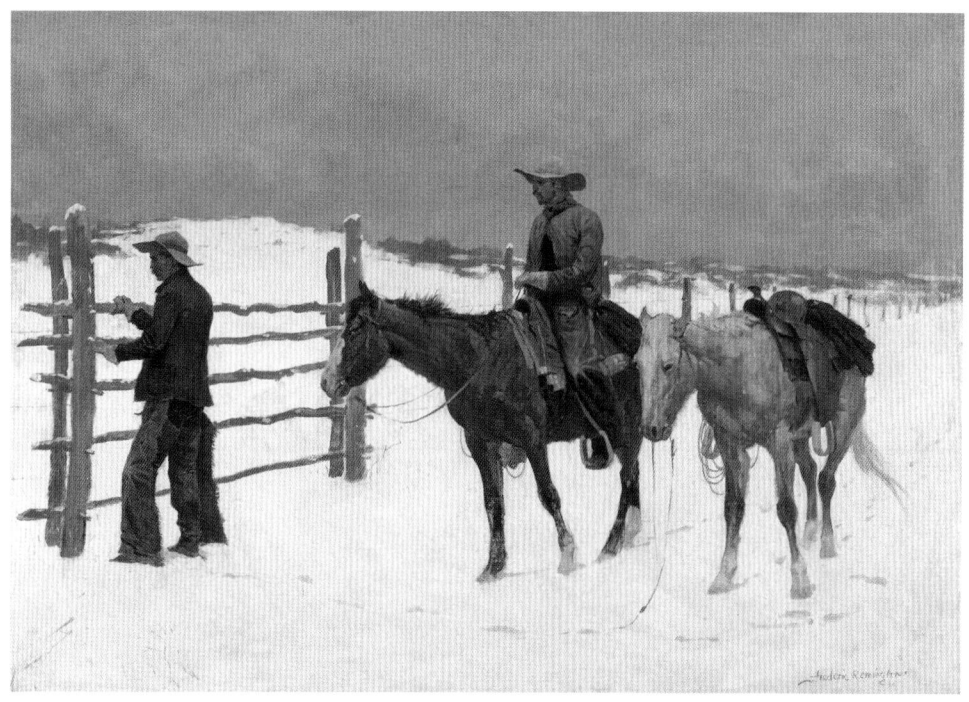

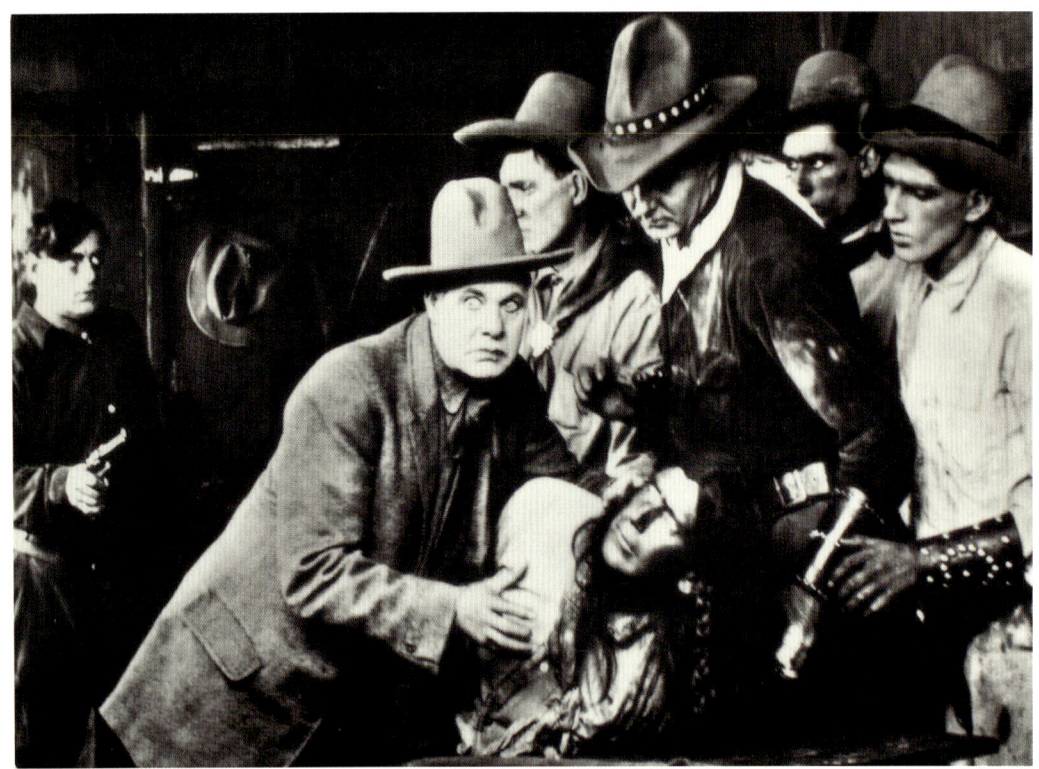

LEFT: Still from *Broncho Billy and the Redskin*, 1914
Billy Rose Theatre Division, The New York Public Library for the Performing Arts, Astor, Lenox and Tilden Foundations

BELOW: Film set for a silent western featuring Broncho Billy at Essanay Film Studio, Chicago, Ill., about 1910. Color reproduction of photographic print, Chicago History Museum, ICHi-16886

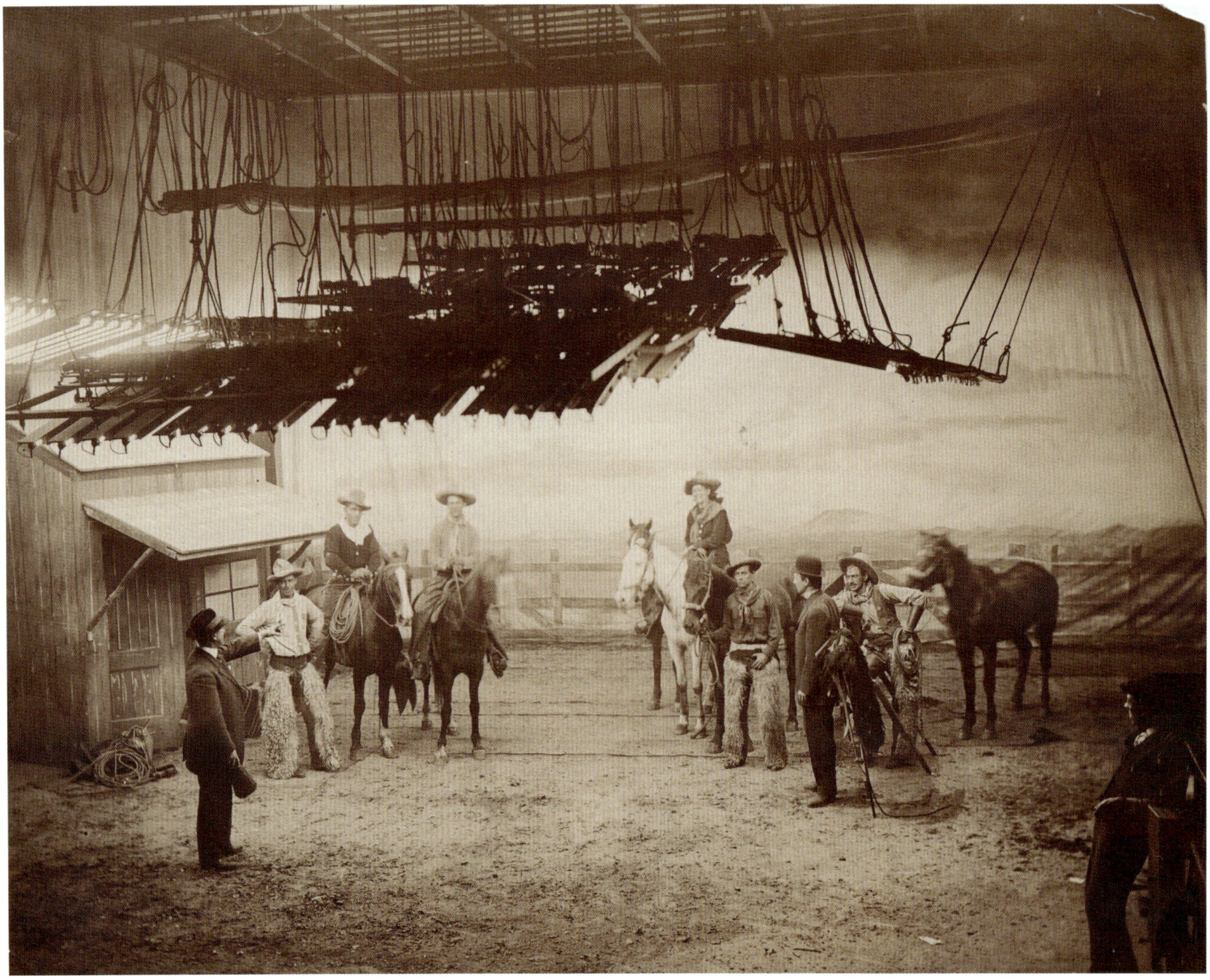

If paint and bronze recorded the cowboy's "fall" in the 1890s, in other media shortly after the turn of the century he appeared very much alive. In 1903 the Edison Studios in New York produced the first narrative film made in America, *The Great Train Robbery*. Its introduction of the cowboy subject into moving pictures thrilled viewers—especially its famous footage of a gunslinger shooting directly at the audience—and in short order led to a new cinematic genre, the western. By 1910, when one out of every five films produced by Americans was a western, a prominent producer acknowledged "it's a funny thing, this moving picture business. It has revivified the decadent cowboy of the frontier and made him live again in the eyes of the people. In the East, a picture of ranch life is one of the biggest drawing cards a film theater can show. They are wanted everywhere."[9]

It was also a funny thing, or so it seemed to some critics, that many of these early "westerns" were filmed in the East, products of studios in or near New York City. By the end of the century's first decade a surfeit of Eastern westerns led to critics' complaints about the evident fiction of posses dashing down New Jersey's leafy lanes, cowboys roaming Connecticut's gentle slopes, or, more egregious yet, studio interiors simulating the great American West. In 1909 one reviewer sagely advised that "cowboys, Indians and Mexicans must be seen in proper scenic backgrounds to convey any impression of reality."[10] In a similar vein, another writer in 1911 mused on the waning enthusiasm for the Eastern westerns and wondered, "Is there any hope for the survival of Western subjects?" He answered his own question with advice to filmmakers: "There is a little, but not much. The Western subject might gain a renewed lease of life if it made a change of base . . . What the markets need is a change of background."[11]

Among the first firms to locate away from the East was Essanay ("S and A") Film Manufacturing Company, established in Chicago in 1907. Essanay's co-founder, Gilbert M. Anderson (the "A" of Essanay), had parlayed a role—actually, several roles—in Edison's *Great Train Robbery* into a career as film actor, writer, director, and producer. By late 1909, he boldly announced his intent to release a western every Saturday.[12] With hundreds of releases to its credit before he left the firm in 1916, Anderson apparently made good on his boast. As an actor Anderson was best known for his leading role in the *Broncho Billy* series, one of the first movie franchises. Today he is remembered on Hollywood's Walk of Fame as the father of the movie cowboy and the first western star.

Anderson believed that "no matter how gifted the actor, he cannot get the true spirit, the life color, and the touches that make for vivid character delineation unless dwelling for some time among the [western] types, immediately before he attempts to impersonate them."[13] In order to get the appropriate spirit for Essanay's popular, fifteen-minute "one-reelers," Anderson planned to film on location in the West. "We have some good stories to put on out there," he explained to a reporter in 1909, suggesting mining tales in Colorado, ranching subjects in Montana or Wyoming, scenic subjects along Oregon's Columbia River or from the Yosemite Valley. "We are taking everything for production purposes with us. We intend to and will break all records in the line of western pictures."[14] His forays proved productive, and profitable too, so much so that in 1912 the company established a western studio at Niles, California, and began shooting numerous films in scenic locales in the San Francisco Bay area and further south.

The decade had begun with worries about the demise of the (Eastern) western, but by its end the cowboy flourished anew in the West. That was, wrote one journalist, "the one domain, which the camera has made distinctively its own . . . It is not a real country," he noted. "It bears about the same relation to the actual West that a Sherlock Holmes story does to an ordinary detective's existence." But it was there that "the moving picture has created its own empire of romance."[15]

Remington's cowboy hadn't fallen after all. If no longer at home on the range, he had found a new home—indeed, a new empire—at the nickelodeon. As one early critic predicted, "there will always be a perceptible demand for these cowboy, ranch life, [and] Indian subjects, which, after all, are racy of the soil; that is to say, typically American."[16]

---

9 William Wright (of Kalem Co., film producers), quoted in "Western Types Are in Vogue," *Los Angeles Times*, December 2, 1910. The number of westerns is given by Robert Anderson, "The Role of the Western Film Genre in Industry Competition, 1907–1911," *Journal of the University Film Association* 31, no. 2 (Spring 1979): 25, note 65.

10 An unsigned critique of Eastern westerns, *New York Dramatic Mirror*, June 5, 1909; quoted in Anderson, "The Role of the Western Film Genre," 24. Foregrounds could also present problems, for instance, costumes. One western cattleman complained, "We've seen too many of these hair-pants heroes from Hoboken" ("Motion Pictures Spoil Wild West Exhibition," *Rocky Mountain News*, April 20, 1919).

11 "The Passing of the Western Subject" (editorial), *The Nickelodeon*, February 18, 1911; quoted in Scott Simmon, *The Invention of the Western Film: A Cultural History of the Genre's First Half-Century* (Cambridge, UK: Cambridge University Press, 2003), 32.

12 *Motion Picture World*, November 6, 1909, 638; cited in Andrew Brodie Smith, *Shooting Cowboys and Indians: Silent Western Films, American Culture, and the Birth of Hollywood* (Boulder: University Press of Colorado, 2003), 49.

13 James S. McQuade, "Essanay's Western Producer G. M. Anderson," *Film Index*, July 23, 1910, 11; quoted in Smith, *Shooting Cowboys and Indians*, 50.

14 Gilbert M. Anderson, quoted in *Views and Films Index*, October 2, 1909, 9; quoted in Smith, *Shooting Cowboys and Indians*, 37.

15 Randolph Bartlett, "Where Do We Ride from Here?" *Photoplay*, February 1919, 36.

16 "Charles Baumann Goes West," *The Moving Picture World* 7, no. 7 (August 13, 1910): 344.

Landscape

Gunfights that punctuated many western films in the 1910s also frequently appeared in American paintings and illustrations, dime novels, and other entertainments of the period. They echoed as well on distant shores as warfare erupted in Europe in the summer of 1914, soon to engulf the continent in multinational conflict. Although the United States remained officially neutral for nearly three years, Americans were preoccupied with events "Over There" and their impact on life at home, concerns that only grew after Congress declared war on Germany in April 1917.

Flanders Fields and other European attractions were closed to American tourists during the war, and most American expatriates, including numerous artists, returned home at the outbreak of the conflict. With European sojourns precluded, attention turned to other attractions in North America, fueling the domestic tourism boom. For many artists, the destination of choice was the American West, not the Western Front. Jan Matulka was but one in a flock of southwestern sojourners, part of an era aptly described as "when New York went to New Mexico."[17]

The war abroad and enhanced facilities for tourism at home gave impetus to a new generation of travelers. The remarkable expansion of the national park system added to the attractions. President Theodore Roosevelt, the great champion of landscape conservation, had added five national parks during his administration (1901–9) and the count increased in the decade after he left office, leading to the creation of the National Park Service in

FACING: N. C. Wyeth, *Gunfight*, about 1916. Oil on canvas, 33½ x 24⅝ Denver Art Museum, William Sr. and Dorothy Harmsen Collection, 2001.443

BELOW: Oscar E. Berninghaus, *A Showery Day, Grand Canyon,* acquired 1915. Oil on canvas, 30 x 40. Reprinted with permission of the BNSF Railway

17 Sanford Schwartz, "When New York Went to New Mexico" (1976), in Schwartz, *The Art Presence* (New York: Horizon Press, 1982), 85–94.

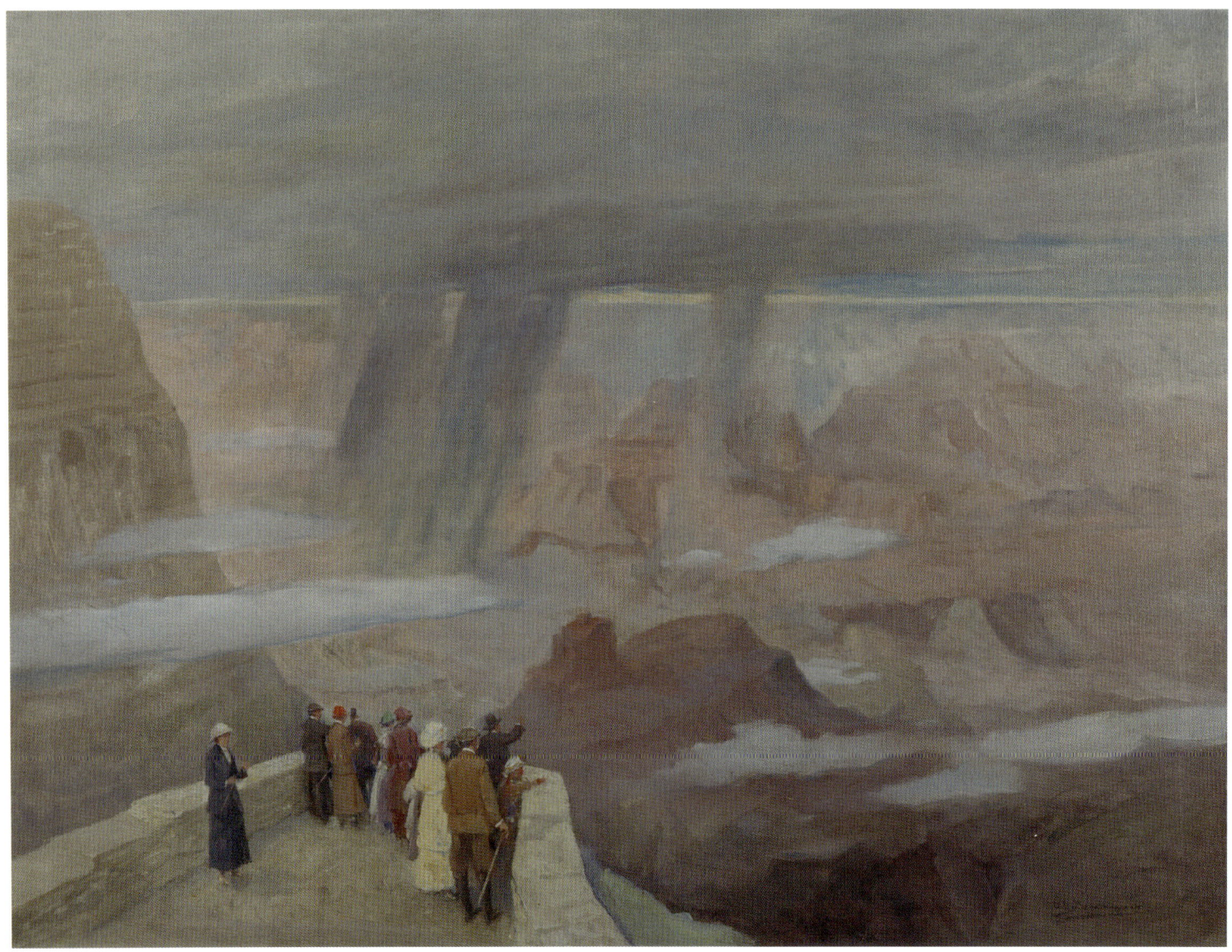

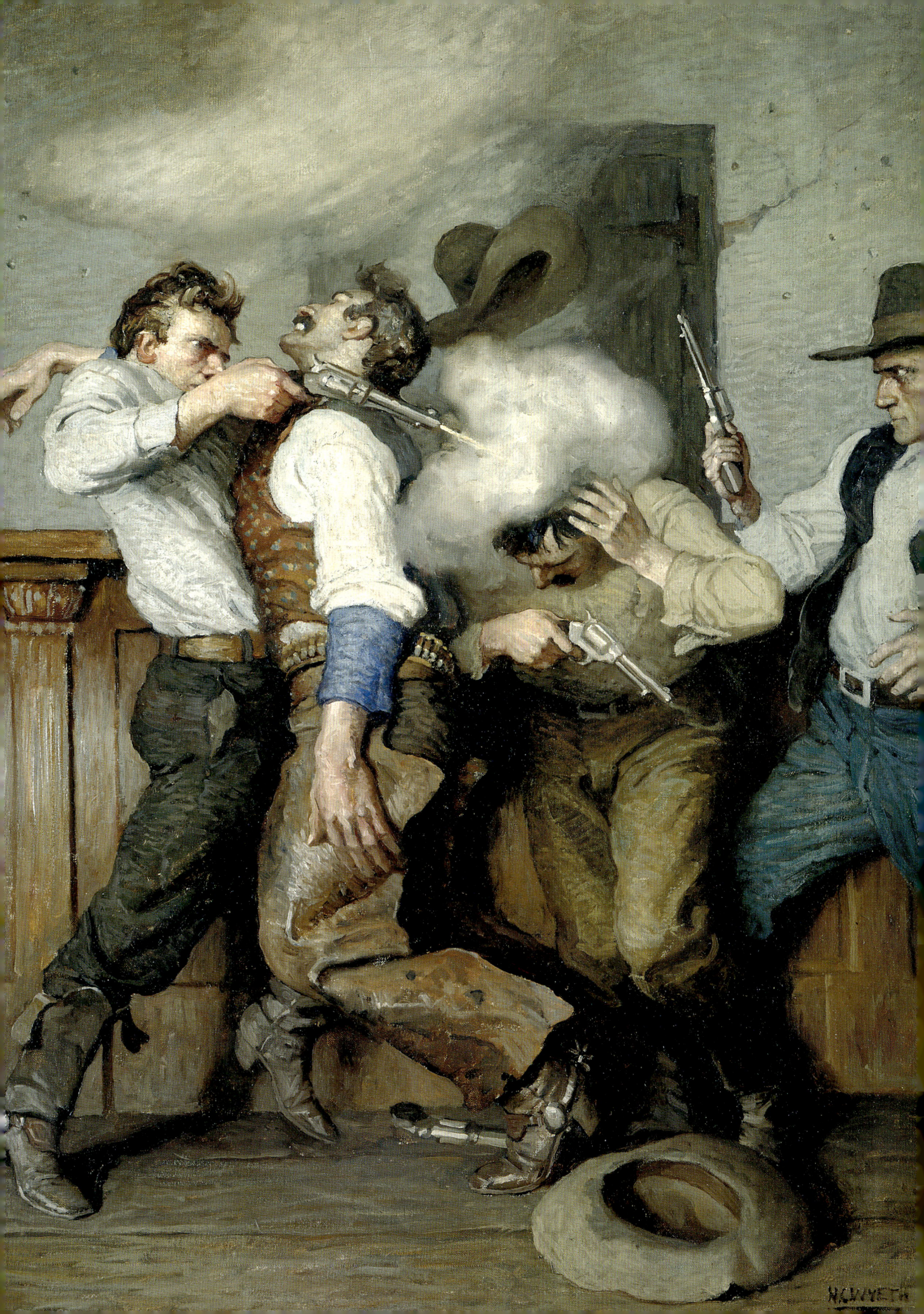

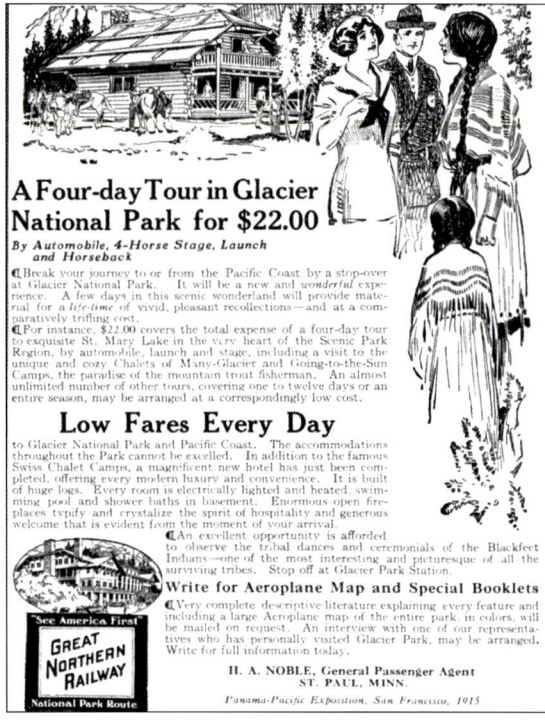
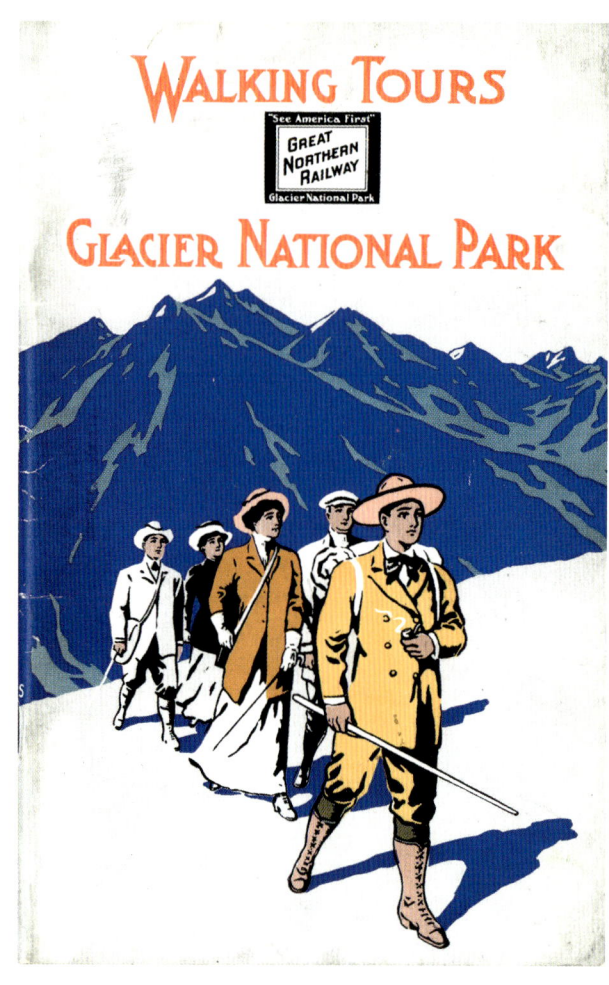

Great Northern Railway advertisement. Reproduced in front matter of *International Railway Journal* 70, no. 3 (June 1913)

Glacier National Park Walking Tours, 1916. Archives & Special Collections, Mansfield Library, The University of Montana

August 1916.[18] The expanded system of national parks provided growing numbers of visitors with scenic opportunities for recreation far from the urban centers that were beginning to dominate modern life. The parks and the railroads promoted this recreational benefit in their advertising campaigns. So too did two scientists from the University of California, Berkeley, who in 1916, the year of the National Park Service's creation, extolled the benefits of exercise in the out-of-doors. The recreation they prescribed could "restore to the human organs the normal balance which special or artificial conditions of [urban] life disturb . . . [T]he type of recreation most urgently needed . . . to-day is to be found in the open country," such as a national park. There the modern urbanite "may find entire relief from the nerve-racking drive of city life, and be brought once more into contact with primitive conditions . . . reawakening his dormant faculties . . . unaffected by the nervous tension so peculiar to town life."[19]

Hikers flocked to mountain trails. Among them were artists, many carrying their drawing materials to sketch the rugged summits or canyon depths. In August 1917 Georgia O'Keeffe joined them, traveling from her teaching position in Canyon, Texas, to the recently designated Rocky Mountain National Park, near Estes Park, Colorado. En route her train crossed New Mexico, and she marveled at the landscape: "Not like anything I ever saw before—I want to stop everywhere—." She was struck by the scale of the place—"There is so much more space between the ground and the sky out here it is tremendous"—and it made her want to stay. "I've wanted to stop [at] most every station," she wrote.[20] But the train continued northward, soon bringing her first glimpse of the Rockies.

O'Keeffe spent several weeks in the Colorado mountains, hiking in the area between Boulder and Estes Park. She wrote ecstatically of one day's trek near Mount Audubon and Stapp Lakes, above the small town of Ward: "It was wonderful—so bare and lonesome—looked over the lake at the snow spotted bare mountain—the ground underfoot covered

18 During Roosevelt's presidency, the following national parks were created: Crater Lake, Oregon (1902); Wind Cave, South Dakota (1903); Sully's Hill, North Dakota (1914, later became a game preserve); Platt, Oklahoma (1906, now part of the Chickasaw National Recreation Area); and Mesa Verde, Colorado (1906). Roosevelt failed in only one attempt, to so designate the Grand Canyon in Arizona, but he declared it a National Monument in 1908. Added to the national parks in the decade after Roosevelt's tenure were Glacier, Montana (1910); Rocky Mountain, Colorado (1915); Lassen Volcanic, California (1916); Denali, Alaska (1917); Zion, Utah (1919); and finally Grand Canyon, Arizona (1919), the year of Roosevelt's death.

19 Joseph Grinnell and Tracy I. Storer, "Animal Life as an Asset of National Parks," *Science* n.s. 44, no. 1,133 (September 15, 1916): 375–76.

20 Georgia O'Keeffe to Alfred Stieglitz, 15 August 1917; in Sarah Greenough, ed., *My Faraway One: Selected Letters of Georgia O'Keeffe and Alfred Stieglitz* (New Haven: Yale University Press, 2011), 181–82.

21 Georgia O'Keeffe to Alfred Stieglitz, 21? August 1917; in Greenough, *My Faraway One*, 182.

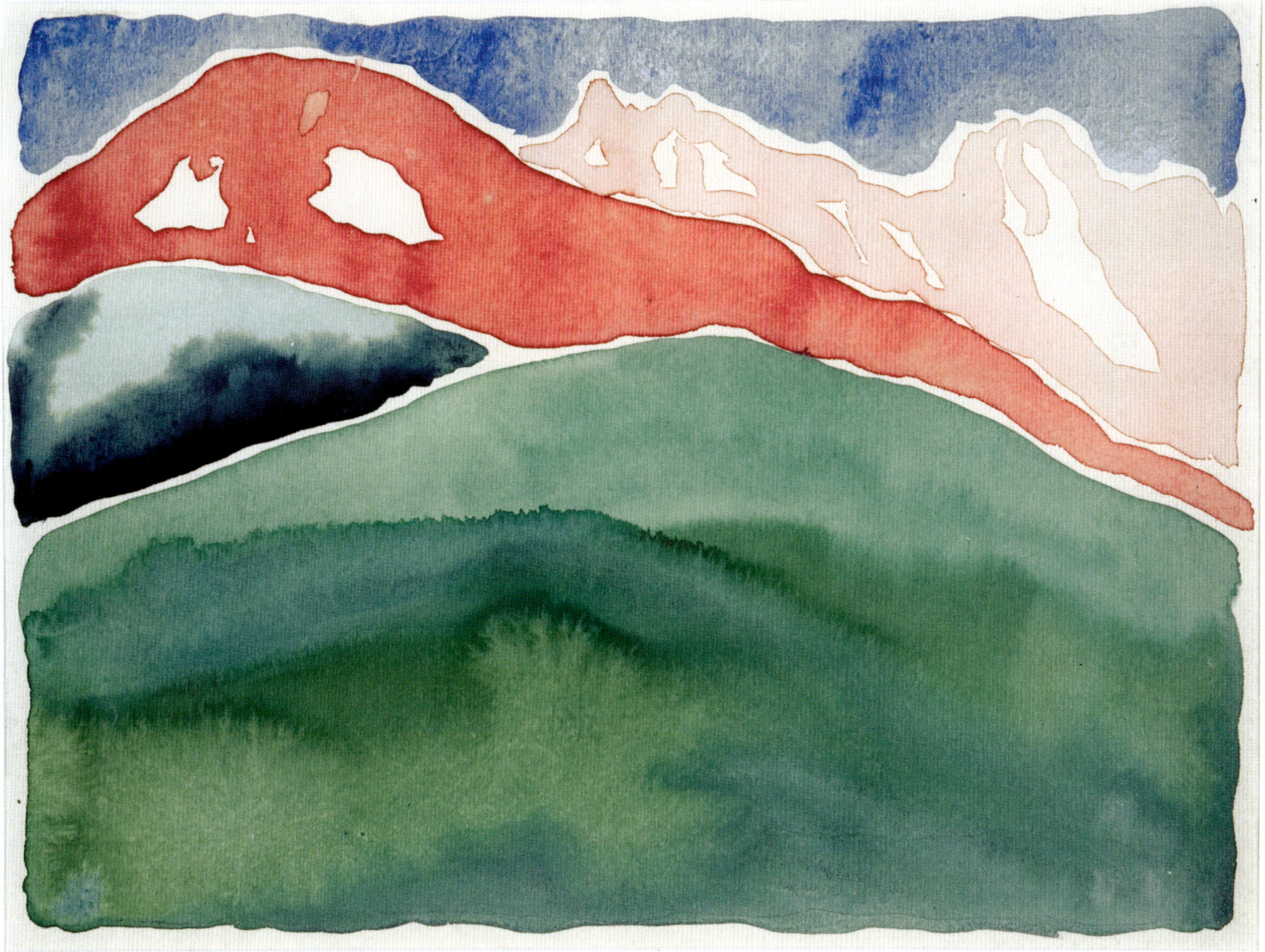

ABOVE: Georgia O'Keeffe, *Pink and Green Mountains, No. 1*, 1917 Watercolor on paper, 8⅞ x 11⅞. Spencer Museum of Art, The University of Kansas, museum purchase: Letha Churchill Walker Memorial Art Fund, 1977.0043. ©2013 Georgia O'Keeffe Museum / Artists Rights Society (ARS), New York

INSET: Unidentified photographer, *Georgia O'Keeffe and Friend in Estes Park, Colorado*, 1917. Photographic print, 2¼ x 3¼. Georgia O'Keeffe Museum, gift of The Georgia O'Keeffe Foundation (2006-06-0751). Image courtesy of the Georgia O'Keeffe Museum

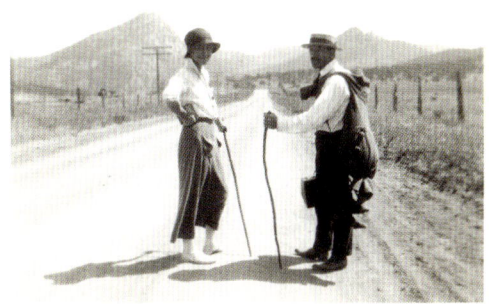

with brilliant flowers—."[21] With pencils she sketched the view, inscribing the simple contours of the land; then she used the drawings as the basis for watercolors that distilled the Rocky Mountain landscape. With saturated washes of brilliant hue, her watercolors initially incorporated the particulars of the site—flowers, pines, snowy peaks—but, as her focus rose from the foreground plane to the lofty summits, the patterns grew simpler, finally resulting in a series of five paintings of pink and green mountains. Nothing in the long history of western landscape painting had prepared viewers for the startling simplicity and assuredness of O'Keeffe's modern vision. No other Rockies looked remotely like hers, miracles of abbreviation in a landscape whose every detail had been painstakingly catalogued by earlier generations of naturalistically inclined artists.

O'Keeffe's watercolors of the western peaks were unique, but hers was not the only attempt to paint the country in a modern manner. In 1914, motivated by the war's outbreak, John E. Thompson returned from a long Parisian residence to his home in Buffalo, New York. That fall, attracted by the railroads' promotional campaigns celebrating Colorado's

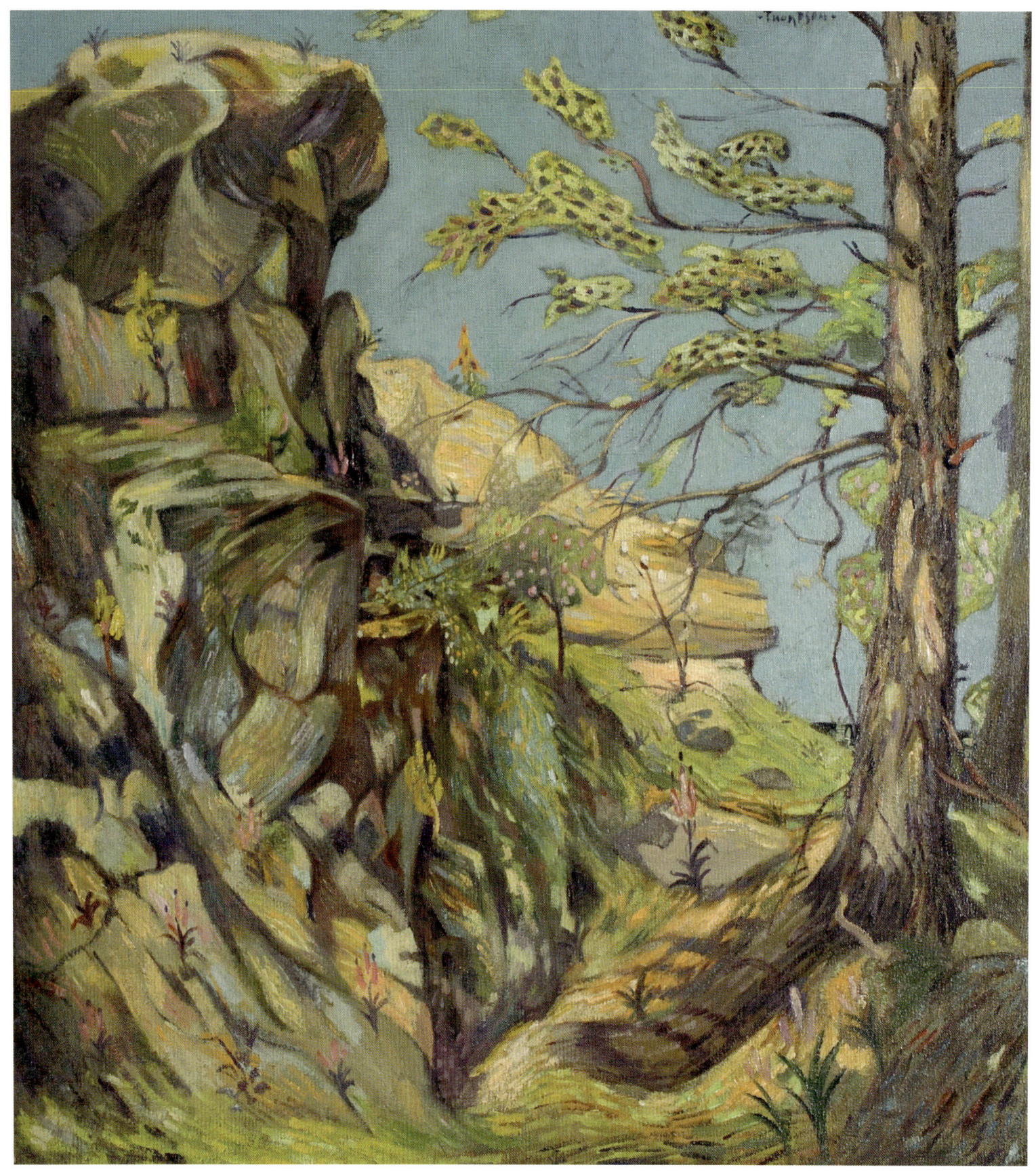

John E. Thompson
Organization of Rocks and Trees, 1919
Oil on canvas, 27 x 25
Collection of Deborah and Warren Wadsworth, Denver

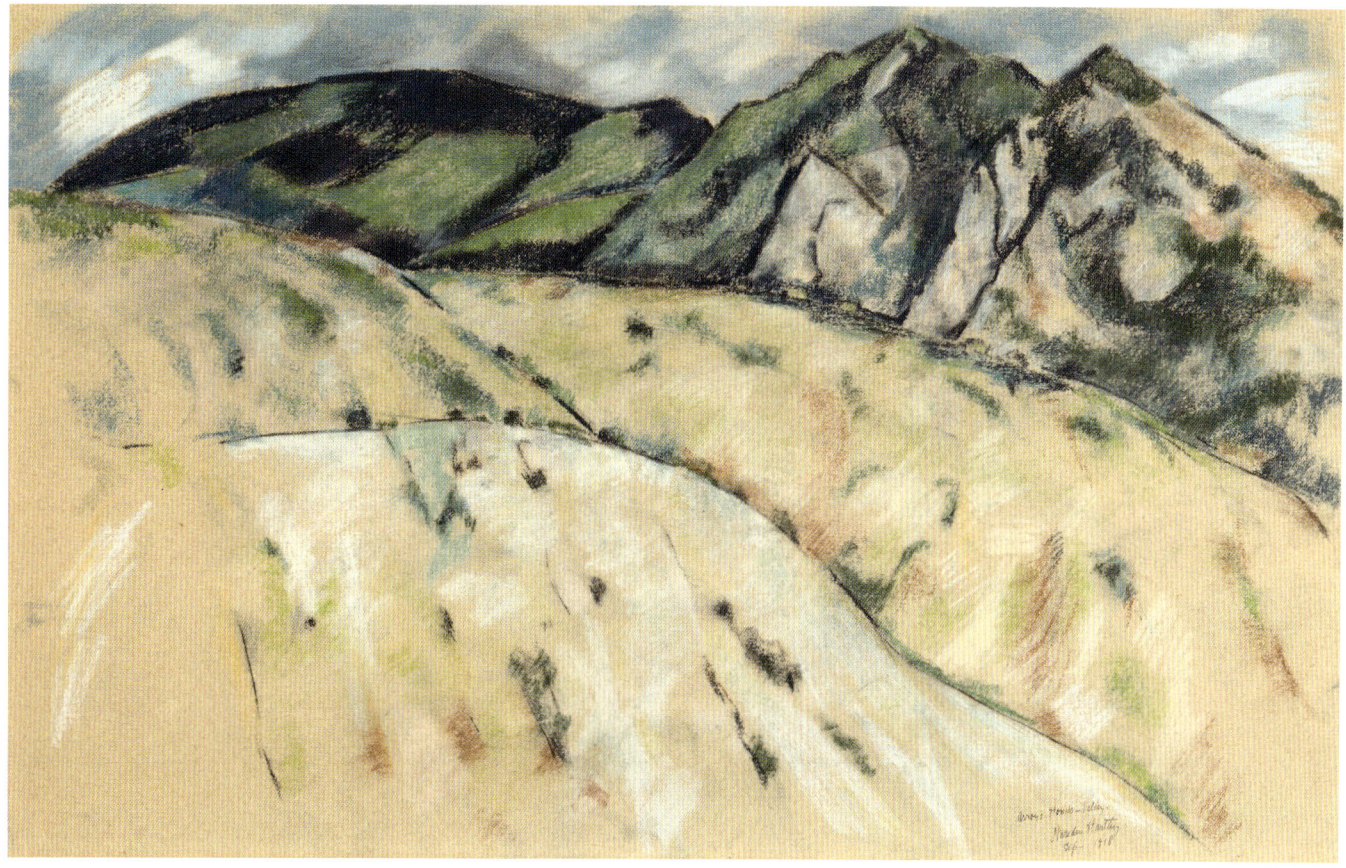

Marsden Hartley
Arroyo Hondo, Valdez, 1918
Pastel on paper, 17 x 27½
Collection of Phoenix Art Museum,
Gift of Mrs. Oliver B. James. Photo by
Ken Howie. ©Estate of Marsden Hartley,
Yale University Committee on
Intellectual Property

22 "Library Art Exhibit Called 'Fraud' and 'Monstrosity' by Two Writers," *Rocky Mountain News*, April 16, 1919.

rugged country and brilliant sunlight, he visited the small mountain town of Pine, southwest of Denver. Inspired by the country, he returned three years later to settle in Denver and devote himself to painting the Colorado landscape. To the subject Thompson brought a vision schooled in the rigors of Paul Cézanne, whose memorial exhibition he had visited in Paris in 1907, and informed by Old Master paintings and artful Asian designs, both of which he studied in the Louvre, plus his familiarity with contemporary innovations, most notably cubism. His distinctive approach yielded an expressive treatment of the landscape unlike earlier western views. In April 1919, Thompson and several of his students and confederates—Walter Mruk, Józef Bakós, and Alexander Korda—included their novel views in the Twenty-fifth Annual Exhibition of the Denver Art Association, where they perhaps predictably aroused great controversy. Letters to the local press dismissed the ensemble as a "fraud upon the public" and a "monstrosity," with Thompson's *Organization of Rocks and Trees* (1919) singled out for its "downright idiocy of conception."[22] Based on this reception, the enterprise earned a local reputation as the "Denver Armory Show."

Further south there were similar departures from tradition by artists in New Mexico. In 1918 Andrew Dasburg accepted an invitation to visit New Mexico from his friend, Mabel Dodge (Luhan), herself a recent arrival in Taos. Dasburg, a veteran of the famous New York Armory Show, brought to the Southwest a sophisticated appreciation of abstraction and shortly began to apply his vision to the inspiring space and scale of New Mexico. His gridded land- and townscapes from the 1920s represent the adaptation of his abstract sensibilities to western place. Other arrivals late in the 1910s similarly responded to the peculiar lay of the land and New Mexico's colors and dazzling light. For instance, in 1917 Leon Kroll painted the Santa Fe landscape with rhymed rotundities suggesting the eroded desert hills, while his friend George Bellows pitched his palette to a higher key in the brightness of a Tesuque morning. But unlike O'Keeffe, Thompson, or Dasburg, who ultimately became committed western residents, Kroll, Bellows, and many others

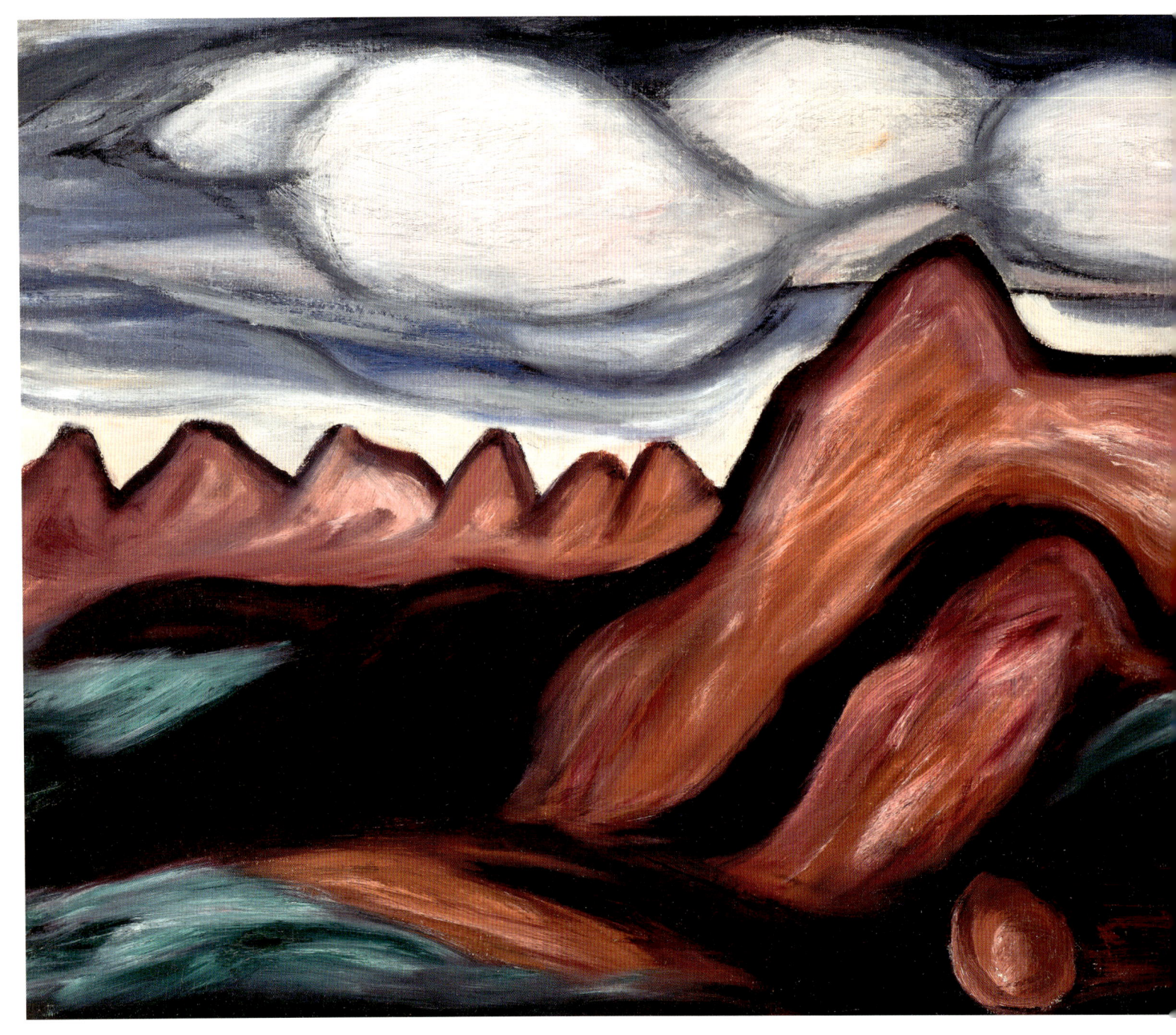

Marsden Hartley
New Mexico Recollections, No. 15, about 1923
Oil on canvas, 23 x 41⅛
Courtesy of American Museum of Western Art—
The Anschutz Collection. Photo by William J. O'Connor
©Estate of Marsden Hartley, Yale University
Committee on Intellectual Property

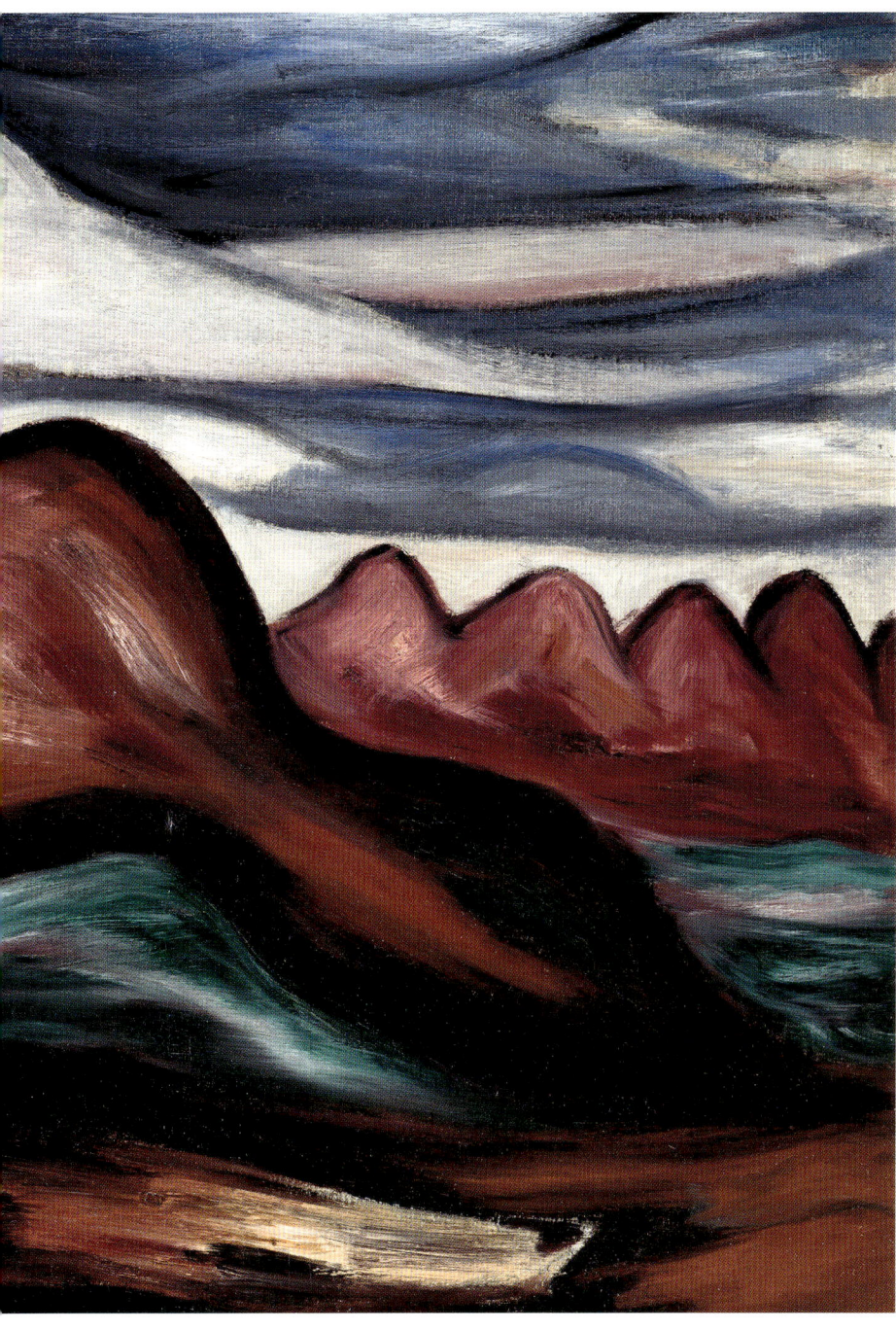

experienced the West as a place of temporary inspiration, a tourist destination.

Nevertheless, even a relatively short visit could produce a very long effect on an artist's work. Marsden Hartley arrived in New Mexico in 1918, another of Mabel Dodge's guests in Taos. One of the last American expatriates to return from wartime Europe, Hartley left his beloved Berlin late in 1915 and resumed a peripatetic career that eventually brought him west. In New Mexico he wrote ecstatically of his repatriation: "I am an American discovering America. I like the position and I like the results."[23] Hartley's exclamation fulfilled the aspirations of the "See America First" boosters, who described their intent to promote "the discovery of America by Americans."[24] But those early champions of western tourism could not have foreseen the pictorial discoveries that Hartley would make in the northern New Mexican landscape. With dazzling pastels—a medium seemingly well suited to the dry country, but surprisingly seldom employed by others—Hartley described the tumescent sand hills, glowing recesses, and serrated skyline of the desert country. On canvases he surveyed the terrain with richly brushed oils, capturing its contours in saturated, expressive hues. The lava-like intensity of his New Mexico views continued after he left the state in 1919. The landscape grew even darker and stormier in a series of *New Mexico Recollections* that he painted in New York and subsequently in Europe, reaching a climax in Berlin where he finally exorcised the memory in 1924.

Hartley was inspired by the same topography that stirred other artists in the West, yet his discoveries—and particularly his *Recollections*—seem fraught with an intensity that is highly personal. His views certainly differ from artists of an earlier generation, like the Society of Men Who Paint the Far West, who, as one of their members explained, sought motifs that "further the National spirit in art."[25] By contrast Hartley's was a very distinctive and modern response to the land, rendered in expressionistic black and bloodred. For him and his modernist cohort, the West was the locus of individual discovery, its image a personal icon more than a national symbol.

For her invaluable help with the preparation of this essay, I am grateful to my research assistant, Samantha Lyons, and I thank the Hall Family Foundation for its generous support of my work through the Kansas University Endowment Association.

23 Marsden Hartley, "America as Landscape," *El Palacio* 5 (December 12, 1918): 340.

24 C. F. Carter to Salt Lake City Commercial Club, 19 October 1905; quoted in Shaffer, "'See America First':" 63.

25 Dewitt Parshall, "Society of Men Who Paint for Far West" [sic], *Exhibition of Paintings by Men Who Paint the Far West, Twelve American Artists and Sandor Landeau*, exh. cat. (Detroit: Detroit Museum of Art, 1916), n.p.

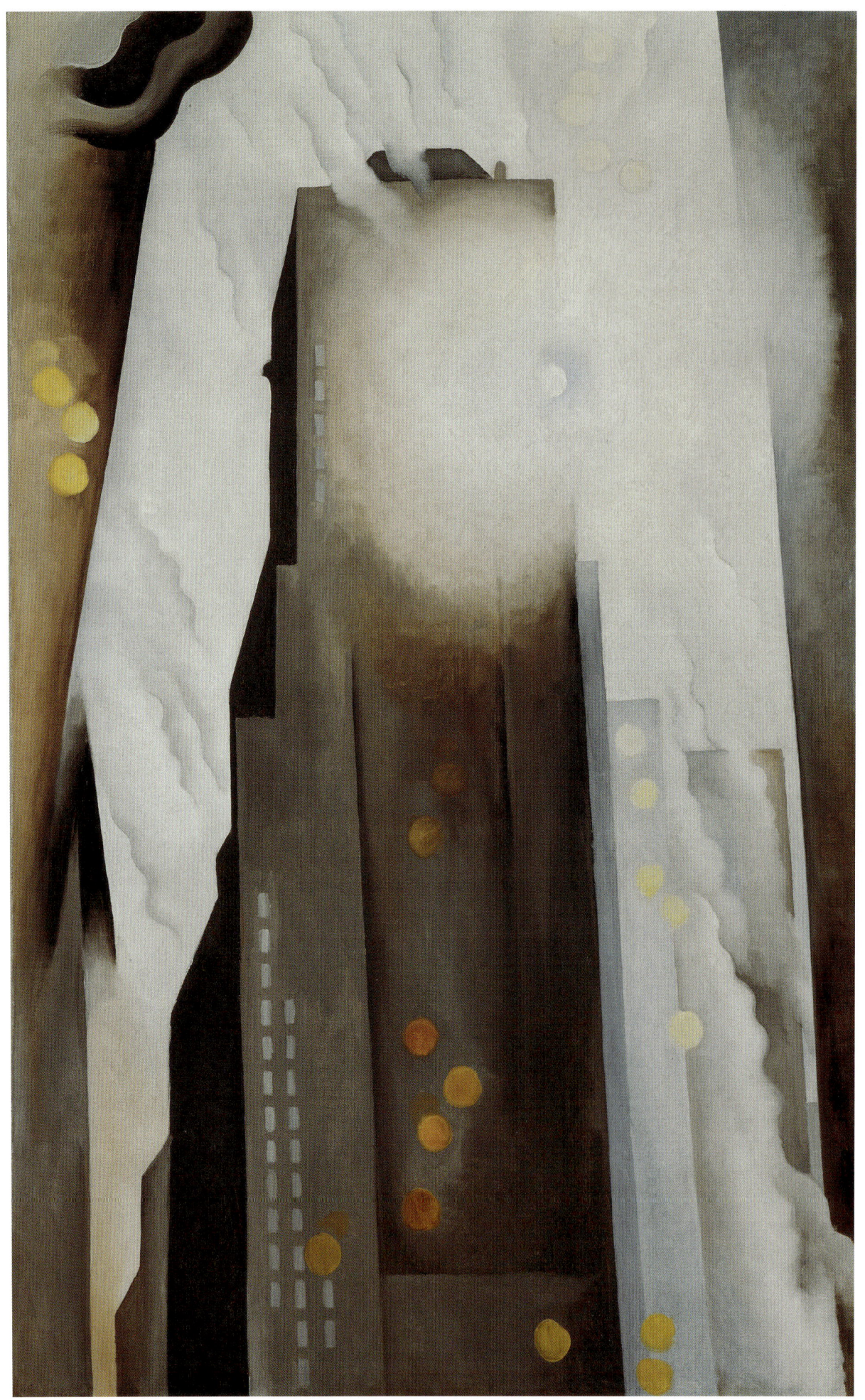

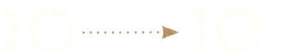

You Ain't ~~Heard~~ *Seen* Nothin' Yet
American Art in the 1920s

RANDALL R. GRIFFEY

TAKING NOTHING AWAY from the artistic accomplishments of Georgia O'Keeffe, John Marin, and others on which this essay will soon focus, the title of this overview of the 1920s takes as its inspiration—riffs on, you might even say—one of the most popular aesthetic spectacles of the decade: the film *The Jazz Singer*. Debuting in New York on October 6, 1927, *The Jazz Singer* tells the story of Jakie Rabinowitz, played by Al Jolson, who in defiance of his strict Jewish father leaves home to pursue his dreams of becoming a successful jazz entertainer. Featuring new Vitaphone technology, which allowed for simultaneous video and audio, *The Jazz Singer* introduced the era of "the talkie" and, at the same time, signaled the gradual demise of the silent film.

An illuminating window on the 1920s, *The Jazz Singer* highlights one of the chief characteristics that defined American culture of the period: a pervasive, optimistic belief in change and, even more, progress. One well-known segment opens with Jolson enticing his audience with his signature line, "You ain't heard nothin' yet," a statement that gained new, perhaps even unintended significance as the first sentence of synchronized speech uttered in a motion picture. The statement introduces "Toot, Toot, Tootsie," a song about lovers saying goodbye at a train station, an exchange overheard and conveyed by Jolson as the song's narrator.

Among other aspects of American culture in the late 1920s, *The Jazz Singer* highlights the degree to which white audiences had enthusiastically appropriated early jazz, interpreting it as a public, communal rejection of puritanical and Victorian values and mores. Rendered considerably more opaque by the passage of time from the early twentieth century to the early twenty-first is the implicit message of Jolson's lighthearted performance, itself a signifier of profound cultural change. Ten years earlier, as thousands of American men decamped for war in Europe, it was inconceivable that a song describing a goodbye between sweethearts at a train station would have exhibited such a jaunty, frivolous flair. The end of the Great War—or, as H. G. Wells erroneously described it, "the war that will end war"—was cause for celebration, and jazz served, among other social functions, as a kind of salve as the nation recovered and a hopeful reminder that, as another song produced two years later put it, "Happy Days Are Here Again." They wouldn't last for long, of course, but that's another story, one told in the essay that follows in this volume.

But for the time being, as much of Europe lay in ruins, progress seemed to many to be America's enviable fate; the country's destiny a seemingly inexhaustible wellspring of new ideas and ceaseless innovation. In the United States, buildings grew taller and taller, automobiles—most notably, Henry Ford's Model T (first released in 1908)—became faster and more affordable, fruits and vegetables became bigger and hardier, and new species of flowers seduced their admirers with larger blooms and more brilliant color.

Georgia O'Keeffe
The Shelton with Sunspots, N.Y., 1926
Oil on canvas, 48½ × 30¼
Gift of Leigh B. Block, 1985.206,
The Art Institute of Chicago. ©2013 Georgia O'Keeffe Museum / Artists Rights Society (ARS), New York

This apparent deluge of invention and innovation bred a particularly excitable brand of hero worship in the 1920s, one made explicit in, among other sources, Eva March Tappan's *Heroes of Progress: Stories of Successful Americans*, a compendium of biographies of thirty then-renowned Americans published in 1921.[1] Some of these names—Alexander Graham Bell, Andrew Carnegie, and Thomas Edison—will ring clearly in twenty-first-century ears; others—Luther Burbank, the "Plant Breeder"; Elias Howe, the "Inventor of the Sewing Machine"; and John Wanamaker, "Founder of the Department Store" perhaps seem less familiar now. Interestingly, Tappan included two artists in this distinguished company: sculptor Augustus Saint-Gaudens, creator of the poignant Shaw Memorial on the edge of the Boston Common, in addition to other memorable works; and illustrator and muralist Edwin Austin Abbey, whose efforts, including his monumental decorations on the theme of the Holy Grail in the Boston Public Library, rarely, if ever, garner even a mention in art history circles today.

Just as they did in fields of industry and science, ideas of progress permeated literary and artistic circles throughout the 1920s. Among the clearest—if, in retrospect somewhat unexpected—manifestations of this phenomenon is the impassioned argument against the Tariff Act of 1921 that the art advocate, collector, and lawyer John Quinn delivered before the Senate Committee on Finance. Asserting that art should not be counted among other imported luxuries and, thus, should not be subject to proposed new tariffs, Quinn emphasized most of all the adverse effects that such impediments to international trade and cultural exchange would have on the arts in the United States. As the collector put it: "New ideas of progress and reform in philosophy, politics, and the fine arts are in the air. To some these new ideas are disquieting. To others, they are liberating and hopeful . . . Progress in the arts as well as in philosophy and in politics is one of the finest and most exhilarating things of our time."[2]

Attesting to the existence and importance of "progress" in contemporary art, the avant-garde Quinn likely had in mind less the creative efforts of Saint-Gaudens and Abbey than the dynamic—indeed, for many "disquieting"—aesthetic ferment that followed in the wake of the International Exhibition of Modern Art, the so-called Armory Show, in 1913, an exhibition that he opened with a triumphant public address.[3] In addition to featuring a respectable survey of recent American painting and sculpture, the Armory Show constituted a veritable master class on European modernism, including the post-impressionist visions of Paul Gauguin and Paul Cézanne and the even more radical creations of Marcel Duchamp, whose *Nude Descending a Staircase (No. 2)* became the exhibition's *cause célèbre*. That Quinn acquired an early version of Duchamp's notorious composition for his renowned collection speaks to his admiration of the French artistic revolutionary, with whom he subsequently became friends.[4] Duchamp himself arrived in New York in 1915, and, in 1920, helped to found the Société Anonyme, a small but influential group devoted to promoting avant-garde art whose activities spanned most of the decade.

However, for most New Yorkers (and many outlying Americans), proof of national progress was nowhere more self-evident than the ever-evolving, ever-growing New York skyline. Almost inevitably, artists and writers were compelled to engage with it. But how to depict the city, a living organism that Duchamp had designated a work of art itself? The proliferation of skyscrapers caused streets to evolve (or, depending on your perspective, to devolve) into canyons with manmade cliffs blocking much of the sky above, and, simultaneously, offered artists views of their surroundings previously bestowed mainly to winged creatures. Thus, the question lingered: was the city best seen and understood from below or from above?

1 Eva March Tappan, *Heroes of Progress: Stories of Successful Americans* (Boston, MA: Houghton Mifflin Company, 1921). For a expansive overview of the 1920s, see Teresa A. Carbone, ed., *Youth and Beauty: Art of the American Twenties* (Brooklyn, NY: Brooklyn Museum), 2011.

2 John Quinn, quoted in *Hearings Before the Committee on Finance, United States Senate, on the Proposed Tariff Act of 1921*, rev. and ed. (Washington, DC: Government Printing Office, 1922), 5,026.

3 For an authoritative account of the Armory Show, see Milton W. Brown, *The Story of the Armory Show* (Greenwich, CT: Joseph H. Hirshhorn, 1963). Brown's study commemorated the fifty-year anniversary of the exhibition's opening. As 2013 marks the Armory Show's centennial anniversary, several scholarly projects this year, including a large exhibition at the New-York Historical Society from October 11, 2013 to February 23, 2014, reexamine the show's impact and legacy.

4 On Quinn, see Judith Zilczer, "The Noble Buyer": *John Quinn, Patron of the Avant-Garde* (Washington, DC: Published for the Hirshhorn Museum and Sculpture Garden, Smithsonian Institution, by the Smithsonian Institution Press, 1978).

5 On O'Keeffe's depictions of New York, see Anna Chave, "'Who Will Paint New York?': 'The World's New Art Center' and the Skyscraper Paintings of Georgia O'Keeffe," *American Art* 5, no.1–2 (Winter/Spring 1991), 87–107.

6 O'Keeffe quoted in Blanche C. Matthias, "Georgia O'Keeffe and the Intimate Gallery: Stieglitz Showing Seven Americans," *Chicago Evening Post Magazine of the Art World*, March 2, 1926, 14; and in Barbara Buhler Lynes, *O'Keeffe, Stieglitz, and the Critics, 1916–1929* (Ann Arbor, MI: UMI Research Press, 1989), 249.

7 Concerning the development of Queens during this period, see *Queens Borough, New York City, 1910–1920; the borough of homes and industry, a descriptive and illustrated book setting forth its wonderful growth and development in commerce, industry and homes during the past ten years . . . a prediction of even greater growth during the next ten years . . . and a statement of its many advantages, attractions and possibilities as a section wherein to live, to work and to succeed* (New York: Chamber of Commerce of the Borough of Queens, 1920).

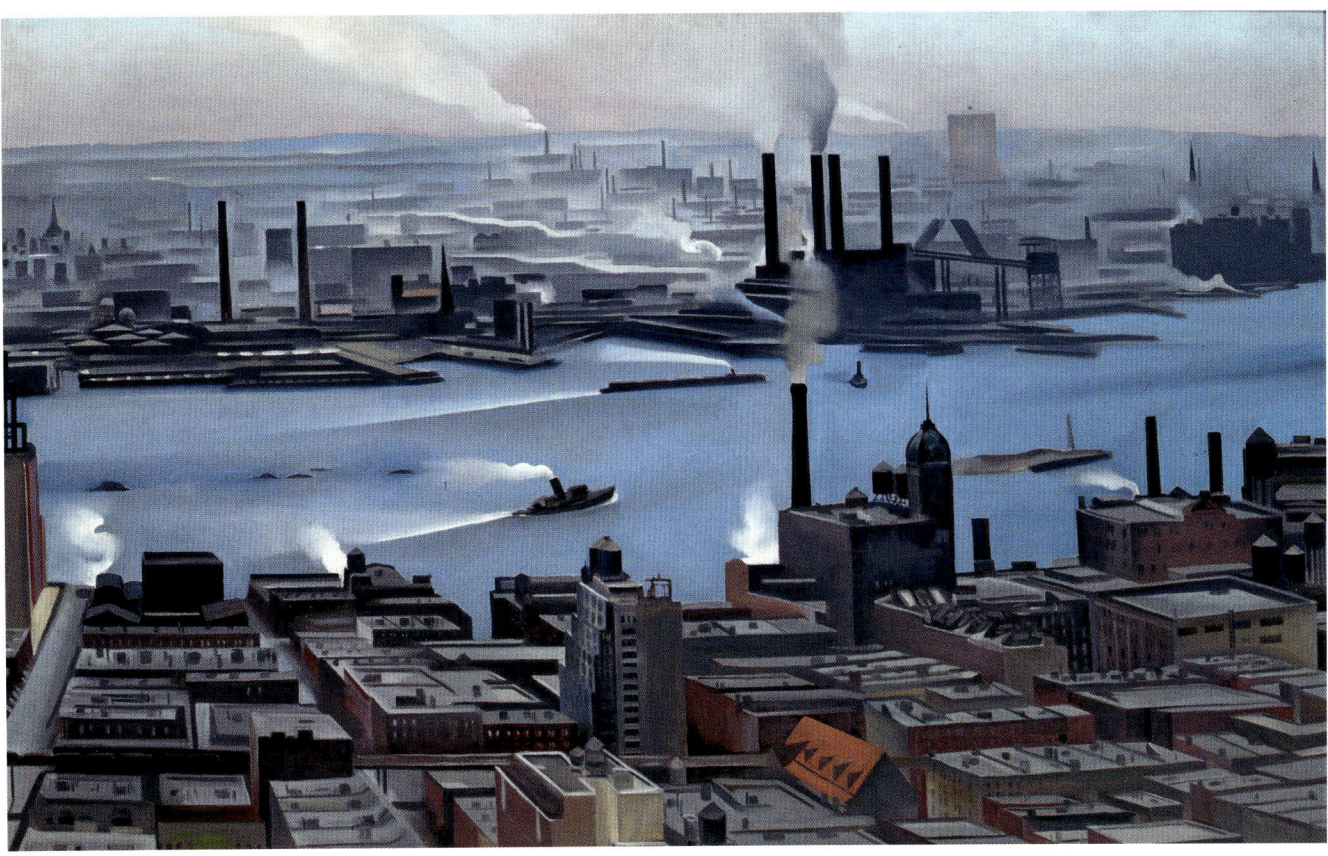

Georgia O'Keeffe, *The East River from the Thirtieth Story of the Shelton Hotel*, 1928. Oil on canvas, 38 x 48⅛. New Britain Museum of American Art, 1958.9. ©2013 Georgia O'Keeffe Museum / Artists Rights Society (ARS), New York

Georgia O'Keeffe, a Wisconsin native who moved to the Big Apple in 1918 by way of Texas, explored both vantage points.[5] In *The Shelton with Sunspots, N.Y.* (1926; see page 44), the painter depicts what might be fairly described as an ant's-eye view of the Shelton Hotel, into which she had moved with her husband, the photographer Alfred Stieglitz. One of the earliest buildings designed in accordance with New York's 1916 step-back law, intended to reduce the amount of shadow cast down onto Manhattan's increasingly dark streets, the Shelton was the tallest hotel in the world when it opened its doors to much acclaim in 1924. O'Keeffe's composition emphasizes the hotel's imposing edifice, which seems to dwarf its admirer, its upward reach reinforced by the canvas's vertical orientation. Scraping the sky, the Shelton partially eclipses the sun, rays from which form a blinding halo around its upper registers. O'Keeffe's smooth brushwork erases detail and all possible signs of conventional subtlety and elegance, transforming the Shelton into an architectural emblem of the cool, rather dehumanizing efficiency of modern American life. "One can't paint New York as it is," the painter once proclaimed, "but rather as it is felt."[6]

In *The East River from the Thirtieth Story of the Shelton Hotel*, painted two years later, O'Keeffe turned her canvas sideways to capture a panoramic, even magisterial view looking toward Long Island City. Rendered in dull tones and punctuated with factory stacks belching smoke into the air, the hazy composition asserts the increasingly industrial character of the spaces running along the river, particularly in the neighboring borough of Queens, which experienced record development in the decade leading up to O'Keeffe's painting.[7] But while borough officials touted Queens' rapid development, trumpeting in public reports that their home turf kept pace with Manhattan's growth next door, O'Keeffe's joyless, detached, and, like *The Shelton with Sunspots*, human-less portrayal of her environs betrays the painter's increasing dissatisfaction with city life, which was accentuated by regular, pleasurable respites to the country home she and Stieglitz maintained upstate near Lake George. Her first visit to New Mexico the year following, in 1929, would further stoke her desire to leave the city behind and to inhabit open, unpaved spaces instead.

Whereas factory stacks appear in O'Keeffe's 1928 depiction of the East River as unsightly and polluting towers marking a seemingly inhospitable industrial landscape, they appear in Aaron Douglas's cover design of November of the same year as inanimate but powerful (if distant) sentinels heralding the dawn of a new day.[8] Introducing a special issue of the *Annals of the American Academy of Political and Social Science* devoted to the topic of the American Negro, Douglas's design, unlike O'Keeffe's depopulated urban scenes, features the human figure prominently. Turned at dramatic, confident profile and holding a shovel, this single male figure symbolizes the New Negro, a key emblem of the political, literary, and artistic movement known as the Harlem Renaissance. Associated closely with the writer and philosopher Alain Locke, whose 1925 publication *The New Negro: An Interpretation of Negro Life* somewhat codified the type, the New Negro evoked a new, socially and politically engaged urban identity for African Americans. In this regard, the New Negro personified scores of disenfranchised blacks who fled discrimination in the Jim Crow South throughout the late nineteenth and early twentieth centuries in search of greater opportunities in northern cities, including New York. This influx of new energy, skill, and talent from other parts of the country (Douglas himself hailed from the Midwest) set the stage for the Renaissance that, in truth, extended far beyond Harlem's boundaries.[9]

Douglas's composition asserts not only the material, but also the symbolic importance of salaried labor for a population whose history bore layered scars of slavery and poverty. More specifically, it attests to the role of black labor in the city's growth. In so doing, it also establishes a parallelism that connected contemporary events with great cultural accomplishment in history: the New Negro builds the new cities, just as the ancient Egyptians had raised awe-inspiring pyramids and temples (leaving aside the inconvenient historical fact that many of the Egyptian buildings were erected by slaves). Indeed, references to ancient Egypt permeated the Harlem Renaissance, evident not least of all in Douglas's signature figurative silhouette, which by the artist's purposeful design recalls the flattened, frontal bodies in Egyptian painting and relief sculpture. In this regard, these distinctive silhouettes, which Douglas would expand into complex mural projects in the 1930s, participated in the widespread, international Egypt-o-mania that followed Howard Carter's discovery of King Tutankhamen's tomb in November 1922. Ultimately, the book cover design's message is cautionary: symbiotically, man erects the city as his new urban habitat makes (or remakes) him, the mounting skyscrapers echoing his proud upright countenance. But the city simultaneously asserts pressure on him, suggesting its capacity not only to empower, but also to overwhelm the New Negro and others in its midst.

Empowering, mesmerizing, and threatening—the city could incite all of these sensations. John Marin's *Lower Manhattan* invokes the metropolis's disorienting effects. Like O'Keeffe's *View of the East River*, Marin adopted an elevated vantage point, looking down and across the city. But, unlike O'Keeffe's pristinely painted view, Marin's depiction of lower Manhattan dissolves into jagged shapes and strokes that suggest dizzying heights, dynamic movement, and endless reverberation. Adapting ideas from European cubism and futurism and translating them into watercolor, the artist rendered a kind of painterly gestalt, suggesting that the city is much more than the sum of its individual parts.

Even so, the foundation of Marin's composition—one that he marked with an irregular star whose points direct the viewer's eye outward—was an unmistakable individual part—indeed, an undeniable star—of the New York skyline. Opened in 1913, the fifty-seven-story Woolworth Building, which Marin painted multiple times, was the tallest skyscraper in the world until 1930. In an article in the *New York Times*, Alan Francis, a visiting Londoner, famously dubbed the Woolworth a "Cathedral of Commerce," suggesting that Americans now worshipped money as much as—as conspicuously as—they worshipped any other god.[10] The nation's postwar boom coupled with economic stagnation throughout Europe sustained—in fact, enhanced—the Woolworth's status as a powerful architectural emblem of not only American progress, but also the nation's newfound international economic might.

FACING: Aaron Douglas, cover design of the *Annals of the American Academy of Political and Social Science*, November 1928. Collection of Richard and C. T. Woods-Powell. Art ©Heirs of Aaron Douglas / Licensed by VAGA, New York, NY. Image courtesy of Spencer Museum of Art, The University of Kansas

8 For a recent study of Douglas's life and art, see Susan Earle, ed., *Aaron Douglas: African American Modernist*, exh. cat. (New Haven, CT: Yale University Press, 2007).

9 For a discussion of the significance of the Harlem Renaissance beyond Harlem's geographical boundaries, see Richard J. Powell, "Enter and Exit the New Negro," in *Black Art and Culture in the 20th Century* (New York: Thames and Hudson, 1997), 41–65.

10 "'Yours is a Land of Contrasts,' Says English Visitor. Alan Francis, Who Came Here in the Interest of British Art, Declares We Do Some Magnificent Things and Tolerate Some Very Disagreeable Ones," *New York Times*, April 27, 1913.

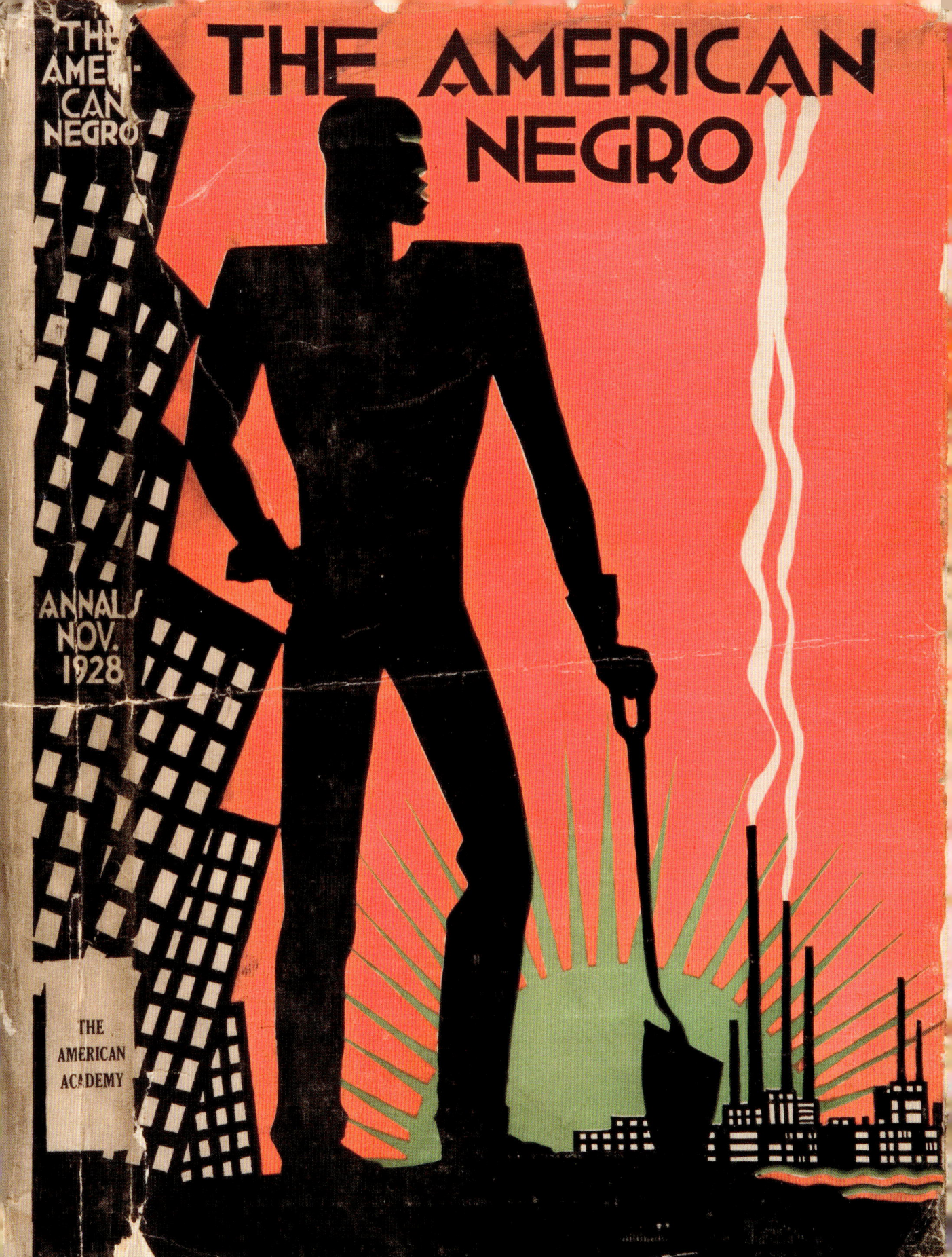

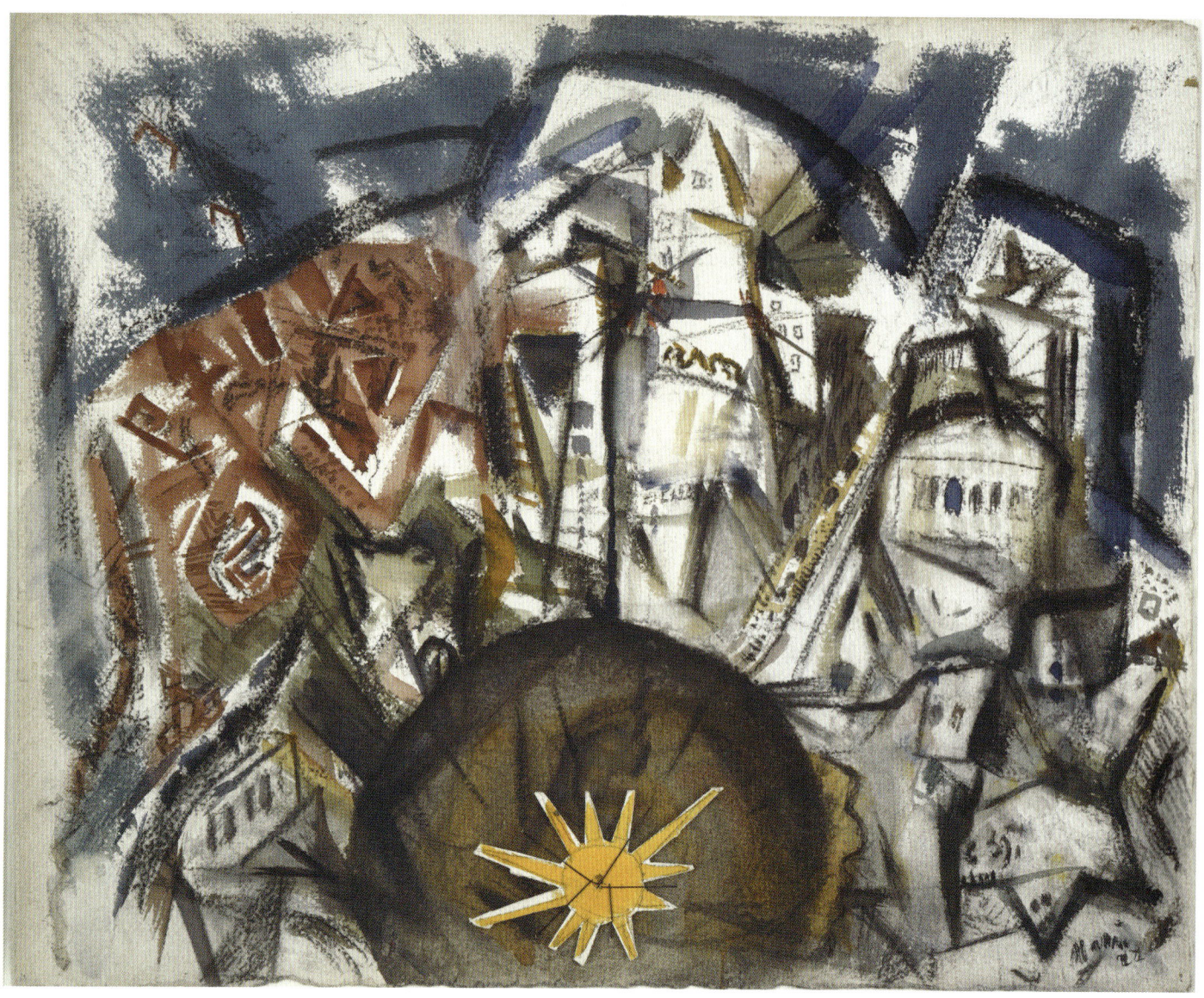

ABOVE: John Marin, *Lower Manhattan (Composing Derived from the Top of Woolworth)*, 1922. Gouache and charcoal with paper cut-out attached with thread on paper, 21⅝ x 26⅞. The Museum of Modern Art, New York, Acquired through the Lillie P. Bliss Bequest, 143.1945. Image ©The Museum of Modern Art / Licensed by SCALA / Art Resource, NY. Art ©2013 Estate of John Marin / Artists Rights Society (ARS), New York

FACING: Charles Sheeler, *Criss-Crossed Conveyors, River Rouge Plant, Ford Motor Company*, 1927. Gelatin silver print, 9¼ x 7⅜. The Metropolitan Museum of Art, Ford Motor Company Collection, Gift of Ford Motor Company and John C. Waddell, 1987 (1987.1100.1). Image ©The Metropolitan Museum of Art / Licensed by SCALA / Art Resource, NY. Art ©The Lane Collection

Whether money was the nation's new god was matter of opinion. More a matter of fact was the widespread belief that America's perceived progress was predicated on its capitalist economy, which fueled the material and technological innovations and amenities that middle- and upper-class consumers enjoyed. "The chief business of the American people is business," President Calvin Coolidge proclaimed in his address to the American Society of Newspaper Editors in January 1925. "They are profoundly concerned with buying, selling, investing and prospering in the world."[11]

Perhaps no single site outside Manhattan manifested Coolidge's dictum more than Henry Ford's sprawling 1,100-acre River Rouge production plant in Dearborn, Michigan. Few artistic projects of the era are more aesthetically analogous with President Coolidge's capitalistic boosterism than the photographs that artist Charles Sheeler took of the plant on commission from the company in 1927. In *Criss-Crossed Conveyors, River Rouge Plant, Ford*

11 "Coolidge Declares Press Must Foster America's Idealism; In Address to Editors, He Warns Them Against the Evils of Propaganda. No Dancer In Prosperity. Financially Strong Journalism, He Says, Is Not Likely to Betray the Nation. News 'Feelers' Deplored. White House 'Official Spokesman' Method of Statement Is Attacked in Editors' Session. American Idealism Mission of Press." *New York Times*, January 18, 1925.

[50]

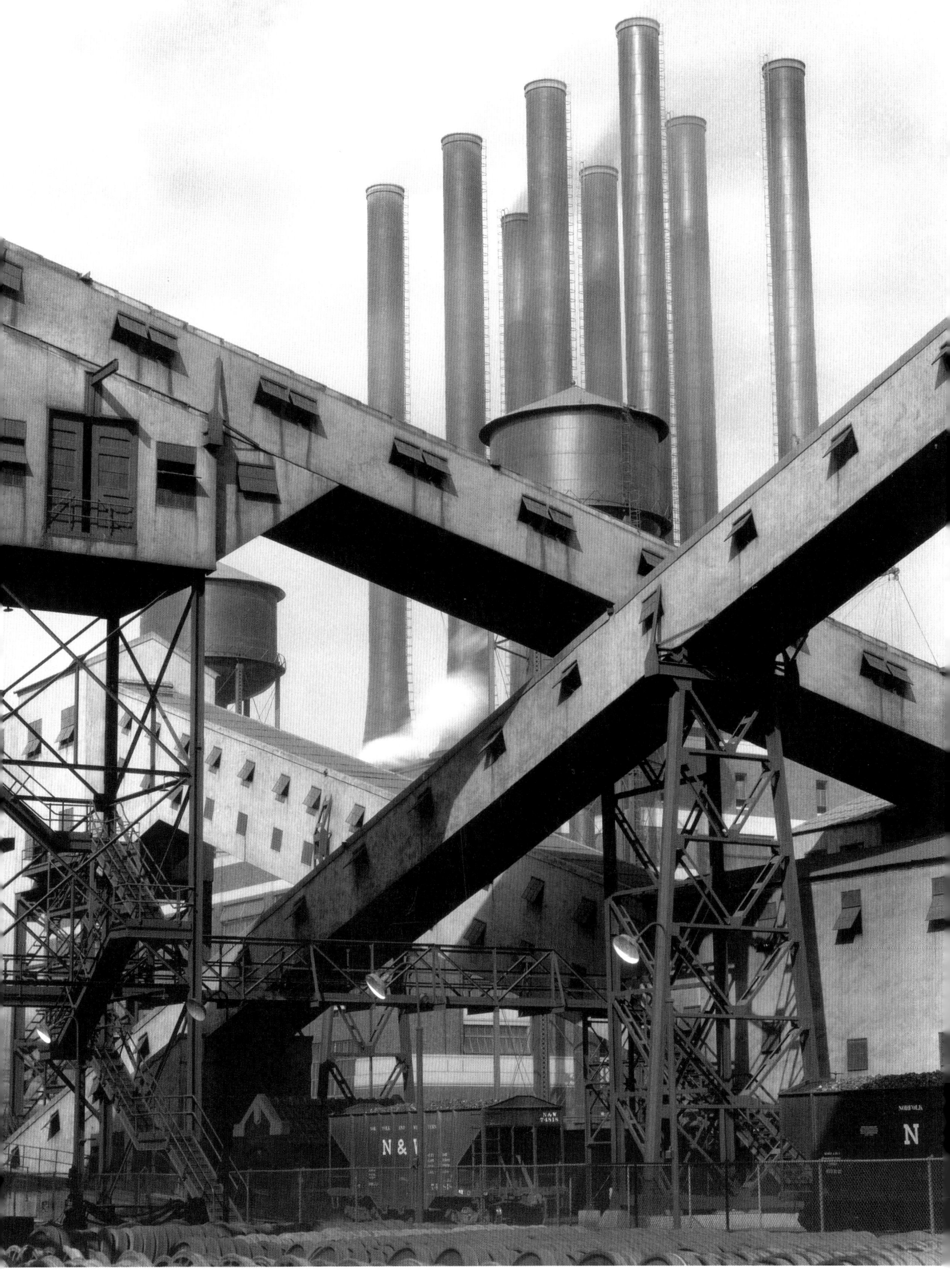

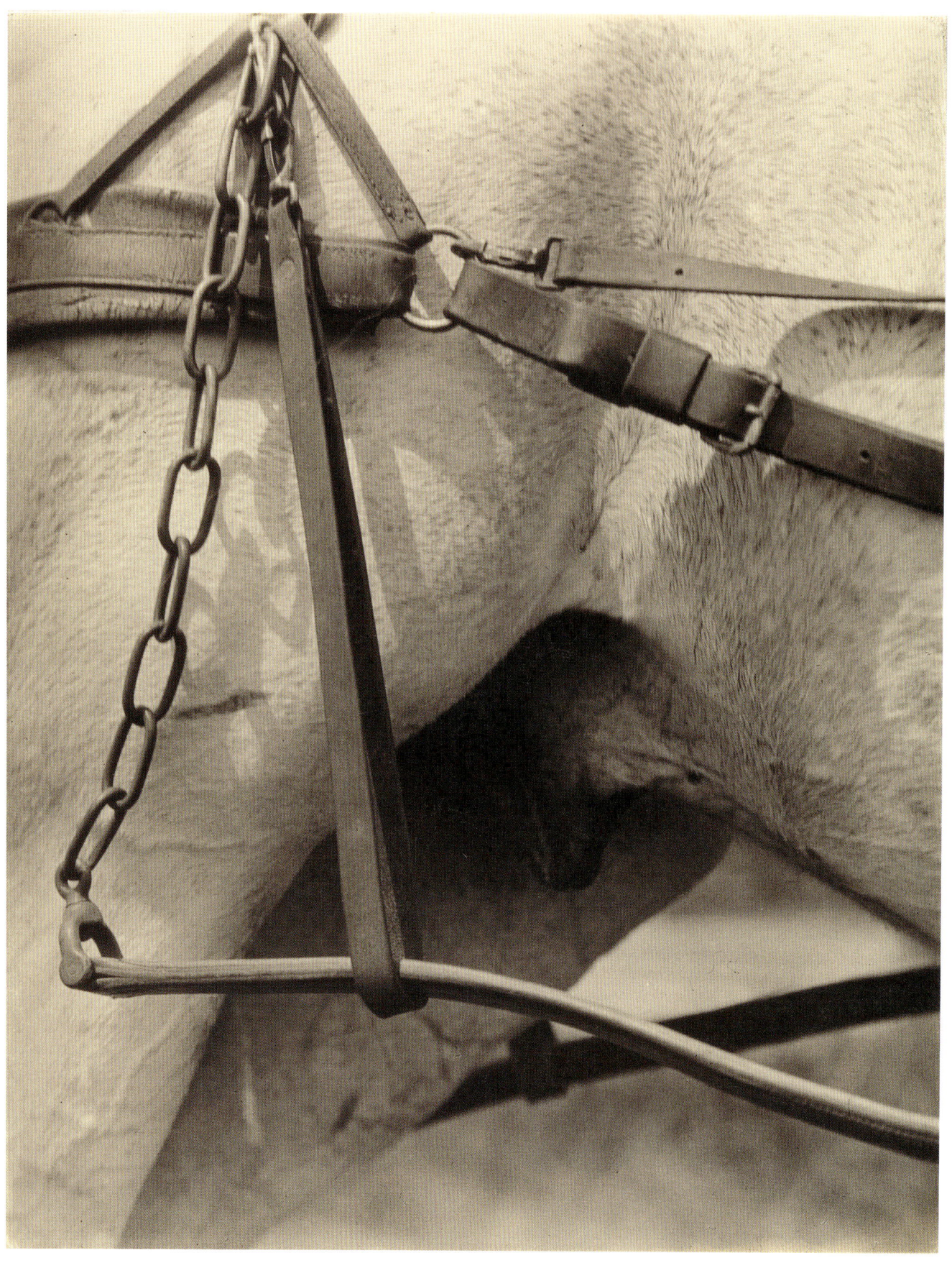

Alfred Stieglitz

Spiritual America, Songs of the Sky A1, 1923

Gelatin silver print, 4 9/16 x 3 5/8

The Metropolitan Museum of Art, Alfred Stieglitz Collection, 1949 (49.55.24).

©The Metropolitan Museum of Art. Image source: Art Resource, NY

12 For a sustained study of what art historian Wanda Corn has described as the "soil and spirit" modernists in Stieglitz's midst, see Corn, *The Great American Thing: Modern Art and National Identity, 1915–1935* (Berkeley, CA: University of California Press, 1999). My interpretation of Stieglitz's *Spiritual America* follows Corn's analysis of the photograph in *Great American Thing*, 32.

13 My description of Russell's painting owes much to Brian W. Dippie, "Charles M. Russell's *In the Enemy's Country*," in Thomas Brent Smith, ed., *Elevating Western American Art: Developing an Institute in the Cultural Capital of the Rockies* (Denver: Petrie Institute of Western American Art, Denver Art Museum [*Western Passages*], 2012), 244–47.

Motor Company, Sheeler takes his viewer deep into the industrial grounds of the plant and exposes much of its inner workings. Like many images from Sheeler's River Rouge series, the photograph calls out the utilitarian elegance of Ford's otherworldly industrial landscape. Crossing one another dynamically right of center, the conveyor belts create a cruciform that divides the composition into four unequal quadrants, each of which contains its own semi-independent visual contents. The smokestacks in the top portion appear like pipes on a church organ, suggesting that the River Rouge plant is like a large-scale, finely tuned instrument, one that likewise produces a kind of beautiful music that inspires reverence.

While Coolidge and his many followers exalted business as the country's characteristic business, many artists and writers in the 1920s recoiled from the uncritical celebration of capitalism as America's essence, fearing that crass, unfettered materialism stifled the cultivation and expression of the national spirit. Concern and resistance along these lines came from many corners of American culture throughout the decade, but nowhere more so than from the artists and writers in the orbit of photographer and gallery director Alfred Stieglitz.[12] One of Stieglitz's most effective photographic ruminations on the compromised state of the nation's spirit is *Spiritual America*, a tightly cropped view of a horse's hindquarters bound by harness straps. The message of Stieglitz's image is direct and resonant: America's spirit, embodied by the white horse, is truncated, its freedom curtailed and innate power subdued by the yoke of rampant white-collar capitalism. In this regard, Stieglitz's photograph exudes a whiff of nostalgia despite the apparent dispassionate, even clinical sensibility of his lens. No doubt the equine symbolism he employed in *Spiritual America* would have harbored particular poignancy for a man like Stieglitz, who belonged to a generation for which the term and concept "horse power" still evoked visions of four legs and hooves rather than four wheels outfitted with Goodyear tires.

Stieglitz's exact contemporary in the West (both men were born in 1864), the Montana-based painter and illustrator Charles Marion Russell, held even more strenuously onto a time before motorcars rolled and ruled the earth. The horses that appear in Russell's *In the Enemy's Country* do not pull taxi carriages, but, rather, they assist a caravan of Kootenai Indians trying to hide in plain sight as they pass into Blackfeet territory to hunt buffalo.[13] Carrying skins over their backs fur side out, the horses, like the cloud cover that throws so much of the scene into shadow, provide necessary camouflage, so that from a distance the troupe could appear like a band of buffalo roaming undisturbed across the landscape. While Russell's caravan moves cautiously forward in space, the artist himself

Charles M. Russell

In the Enemy's Country, 1921

Oil on canvas, 24 x 36

Denver Art Museum, gift of the Magness Family in memory of Betsy Magness, 1991.751

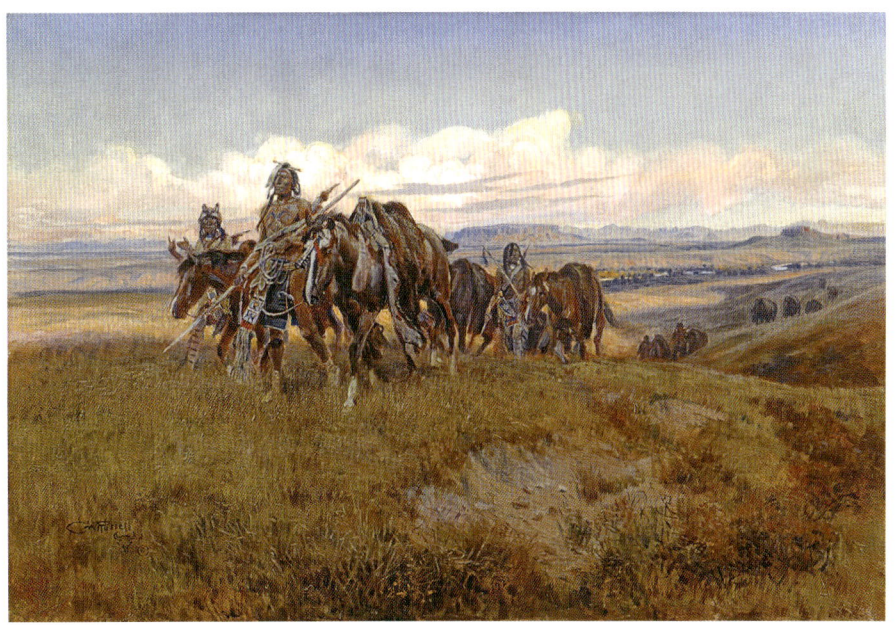

looked concertedly backward in time: decades had passed since the Kootenai, the Blackfeet, and the buffalo had moved freely throughout the northern plains.

By the 1920s, the American West was, like many other parts of the country, increasingly populated by Scouts and Chiefs of a decidedly different, mechanical variety. Throughout the early twentieth century, while most American Indians endured life on reservations, the burgeoning motorcycle and automobile industries eagerly appropriated both generic and specific names associated with Native American history and culture to sell their products.[14] Founded in 1901, Springfield, Massachusetts–based Indian Motocycles Manufacturing Company was among the first to seize on Indian iconography to this end. As one memorable poster from 1914 asserts, an Indian motocycle possesses the speed, reliability, and flexibility that even an Indian chief could appreciate, so much so that he happily mounts this modern marvel instead of his trusty steed.

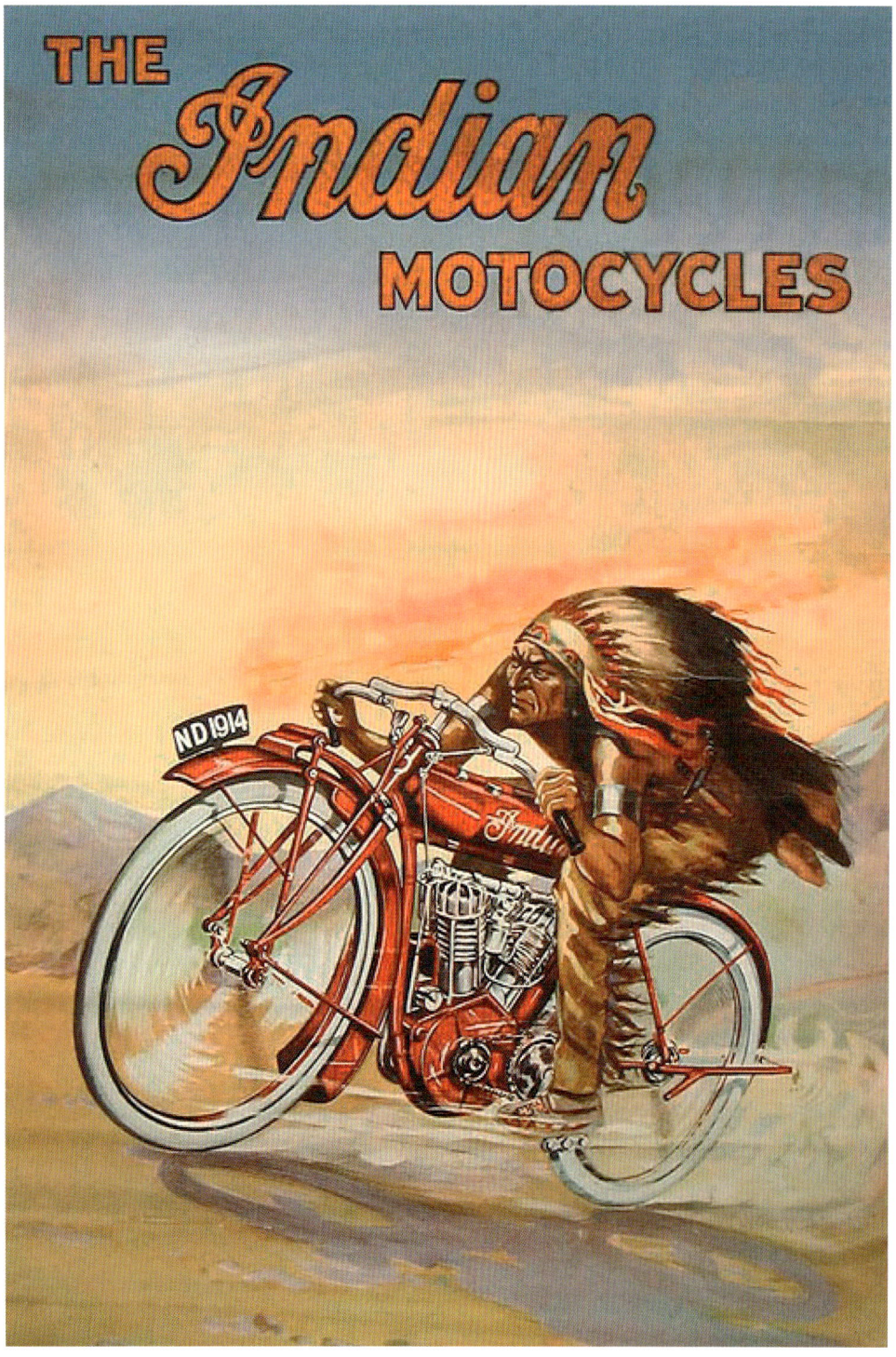

Indian Motocycles poster, 1914

Image courtesy of the Baer Family Library

[54]

As it was for many industrial manufacturers, the 1920s were a boom time for Indian Motocycles, largely due to two historically successful models. In 1920, the same year in which Russell painted *In the Enemy's Country*, the company introduced the Scout, which became, as an ad in *Popular Mechanics* touted, "the favorite among red-blooded fellows everywhere."[15] Two years later, the same company introduced the even more popular and successful Chief, which could reach unprecedented speeds up to ninety-five miles per hour.

In 1926, General Motors got in on the action by launching its Pontiac brand, whose namesake harkened back not only to the car's home base of manufacture in Pontiac, Michigan, but also further back in time to Chief Pontiac, who famously resisted the British occupation of the Great Lakes region following the French and Indian War. While Indian Motocycles legitimized the company's appropriation of Native American culture by asserting that they were producing the modern equivalent of horses, Pontiac's claims to Indian iconography were even more tenuous, extending merely to the automobile's color, an oblique reference, one assumes, to the so-called "Red Man," and the hood ornament, a stylized, Art Deco depiction of the legendary chief.

General Motors' release of the Pontiac in 1926 coincided with the publication of the first official map of the fully integrated U.S. Highway System, a document that illuminates the degree to which America's roadways now crisscrossed all regions of the country, including Russell's once-remote northwestern plains. In fact, the artist's hometown of Great Falls resided at the confluence of U.S. Routes 87 and 91, major east-west, north-south thoroughfares respectively. *In the Enemy's Country* omits all such signs of modernity, preserving in paint a time when Chiefs and Scouts hunted on two feet rather than sped through the countryside noisily on two or four wheels. Russell's death in the same year as the Pontiac's debut and official highway map's publication marks a poignant historical coincidence.

Whatever form it took, the artistic disavowal of capitalist, urban consumerism encouraged and even necessitated a renewed engagement with nature, however vaguely and variously it was defined. But even nature itself was not immune from modern "progress," as an examination of O'Keeffe's renowned flower paintings reveals. *Yellow Hickory Leaves with Daisy* (1928) constitutes a useful case study to this end. Showing a single Shasta daisy resting atop a bed of hickory leaves, the painting focuses closely on the group of leaves and accompanying bloom, encouraging scrutiny, even as O'Keeffe's smooth application of paint omits minute detail that one would see if the same objects were actually viewed up close. Beautiful and discreet, the single Shasta daisy in O'Keeffe's painting serves not only as a floral icon, but also as a kind of porthole to new understanding of her still-life painting and, by extension, to unexplored dimensions of American still-life imagery throughout this period.

The floral star of O'Keeffe's painting, the Shasta daisy was one of Luther Burbank's most prized creations. Little remembered today outside his adopted home of Santa Rosa, California, the Massachusetts-born "Plant Wizard" was an international celebrity throughout the early twentieth century, responsible for dozens of vegetables and flowers that became ubiquitous in American life.[16] Not the least of these was the Burbank potato, the forerunner of the russet potato, which he developed to resist rot and blight. His accomplishments earned him a profile in, among other numerous period publications, Tappan's *Heroes of Progress*, which celebrated the broad scope and impact of his vision and work, from the ornamental to the practical: "Many people who know the Shasta daisy, the sweet-scented verbena and calla lily, and the dahlia with the fragrance of the magnolia, have heard less about Mr. Burbank's more practical work. He never forgets his aim to make food better, and cheaper, and, in the case of the daisy, he sends all over the world, if necessary, for plants that possess the qualities needed. The results are marvels."[17]

As Tappan's glowing profile of Burbank suggests, the daisy was one of the Plant Wizard's most miraculous creations and the one with which he was most associated among his adoring followers. At the very least, its appearance in O'Keeffe's painting attests to

14 Among numerous studies devoted to the topic of the corporate and commercial appropriation of American Indian culture, see Meta G. Carstarphen and John P. Sanchez, eds., *American Indians and the Mass Media* (Norman: University of Oklahoma Press, 2012). In this anthology, Selene G. Phillips addresses specifically General Motors' appropriation of Pontiac during World War II. Phillips, "'Indians on Our Warpath': World War II Images of American Indians in LIFE Magazine," 33–55.

15 *Popular Mechanics*, March 1924, Advertising Section, 172.

16 For a recent biography of Burbank, see Jane S. Smith, *The Garden of Invention: Luther Burbank and the Business of Breeding Plants* (New York: Penguin Press, 2009).

17 Tappan, *Heroes of Progress*, 111.

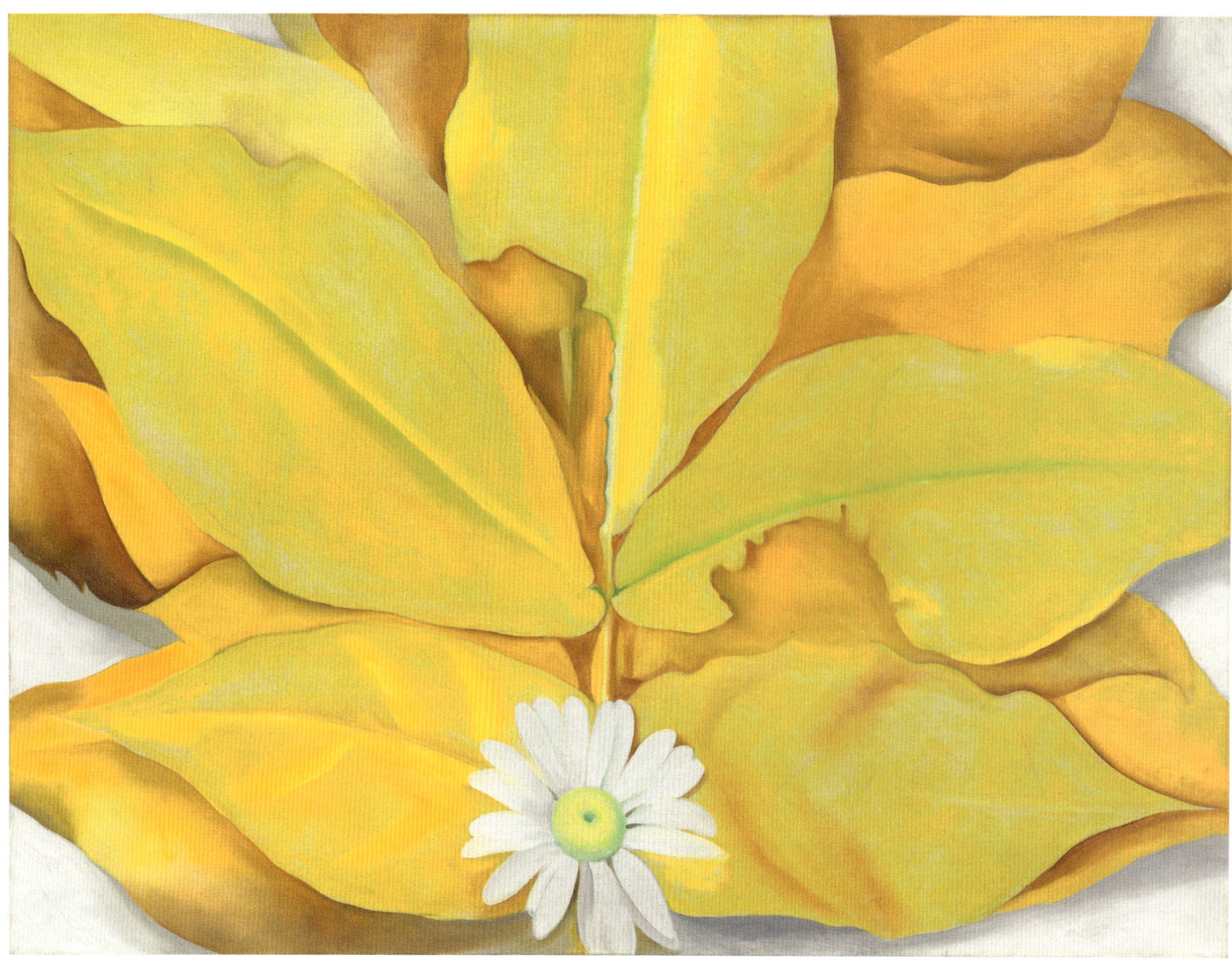

the bloom's immense popularity and, by extension, to Burbank's ubiquity in American culture. Indeed, viewed through the lens of Burbank's widespread impact on American culture in the early twentieth century, still-life painting and photography begin to appear like a veritable catalog of his wondrous inventions. In addition to the Shasta, Burbank was the inventor of the yellow calla, which makes appearances in works by O'Keeffe, Preston Dickinson, and other early modernist still-life artists. The botanist also bred the more robust gladiolus, which might be the same flower that turns up in paintings by O'Keeffe and Charles Demuth, in addition to large Oriental poppies, which may be the variety that O'Keeffe immortalized in paint.[18]

Burbank's ubiquity in American culture made the appearance of his creations in early modernist still-life painting and photography almost inevitable. But the Shasta daisy's iconic appearance in O'Keeffe's painting seems more than coincidental. Indeed, the painting might even be fairly interpreted as a symbolic portrait of the famed breeder of plants. O'Keeffe was herself an avid gardener, as were other artists in Stieglitz's orbit, including Charles Demuth and Edward Steichen, and so likely knew of Burbank's reputation. Steichen, in fact, bought seeds directly from Burbank, and, to a degree, modeled his career after the master gardener.

Burbank's widespread association with the Shasta suggests that O'Keeffe's painting from 1928 could be counted among the many symbolic portraits created by Stieglitz circle artists, extending a line of pictures including Francis Picabia's *Here, This is Stieglitz,* in which the photographer appears in the form of a mechanized equivalent, a camera with a broken

Georgia O'Keeffe
Yellow Hickory Leaves with Daisy, 1928
Oil on canvas, 29⅞ x 39⅞
Alfred Stieglitz Collection, gift of Georgia O'Keeffe, 1965.1180, The Art Institute of Chicago. Photography ©The Art Institute of Chicago

18 These assertions are based on a thorough review of the authoritative and illustrated *Luther Burbank: His Methods and Discoveries and Their Practical Application / Prepared from His Original Field Notes Covering More Than 100,000 Experiments Made During Forty Years Devoted to Plant Improvement; with the Assistance of the Luther Burbank Society and its Entire Membership; Under the Editorial Direction of John Whitson and Robert John and Henry Smith Williams,* 12 vols. (New York: Luther Burbank Press, 1914–15).

19 Luther Burbank, with Wilbur Hall, *The Harvest of the Years* (Boston: Houghton Mifflin Company, 1927).

20 For an illuminating discussion of Kahlo's portrait, see Lucretia Hoover Giese, "A Rare Crossing: Frida Kahlo and Luther Burbank," *American Art* 15, no. 1 (Spring 2001): 53–73.

21 Van Wyck Brooks, *Days of the Phoenix: The Nineteen-Twenties I Remember* (New York: E. P. Dutton & Company, 1957), 2.

bellows, and Marsden Hartley's *One Portrait of One Woman*, an evocation of Gertrude Stein's formidable presence through the depiction of her teacup.

Burbank's death in 1926 and the publication of his memoirs, *The Harvest of the Years*, the following year spurred a floodtide of commemorative tributes that extended into the next decade.[19] In this regard, O'Keeffe's painting might also be grouped with slightly later posthumous portrayals of the Plant Wizard by Diego Rivera, who featured Burbank in his mural *Allegory of California* (1930–31), and Frida Kahlo, whose 1931 surrealist portrait shows him like a tree with roots extending into the earth and into his interred corpse.[20] Burbank continues to bring life to earth even from beyond the grave.

Like Burbank, many American artists and writers in the 1920s aspired to produce new, original creations that grew from the soil. But for these artists and writers "the soil" was a powerful philosophical, aesthetic metaphor that connoted homegrown antidotes to the imported cultural values and artistic modes, both past and present, to which American culture had long been subject. As the cultural critic Van Wyck Brooks recalled in his memoirs, "no word was more constantly on [artists'] lips [than *roots*] unless it was the native 'soil' or 'earth,' and this obsession lay deep in the minds of urban cosmopolitans whom one saw toiling now with spade and pick."[21]

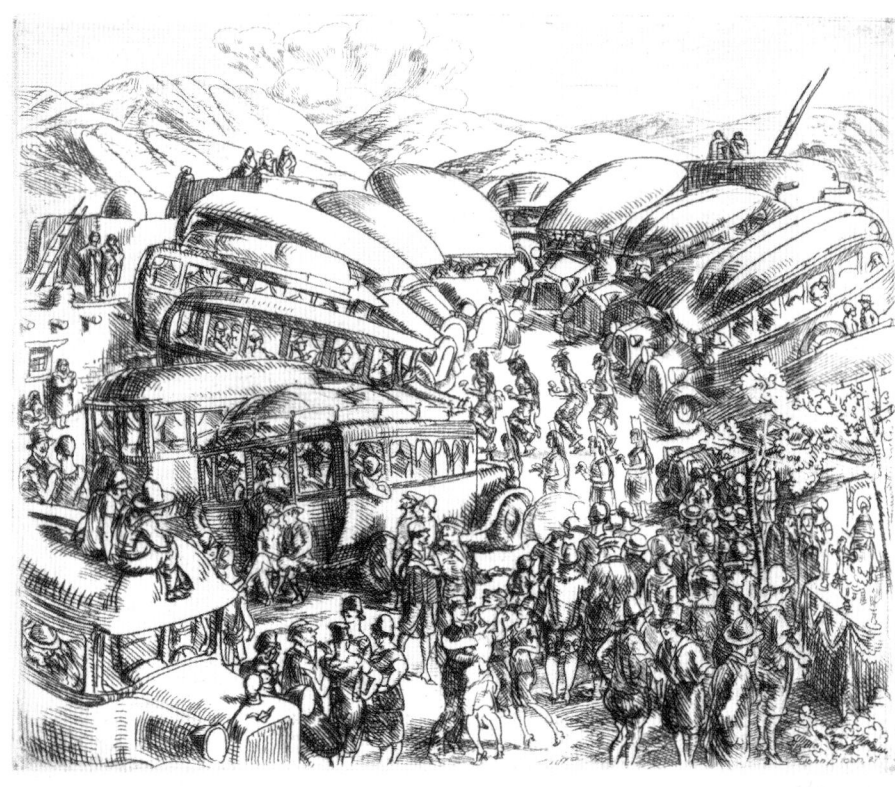

John Sloan
The Indian Detour, 1927
Etching, Plate: 6 x 7⅛; Sheet: 9½ x 12⅝.
Philadelphia Museum of Art: purchased with funds contributed by Lessing J. Rosenwald and with the Katharine Levin Farrell Fund, 1956.
©2013 Delaware Art Museum / Artists Rights Society (ARS), New York

Among other aesthetic effects throughout the 1920s, artistic obsession with "the soil" both sustained and enhanced the allure of the southwestern United States, particularly New Mexico, where Euro-American painters and sculptors from many parts of the country had been congregating and working in Taos and Santa Fe since the turn of the century. Within the particular cultural conditions of the period, native cultures of the Southwest radiated with perceived authenticity and "nativeness," largely because many city-dwelling Anglos continued to imagine them coexisting peacefully with nature and making their art out of a kind of inner spiritual necessity, surprisingly along lines similar to those endorsed by the European modernist Wassily Kandinsky in his influential treatise *Concerning the Spiritual in Art*, first published in 1911.

In fact, *economic* necessity fueled the production of native art as much as or more than spiritual necessity, as many impoverished Pueblo artists and performers increasingly accommodated a growing tourist market, which came originally from the railroad. Thanks to increasing motor vehicles and the roads that carried them (Route 66 was established officially in November 1926), Santa Fe, Taos, and their surrounding pueblos became—like Russell's Montana— more accessible and popular among artists and non-artists alike. John Sloan, who arrived in New Mexico in 1919, parodied the area's booming tourism industry in 1927 with his memorable prints *The Indian Detour*, which the artist described as "a satire on the Harvey Indian Tour" and *Knees and Aborigines*, a playful meditation on relative modesty between the attendees and the performers of a traditional Pueblo Indian dance.

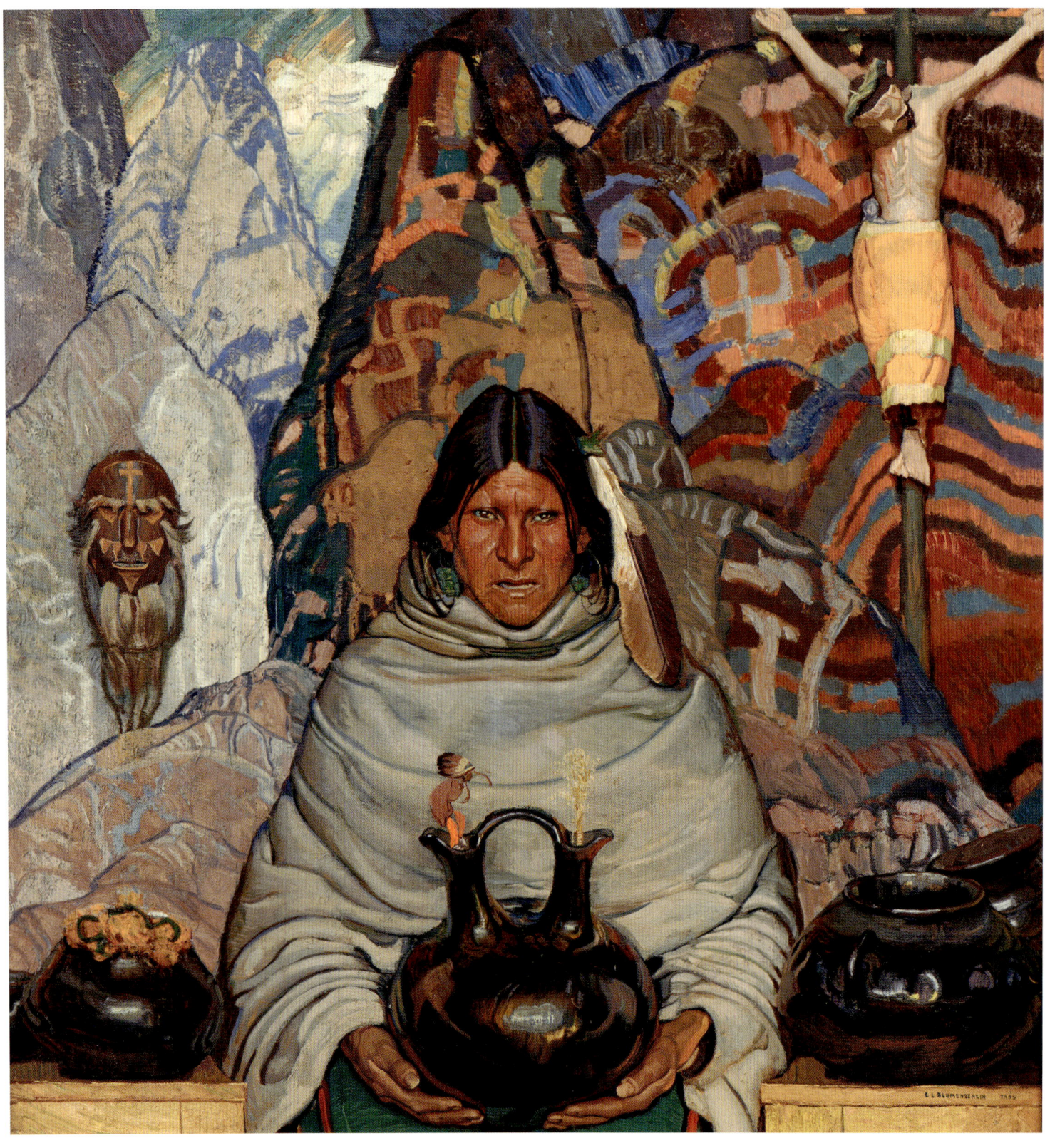

ABOVE: Ernest L. Blumenschein
Superstition, 1921
Oil on canvas, 50¼ x 49
Gilcrease Museum, Tulsa, Oklahoma, 0137.531

FACING: William Penhallow Henderson
Walpi Snake Dance, about 1920
Oil on canvas, 42 x 55
The Eugene B. Adkins Collection at the Fred Jones Jr. Museum of Art, the University of Oklahoma, Norman, Oklahoma and the Philbrook Museum of Art, Tulsa, Oklahoma

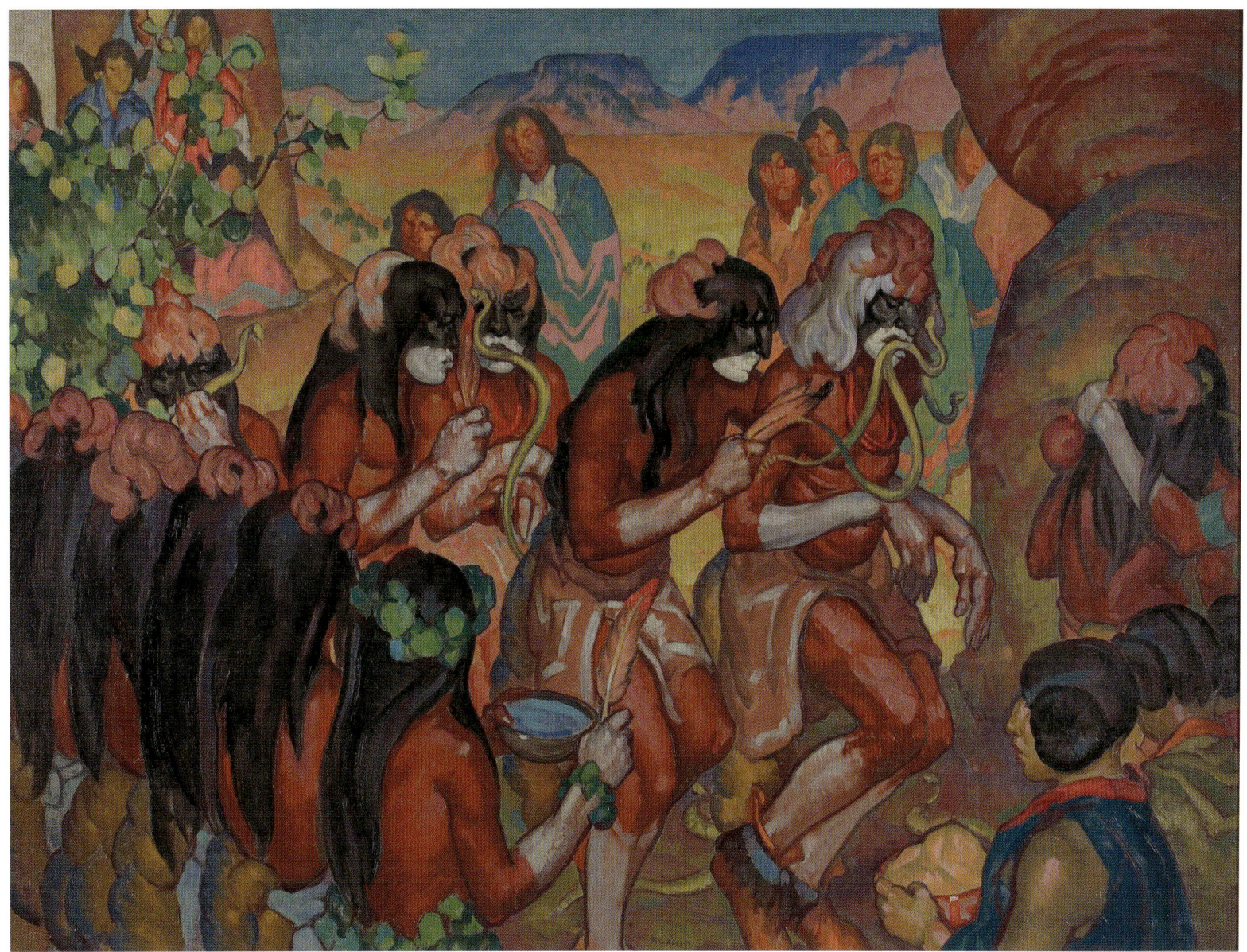

22 For a useful examination of the art colonies of Taos and Santa Fe and the generational shift throughout the 1920s, see Charles C. Eldredge et al., *Art in New Mexico, 1900–1945: Paths to Taos and Santa Fe* (Washington, DC: National Museum of American Art, Smithsonian Institution, 1986).

23 My discussion of Blumenschein's painting is indebted to Skip Keith Miller, "*Superstition* and the Artist's Native Rights," in Peter H. Hassrick and Elizabeth J. Cunningham, *In Contemporary Rhythm: The Art of Ernest L. Blumenschein*, exh. cat. (Norman: University of Oklahoma Press, 2008), 119–27.

24 For a discussion of Henderson's painting, see Mark A. White, "Time and Modernity in the Art of the American Southwest" in Byron Price et. al., *The Eugene B. Adkins Collection* (Norman: University of Oklahoma Press, 2011), 25.

Artistically, the 1920s constituted somewhat of a generational shift in New Mexican modernism, from academically trained figure painters (most of them associated with the Taos Society of Artists, which was active from 1915 to 1927) to the more abstract concerns of somewhat younger artists interested more in landscape.[22] Ernest Blumenschein's *Superstition* (1921) and William Henderson's *Walpi Snake Dance* (about 1920) testify to the enduring artistic and political viability of their figurative imagery. Blumenschein's dense and vibrant composition features model Jim Romero in the guise of a chief staring somewhat defiantly out at the viewer. He is surrounded by a wide range of religious objects representing the potent blend of European and indigenous traditions that contributed to the region's character and appeal.[23] The chief holds a Tewa "wedding vase," symbolizing a metaphoric and unique union of cultures. By contrast to Blumenschein's static, iconic image, Henderson's composition, filled with bodies in motion, pulsates with color and organic form.[24] The dancers' collective intimate relationship with nature is suggested by the fact that their bodies reside below the horizon line.

> Artistically, the 1920s constituted somewhat of a generational shift in New Mexican modernism.

[59]

Despite their compositional and stylistic differences, both paintings gained political, even propagandistic significance in light of the aggressively assimilationist policies advanced by the Bureau of Indian Affairs, headed throughout the decade by Charles Burke. As Commissioner of Indian Affairs, Burke issued, among other repressive actions, directives against ceremonial dancing in 1921 and in 1923 (many outsiders considered the Snake Dance, which Henderson depicts, to rank among the most "barbaric" of ceremonies).[25] The passage of the Indian Citizenship Act in 1924, about which many native peoples were themselves conflicted, did provide Indians and their Anglo supporters a foundation for resistance by claiming that the bureau's actions violated Indians' First Amendment rights to free religious and personal expression. While Blumenschein's and Henderson's paintings may appear somewhat *retardataire* when compared to other art from the 1920s, *Superstition* and *Walpi Snake Dance* can be fairly interpreted as artistic responses to official government actions, assertions in paint that the Pueblo peoples have the right to be and remain as they are.

In this context, the efforts of painters more recently arrived in Taos and Santa Fe may appear more artistically avant-garde but less politically engaged. Invited to New Mexico by New York socialite and Taos transplant Mabel Dodge, Marsden Hartley had, by 1920, already come and gone. Initially, he heralded the region as "a country of things in light," but he concluded upon departure that it was "the stupidest place I ever fell into." Nevertheless, images of the New Mexican desert haunted his imagination, and he recorded these in a series

John Marin, *Mountains near Taos*, 1929 Watercolor over pencil on paper, 16¹⁵⁄₁₆ x 22⅛. Mead Art Museum, Amherst College, gift of Dorothy and James Schramm (Class of 1926), AC 1991.30.1. Art ©2013 Estate of John Marin / Artists Rights Society (ARS), New York

25 On Burke, see Leonard Schlup, "Charles Henry Burke and the Department of Indian Affairs in the Harding and Coolidge Administrations," *International Review of History and Political Science* 17 (1980): 1–14.

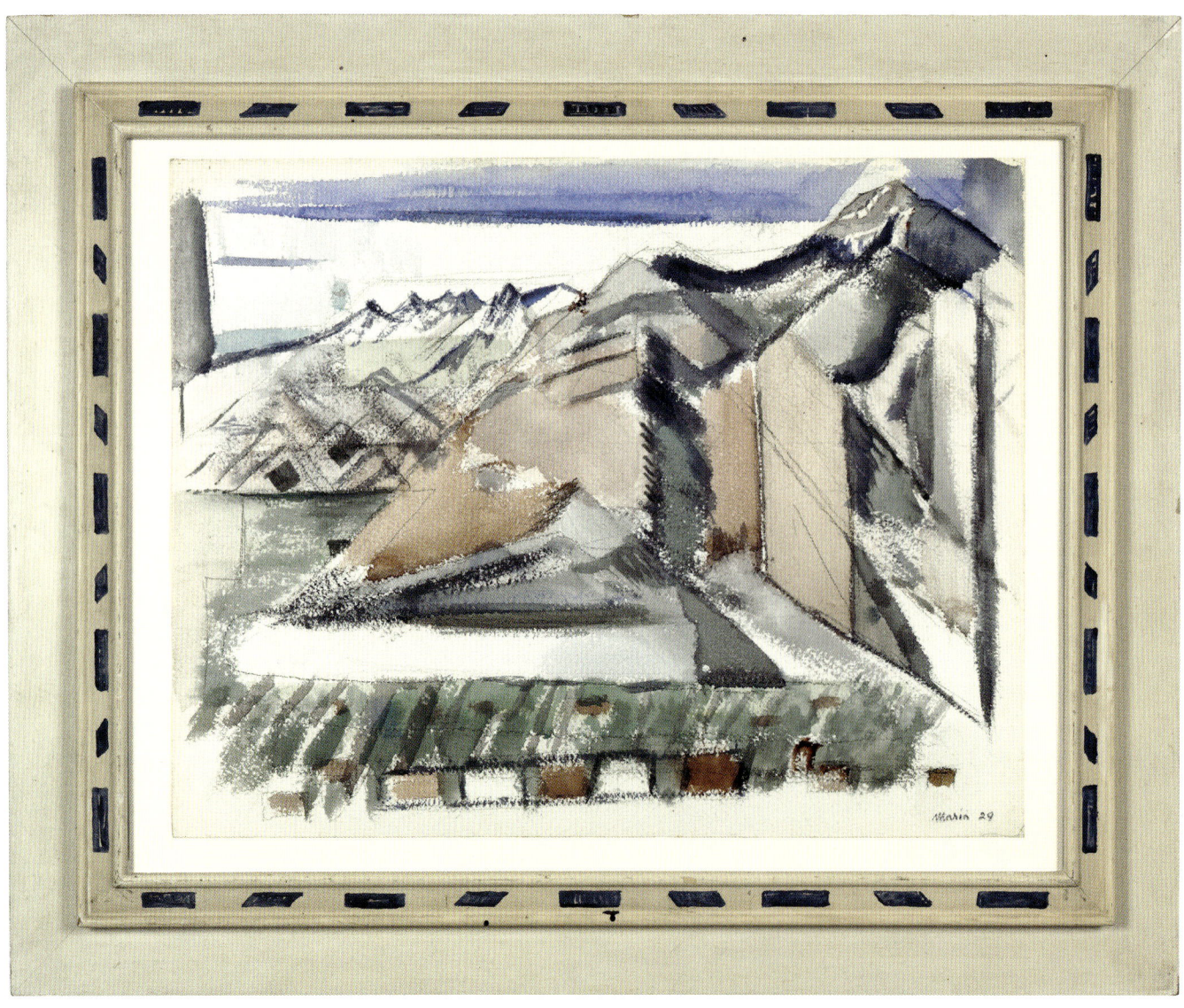

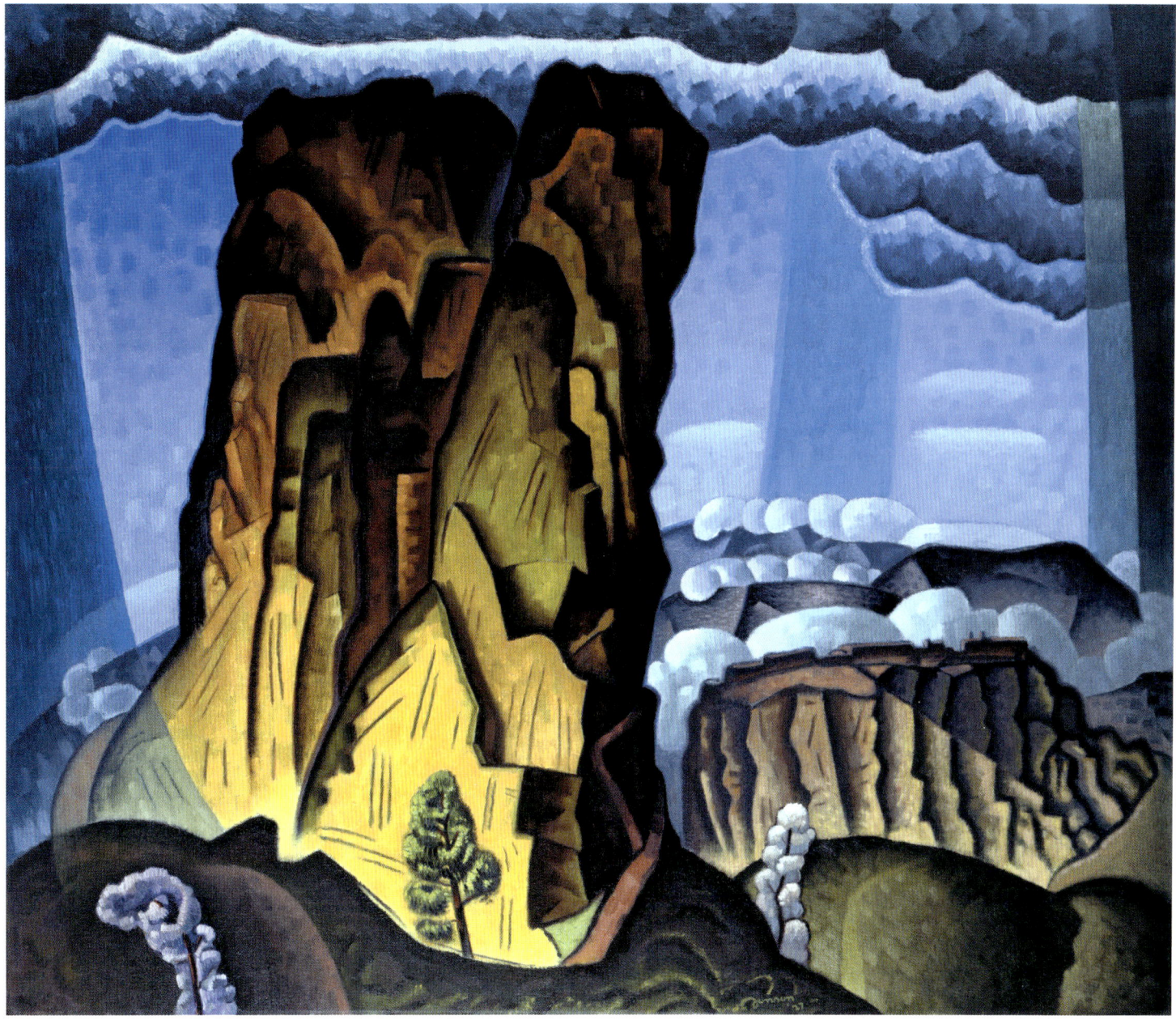

Raymond Jonson
Pueblo Series, Acoma, 1927
Oil on canvas, 36½ x 43½
Denver Art Museum, William Sr. and
Dorothy Harmsen Collection, 2001.44

26 For a sustained analysis of Hartley's *Recollections*, see Heather Hole, *Marsden Hartley and the West: The Search for an American Modernism* (New Haven: Yale University Press, 2007).

of mostly murky, lugubrious *Recollections* that he painted after returning to Germany, compositions that seem to express more about the painter's bleak state of mind in postwar Berlin than they do anything about the southwestern landscape he renounced.[26]

Mabel Dodge also lured John Marin to New Mexico. Arriving in 1929, he explored the region in the Ford car that Dodge lent him and recorded his impressions in about one hundred watercolors. *Mountains near Taos* likely depicts the Sangre de Cristo Range, the angular geometries of which the painter emphasized through charcoal lines and washes of green-blue and warm beige. Marin's deft aqueous technique, which activates the white of the paper, also captures the unique New Mexican light. A band of rectangles running along the bottom of the composition and around its painted perimeter can be read metaphorically: abstraction serves as the essential foundation of and frame for Marin's representation of nature, which, like Russell's *In the Enemy's Country*, actively omits any clear sign of the automobile's presence.

Compared to Marin's calligraphic *Mountains Near Taos*, Raymond Jonson's *Pueblo Series, Acoma* (1927) appears to be more in keeping stylistically with the industrial aesthetics of the period despite his landscape subject. A protégé of B. J. O. Nordfeldt, Jonson simplified the contours of his forms by painting thick, clean outlines while he energized his

[61]

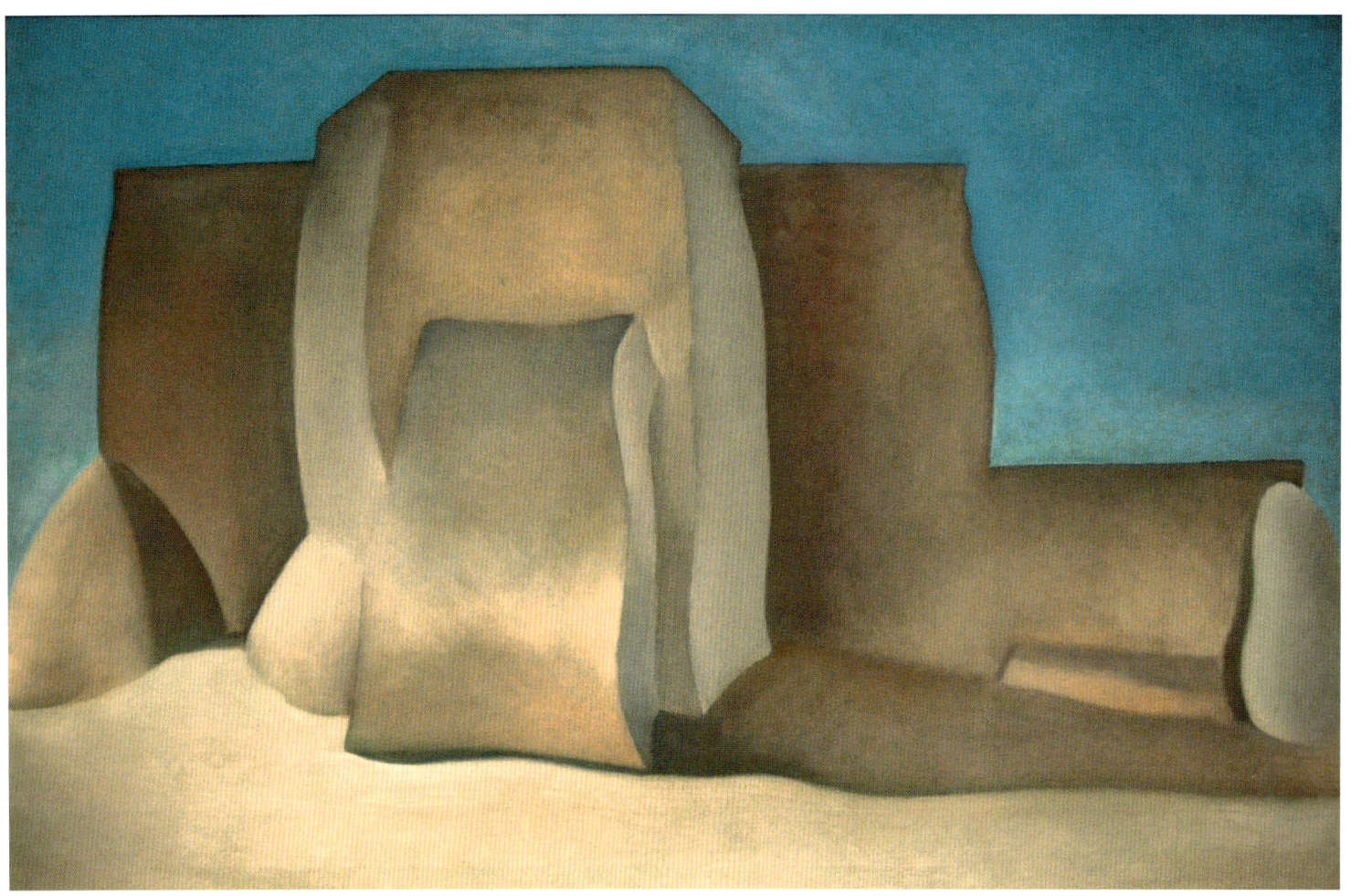

composition by adopting a deeply saturated palette. Seemingly propelled by some unseen, volcanic force from below ground, the large mesa in the foreground rises to the sky like a tall building, forming a physical connection between the earth and the heavens. Harkening back to romantic depictions of western geological wonders in the nineteenth century, such as Thomas Moran's numerous depictions of Castle Rock along Wyoming's Green River, *Pueblo Series, Acoma* celebrates nature's geological architecture and inspires private rumination on the identity of nature's architect. And, like the recently deceased Moran (he died in 1926), Jonson manipulated scale for dramatic effect, an extreme exaggeration that is laid bare when one compares the painting to the actual site, impressive on its own terms.

Perhaps Jonson's manipulation of scale, which far exceeds even Moran's, can be attributed to the pervasive impact of the skyscraper on American life and aesthetics of the period, which the artist would have known not only from famous examples in New York, but also as a result of the evolving skyline of his earlier adopted home of Chicago. Whatever the underlying causes of the artist's aesthetic choices, the painting aspires to evoke the Acoma Pueblo's historical and spiritual resonance as one of the earliest inhabited sites in North America on record.

While Jonson's mesas reach to the heavens like skyscrapers, O'Keeffe's depiction of the famed Spanish mission church of Saint Francis near Taos collapses completely the boundary between earth and architecture, the natural and the manmade. Like many before and after her, O'Keeffe was, upon her first extended stay in New Mexico in 1929, drawn to the region's historic sites. Inventively, the painter isolated the building from its environment and, rather than paint the church's façade, which renders its origin and function explicit, she gravitated to its more nondescript altar end. In these respects, O'Keeffe's approach was much like that

Georgia O'Keeffe
Ranchos Church, No. II, NM, 1929
Oil on canvas, 24⅛ × 36⅛
The Phillips Collection, Washington, D.C.,
Acquired 1930

of the young photographer Ansel Adams, who was working in Taos around the same time. Both the painter and the photographer depicted the church as a kind of large-scale abstract sculpture, strangely historic and simultaneously modern. In this way, *Ranchos Church* testified to the naturalness of abstract design and to the native genius of artistic expression that grows directly from the soil—quite literally, in this case.

O'Keeffe, who began visiting New Mexico almost annually after her first visit in 1929 and relocated there permanently in 1949, was back home in New York in October 1929, when, on the twenty-ninth day of the month, the Stock Market crashed, ushering in the Great Depression. Black Tuesday brought the so-called Roaring Twenties to a screeching halt. The pervasive belief in progress that marked much of the decade gave way to widespread pessimism, a feeling expressed powerfully by an unidentified author writing in the African American journal *The Crisis* in August 1931: "Surely prosperity will come again but not to everybody. Every slump, every depression, like every war, leaves the dead, the wounded, the maimed and the discouraged. For them prosperity will never come again."[27] Harkening back to World War I, the author's war analogy was also unintentionally prescient: looking ahead to not only the economic, but also the ecological, political, and military challenges that the nation would face in the next decade, the American public truly hadn't seen nothin' yet.

27 Unidentified author, quoted in "As the Crow Flies," *The Crisis: A Record of the Darker Races* 40, no. 8 (August 1931): 260.

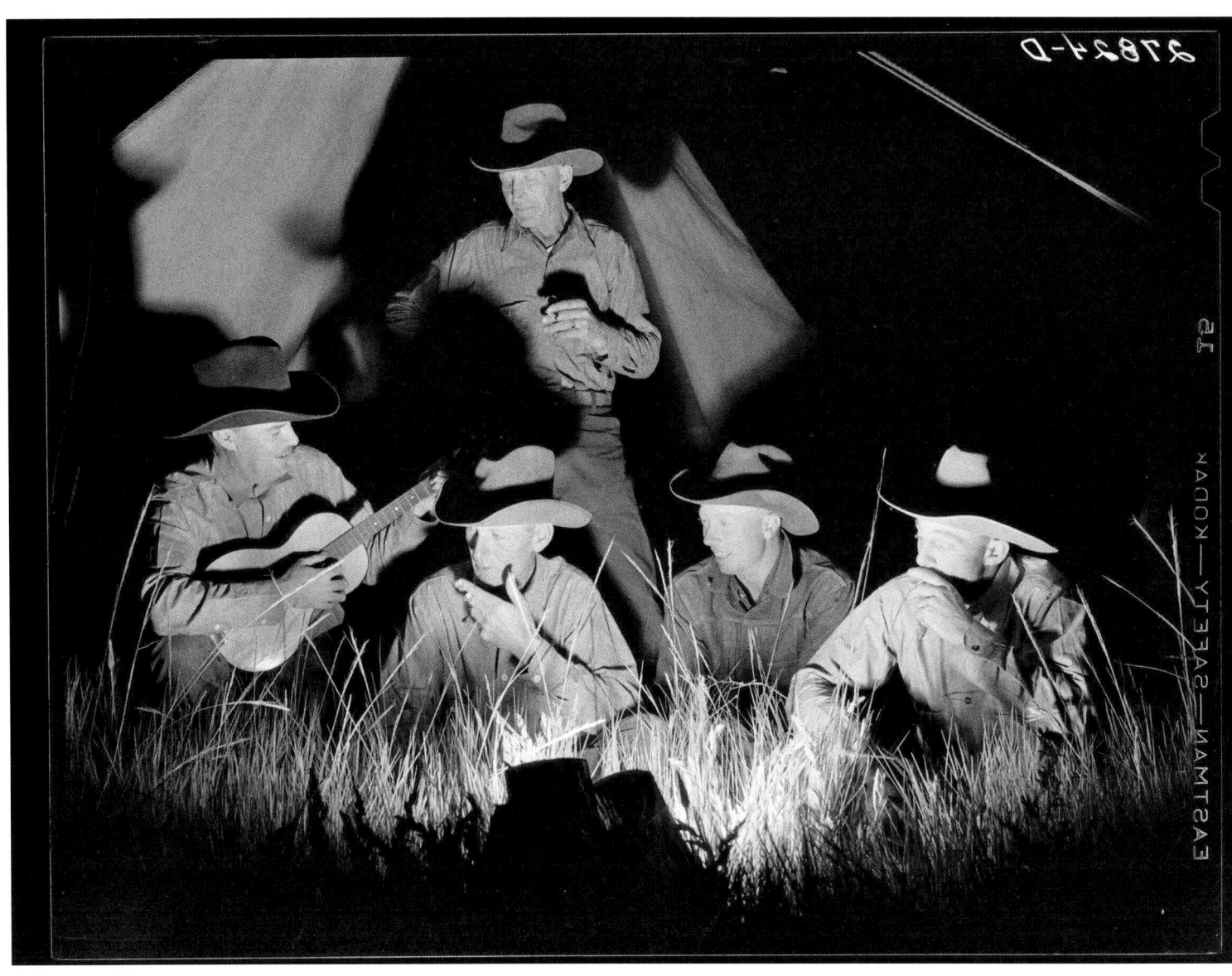

Arthur Rothstein
Cowhands singing after a day's work, Quarter Circle "U" Ranch roundup, Big Horn County, Montana, June 1939
Black & white film negative, 3¼ x 4¼ or smaller
Library of Congress, Prints & Photographs Division, FSA/OWI Collection [LC-USF346-027824-D]

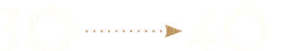

Tumult and Triumph:
Taking the Pulse of Western American Art in the 1930s

BETSY FAHLMAN

THE DECADE OF THE 1930S represents the heart of the Depression era, a period of nationwide economic devastation. Yet because of government-funded art programs, it was also a time of artistic vibrancy, in the West as in the rest of the United States. Franklin Delano Roosevelt became president in 1933 and by 1935 had established a series of initiatives collectively known as the New Deal. Best known is the Works Progress Administration (WPA), which served as the umbrella for agencies designed to bring relief and recovery.

The federal government became a significant arts patron during this period. Washington, D.C., agencies set up regional offices for more efficient administration, though officials in the nation's capital supervised art commissions surprisingly closely. With some short-lived programs, like the Public Works of Art Program (PWAP), federal funds were locally administered. Photographers from the Farm Security Administration (FSA) and its successor agency, the Office of War Information (OWI),[1] traveled to every state. An implicit national cultural agenda of placing art in public places that highlighted American history and contemporary achievements, as well as documenting the accomplishments of government programs, was reinforced by a remarkable stylistic and thematic consistency that simultaneously fostered and highlighted regional culture. Never before had the nation given such broad support to the arts. Federal support, however, is only part of the story, and there were many artists who did not seek government commissions, although they often explored themes parallel to those artists who did receive funding.

The classic symbols of the Old West—cowboys and Indians and the immense and typically sublime landscape—are primarily masculinist constructs. This essay is focused on the "New West," one shaped by talented women artists and by mining and dams (signifiers of a modern West), and whose iconography was enriched by new archetypes, including farmers, miners, and migrants. The New West embraces both a gendered approach and a landscape of enterprise.

But artists could hardly avoid iconic themes. FSA photographers regularly recorded scenes of ranching and cowboys. Arthur Rothstein's handsome image of cowhands singing and telling stories after a day's work at the roundup at the Quarter Circle "U" Ranch in June 1939 near Birney, Montana, is steeped in the visual conventions of Frederic Remington's late paintings. It also references the gradual economic reinvention of working outfits as dude ranches. Cowhands now doubled as entertainers, giving the open range an overlay of tourism to sustain tradition.

---

1 Roy Stryker headed first the FSA and then the OWI. Many of the same photographers continued with the renamed agency, and additional ones were hired. The purpose changed from one focused on the problems of agriculture to imaging a strong America capable of winning the war. Pictures of desolate farms were replaced by those of mining and railroads.

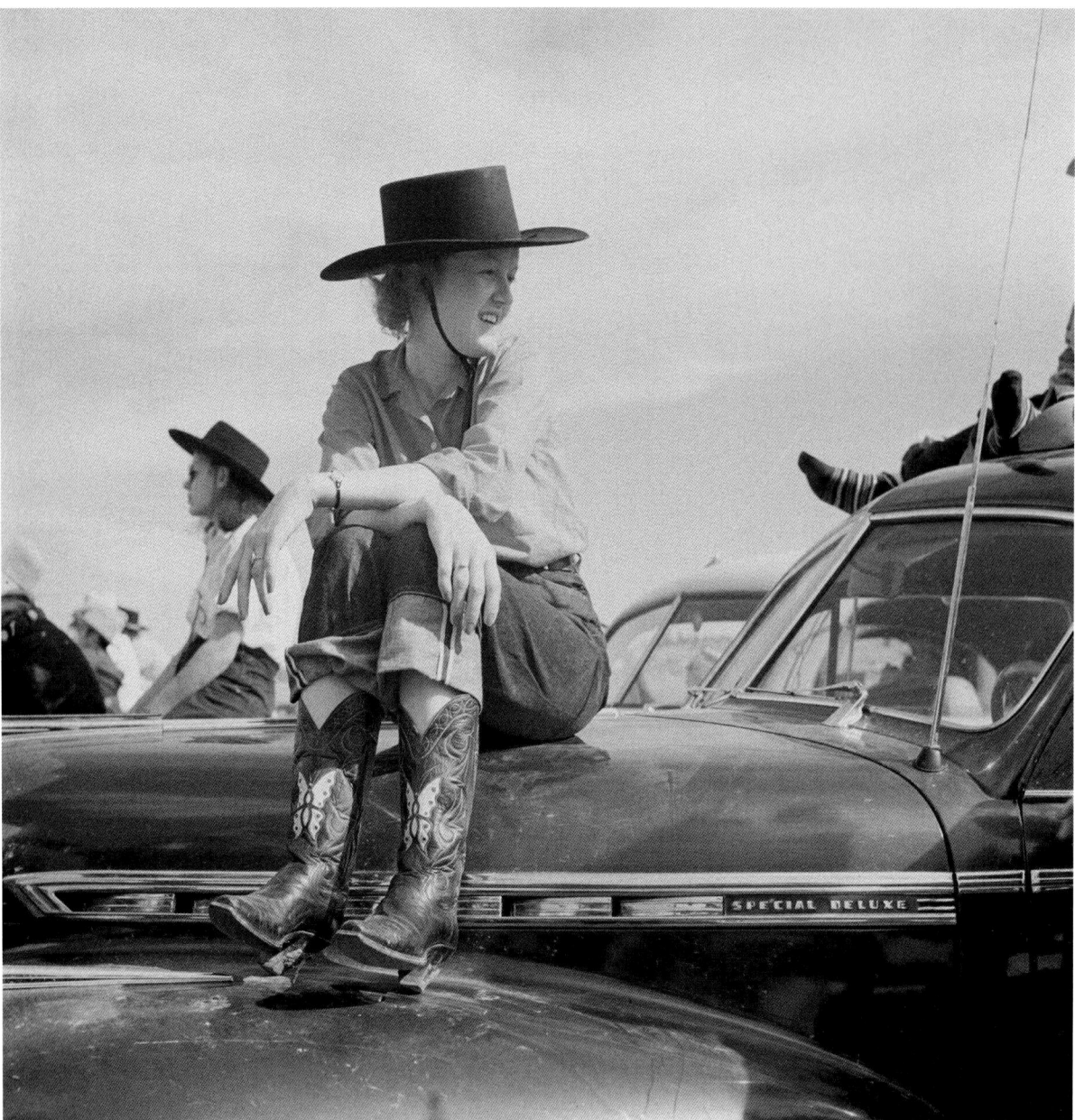

Marion Post Wolcott *Dude at rodeo, Ashland, Montana*, September 1941. Black & white nitrate negative, 2¼ x 2¼ or smaller. Library of Congress, Prints & Photographs Division, FSA/OWI Collection [LC-USF34-058902-E]

Such a change is evident in another FSA photograph. In September 1941, Marion Post Wolcott photographed a rodeo in Ashland, Montana. A young woman "dude" wearing new jeans and cowboy boots is seated on the hood of a shiny new Chevrolet Special Deluxe. In the New West, modern horsepower trumps the four-legged version.

The response to the question posed by Thomas Hart Benton—"Where does the West begin?"[2]—proved to be artistic as well as geographical. Two emblematic works serve as veritable banners for this era: *The Arts of Life in America: Arts of the West* (1932) by Thomas Hart Benton and *Cow's Skull: Red, White, and Blue* (1931) by Georgia O'Keeffe. This pair of powerful canvases exemplifies the Regionalist and modernist styles of the decade. Benton's work is typical of Regionalism in its representational style and its grounding in rural folk culture. While Benton portrayed urban themes, it was the sense of place of middle America that most fascinated him. O'Keeffe's aesthetic derived from an understanding of abstraction, a minimized palette, and emphasis on line and form. The styles have considerable overlap; Benton's muscular composition would have been impossible without his encounters with American modernism, while O'Keeffe's southwestern paintings are inextricably tied to place.

Benton's painting is part of a series of five murals executed for the library of the Whitney Museum of American Art in 1932 and now at the New Britain Museum of

2 Thomas Hart Benton, *An Artist in America* (Columbia: University of Missouri Press, 1983 [1951]), 199. See "The West," 199–245.

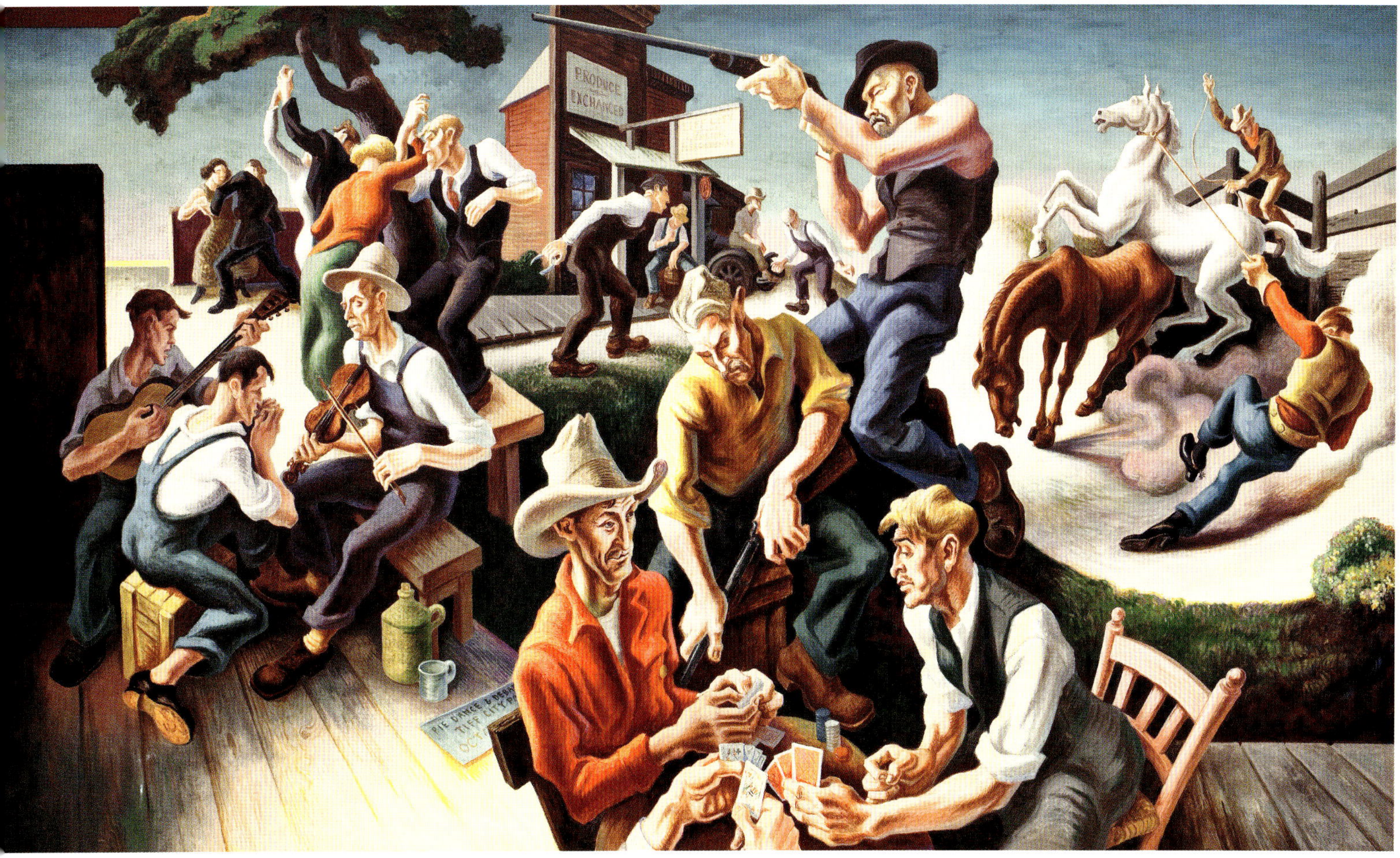

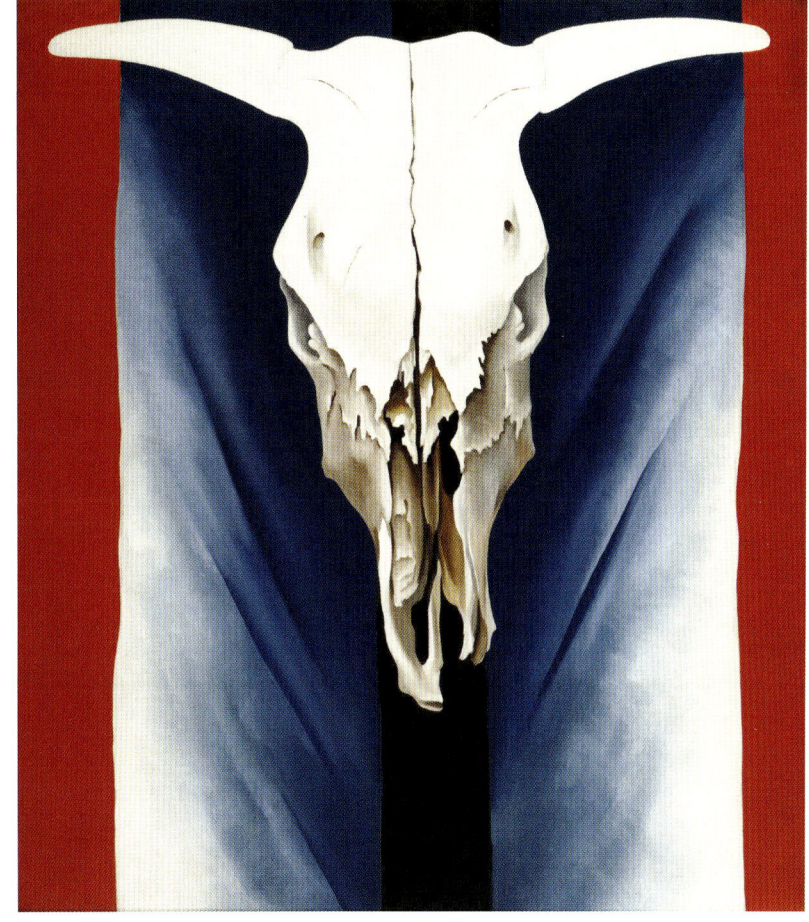

Thomas Hart Benton
The Arts of Life in America: Arts of the West, 1932
Tempera with oil glaze on linen mounted on panel, 96 x 156. New Britain Museum of American Art, Harriet Russell Stanley Fund (1953.21). Art ©T. H. Benton and R. P. Benton Testamentary Trusts / UMB Bank Trustee / Licensed by VAGA, New York, NY

Georgia O'Keeffe
Cow's Skull: Red, White, and Blue, 1931
Oil on canvas, 39⅞ x 35⅞
The Metropolitan Museum of Art, Alfred Stieglitz Collection, 1952 (52.203). ©The Metropolitan Museum of Art.
Image source: Art Resource, NY

American Art. They represent, in the artist's words, "a conglomerate of things experienced in America,"³ and in addition to the *Arts of the West* are made up of the *Arts of the City*, the *Arts of the South*, *Indian Arts*, and *Intellectual Business and Political Ballyhoo*.

The artist's firsthand experience of the West by the time he executed the Whitney murals was rather selective. In the late 1920s, he traveled through Texas, New Mexico, Colorado, and Wyoming, trips that inspired a significant body of work. There he found himself, as his biographer Henry Adams has observed, at "the juncture of crude reality and fabulous Western myths."⁴ Feeling as if he was "on the great curve of the world," Benton was impressed by the scale of the West. His encounter with a region where "there are no limits" introduced him to rugged individuals who actively embraced the "largeness of their surroundings." And his recognition that "the West clings to its past"⁵ grounded his images in historical precedent despite their evident contemporaneity.

Arts of the West is a vigorous and lively composition. At right, two cowboys rope one of a pair of horses. In the center, three men seated at a small table are engaged in a game of poker: one warily watches the other, while only the hands of the third player are visible. Above them is a pair of men with rifles, one of whom loads his gun while the other aims at some unseen target, preparing to shoot. In the center background, a group of men play horseshoes in front of the produce exchange of the Tiff City General Merchandise store. At far left, a trio plays the guitar, fiddle, and harmonica (the model for the harmonica player was Benton's student Jackson Pollock), with a jug of moonshine on the floor placed close to the fiddler's bench for ready refreshment. A poster on the floor announces the dance that takes place in the left background, suggested by three couples. It is definitely a view of the masculine West, with women playing minor roles compared to the more engaged activity of the seventeen men who are pictured.

The work of Georgia O'Keeffe, who saw the West through sharp modernist eyes, expands Benton's Regionalist evocation of western America. *Cow's Skull: Red, White, and Blue* references a powerful western symbol. Her image has deep historical roots—for instance, Frederic Remington emblazoned his bookplate with a buffalo skull, and Charles M. Russell used one as a kind of signature or logo on his paintings. O'Keeffe recalled the bones she found regularly in the Southwest: "The first summer I spent in New Mexico I was a little surprised that there were so few flowers. There was no rain so the flowers didn't come. Bones were easy to find so I began collecting bones." At the end of the season, she shipped a barrel of them back to New York, where she painted a series of horse's skulls before tackling cow skulls: "In my Amarillo days cows had been so much a part of the country I couldn't think of it without them."⁶

O'Keeffe's work is located within a broad discourse of cultural nationalism focused on defining distinctive American subjects and cultural iconography emphatically grounded in place. For her, skulls were a regional symbol emblematic of the American West. Furthermore, the red stripes on either side of the painting were inspired by a Navajo blanket she owned.⁷ American modernists often used indigenous art forms to gain a more direct visual language for modernism.

For many artists, the skull was a symbol of the Dust Bowl. Arthur Rothstein's bleached steer skull set on the cracked, parched alkali flats in the remote Badlands of South Dakota serves as a stark memorial to the conditions he found. In this series of photographs, he used the skull as a handy prop, moving it several times, to demonstrate how drought had nearly destroyed the cattle industry of the Great Plains. This most famous of his published photographs of skulls is also the most visually dramatic. That he had moved the skull caused considerable controversy, leading critics of Franklin Delano Roosevelt's programs to accuse the president of exaggerating conditions. In truth, all FSA photographers were skilled artists who rearranged, posed, and directed subjects, making use of a range of common studio techniques to achieve the most effective composition.

Painter Alexandre Hogue believed that grazing land had been decimated "first by the fence, then by overplowing, now by drought."⁸ In his lithograph *End of the Trail* (1938), he

---

3 Thomas Hart Benton essay: http://www.nbmaa.org/index.php?option=com_content&task=view&id=112. Last accessed 3/5/13.

4 Henry Adams, *Thomas Hart Benton: An American Original* (New York: Alfred A. Knopf, 1989), 153.

5 All quotations from Benton, *An Artist in America*, 199–201, 211.

6 Both quotations from *Georgia O'Keeffe* (New York: Penguin Books, 1977), n.p.

7 See Wanda M. Corn, *The Great American Thing: Modern Art and National Identity, 1915–1935* (Berkeley: University of California Press, 1999).

8 Lea Rosson DeLong, *Nature's Forms, Nature's Forces: The Art of Alexandre Hogue* (Norman: University of Oklahoma Press, and Tulsa: Philbrook Museum, 1984), 116, quoting Hogue in "U.S. Dustbowl," *Life* 2 (June 21, 1937): 60. See also Susie Kalil, *Alexandre Hogue: An American Visionary—Paintings and Works on Paper* (College Station: Texas A&M University Press, 2011); and Mark Andrew White, "Alexandre Hogue's Passion: Ecology and Agribusiness in The Crucified Land," in Alan C. Braddock and Christopher Irmscher, eds., *A Keener Perception: Ecocritical Studies in American Art History* (Tuscaloosa: University of Alabama Press, 2009), 168–88.

9 See Timothy Egan, *The Worst Hard Time* (New York: Houghton Mifflin, 2006) and James Curtis, *Mind's Eye, Mind's Truth: FSA Photography Reconsidered* (Philadelphia: Temple University Press, 1989).

10 Paul Taylor, "Again the Covered Wagon," *Survey Graphic* 24 (July 1935): 348–51; http://newdeal.feri.org/survey/35348.htm. Last accessed 3/5/13.

11 Ibid.

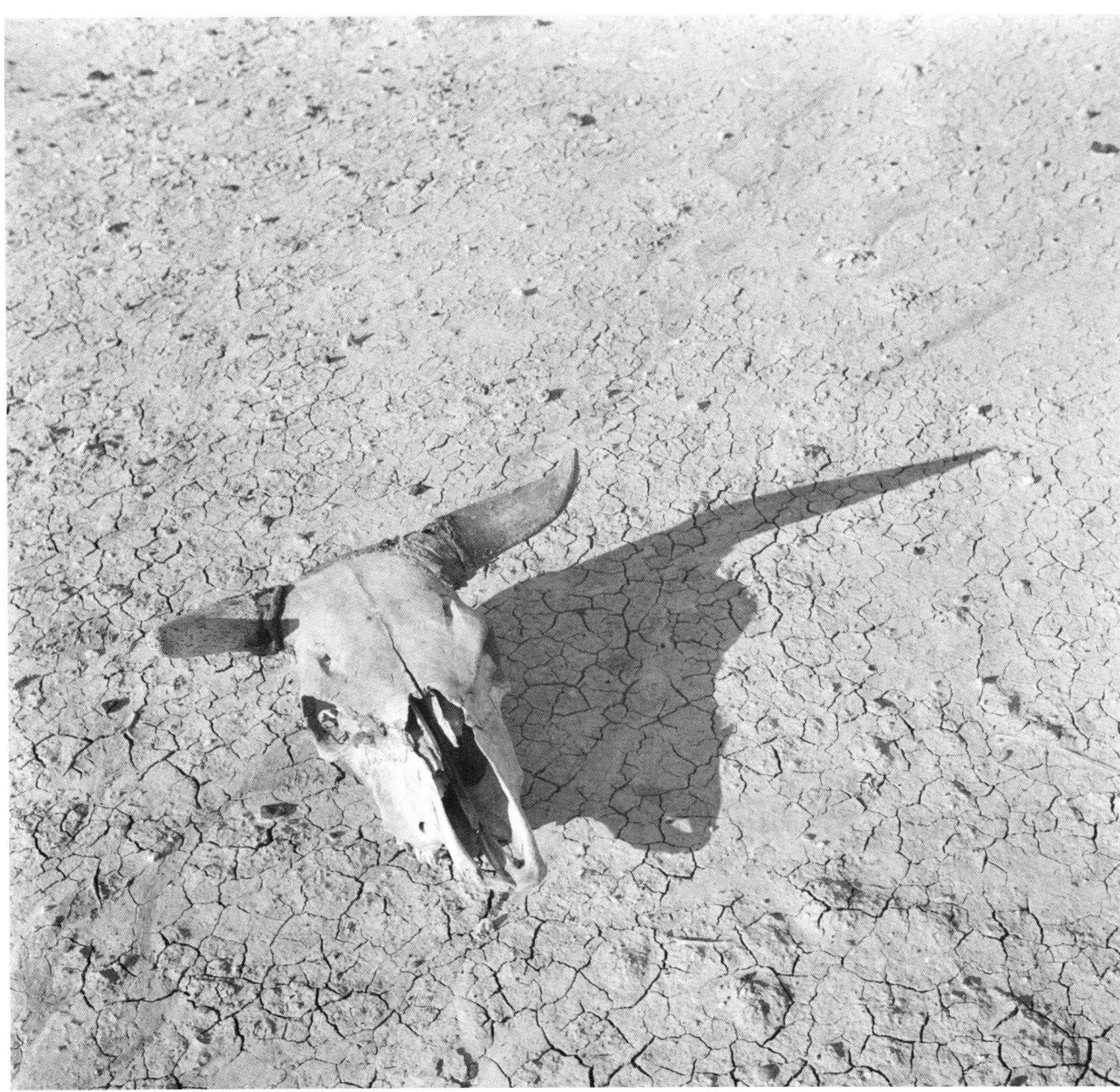

Arthur Rothstein
Bleached skull of a steer on the dry sun-baked earth of the South Dakota Badlands, May 1936
Black & white nitrate negative, 2¼ x 2¼ or smaller
Library of Congress, Prints & Photographs Division, FSW/OWI Collection [LC-USF34-004507-E]

arranged a skull, snapped barbed wire, and a broken plow to reinforce Rothstein's view of environmental disaster.

The Dust Bowl conjures up indelible images of what is characterized as "the Dirty Thirties," and it was dramatically pictured in a series of famous photographs Rothstein shot of a dust storm in April 1936 in Cimarron County, Oklahoma.[9] The relentless dust blew through the plains, swept up soil, covered machinery and buildings, and filled the lungs of people and animals. That Rothstein directed his subjects as he created his visual narrative parallels the actions of Pare Lorentz in his documentary *The Plough that Broke the Plains* (1936). Conditions were characterized as the "bleak winds of adversity"[10] by Berkeley political economist Paul Schuster Taylor:

> Vast clouds of dust rise and roll across the Great Plains, obscuring the lives of people, blighting homes, hampering traffic, drifting eastward to New York and westward to California. They carry the natural riches of the plains and deposit them broadcast over the nation. Exposed by cultivation which killed the protecting grasses, and powdered by protracted drought, the rich topsoil is being stripped from tens of thousands of acres by wind erosion, leaving land and life impoverished.[11]

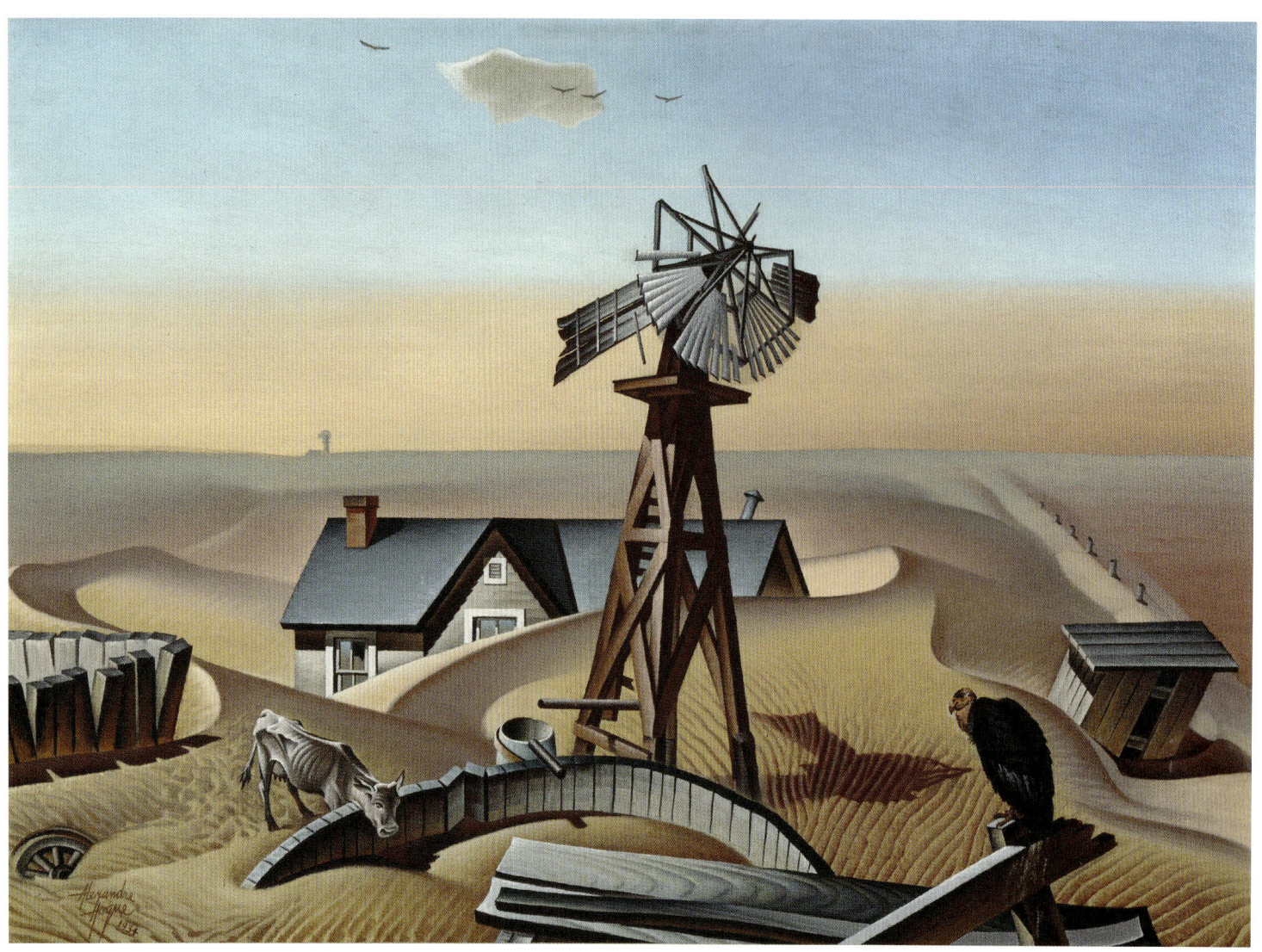

Painters created compelling images of the devastation caused by these immense climatic events, as well as chronicling the unequal battle fought between farmers and the dust storms and clouds of rapacious locusts that ravaged their crops. Hogue produced a series of Dust Bowl canvases whose titles, like *The Crucified Land* (1939) and *Erosion No. 2, Mother Earth Laid Bare* (1936), convey the biblical proportions of this environmental disaster. One of Hogue's most striking paintings is *Drouth Stricken Area* (1934). An abandoned farm is nearly swallowed up by a sea of dust. The windmill is broken, and a lone steer, gaunt and skeletal, appears near death, closely watched by a vulture perched nearby.

Apocalyptic dust storms put economic refugees from the Plains states—the so-called Okies, Arkies, and Texies—on the move, and FSA photographers followed them. Dorothea Lange and Paul Schuster Taylor (her second husband) published *An American Exodus: A Record of Human Erosion* (1939), a landmark book about the drought-impelled migration westward and its human cost. The rickety, slow-moving, overloaded cars of refugees on western highways became a familiar sight. Taylor described them in a 1935 article titled "Again the Covered Wagon":

> The refugees travel in old automobiles and light trucks, some of them home-made, and frequently with trailers behind. All their worldly possessions are piled on the car and covered with old canvas or ragged bedding, with perhaps bedsprings atop, a small iron cook-stove on the running board, a battered trunk, lantern, and galvanized iron washtub tied on behind. Children, aunts, grandmothers and a dog are jammed into the car, stretching its capacity incredibly.[12]

Alexandre Hogue
Drouth Stricken Area, 1934
Oil on canvas, 30 x 42¼
Dallas Museum of Fine Arts,
Dallas Art Association purchase

12 Ibid.

13 The FSA photographers wrote captions for the images they sent to Washington, and Lange included this quotation in hers (LC-USF34-009667-E). The FSA/OWI photographs may be found online on the American Memory site maintained by the Library of Congress: http://memory.loc.gov/ammem/fsahtml/fahome.html. Last accessed 3/5/13.

14 Franklin D. Roosevelt, "The Forgotten Man," radio address, Albany, NY, April 7, 1932; http://newdeal.feri.org/speeches/1932c.htm. Last accessed 3/5/13.

Lange's *Migrant Mother* (see page 7), shot in California in 1936, became one of the icons of the Depression. Two other FSA images from 1936 also capture Taylor's words. Arthur Rothstein encountered Vernon Evans and his family on Highway 10 near Missoula, Montana. They had left the grasshopper-ridden and drought-stricken area of Lemmon, South Dakota, hoping for a new start on the West Coast. On the back of his car is written in large letters: "Oregon or Bust." Another photograph, this one by Lange, shows drought refugees from Abilene, Texas—migratory laborers who were following the harvest in California. When Lange interviewed the father, he told her: "Two year drought, then a crop, then two years drought and so on."[13]

In a radio address delivered on April 7, 1932, Franklin Delano Roosevelt used the term "forgotten man" to describe these desperate people on the move:

> These unhappy times call for the building of plans that rest upon the forgotten, the unorganized but the indispensable units of economic power, for plans like those of 1917 that build from the bottom up and not from the top down, that put their faith once more in the forgotten man at the bottom of the economic pyramid . . . It is high time to get back to fundamentals. It is high time to admit with courage that we are in the midst of an emergency at least equal to that of war. Let us mobilize to meet it.[14]

Lange's first husband, Maynard Dixon, to whom she was married at the time, painted a series of canvases on the theme of the "forgotten man" that resonate with Roosevelt's words. The artist portrayed men whose prospects are bleak, as well as the social unrest that resulted from their frustration. In several works he recorded urban scenes of the sort that were the subjects of Lange's earliest Depression photographs. He imagined these were individuals with no place to go, whose destinations were "nowhere" and "unknown."

Maynard Dixon, *Forgotten Man*, 1934
Oil on canvas, 40 x 50⅛
Brigham Young University Museum of Art, gift of Herald R. Clark, 1937

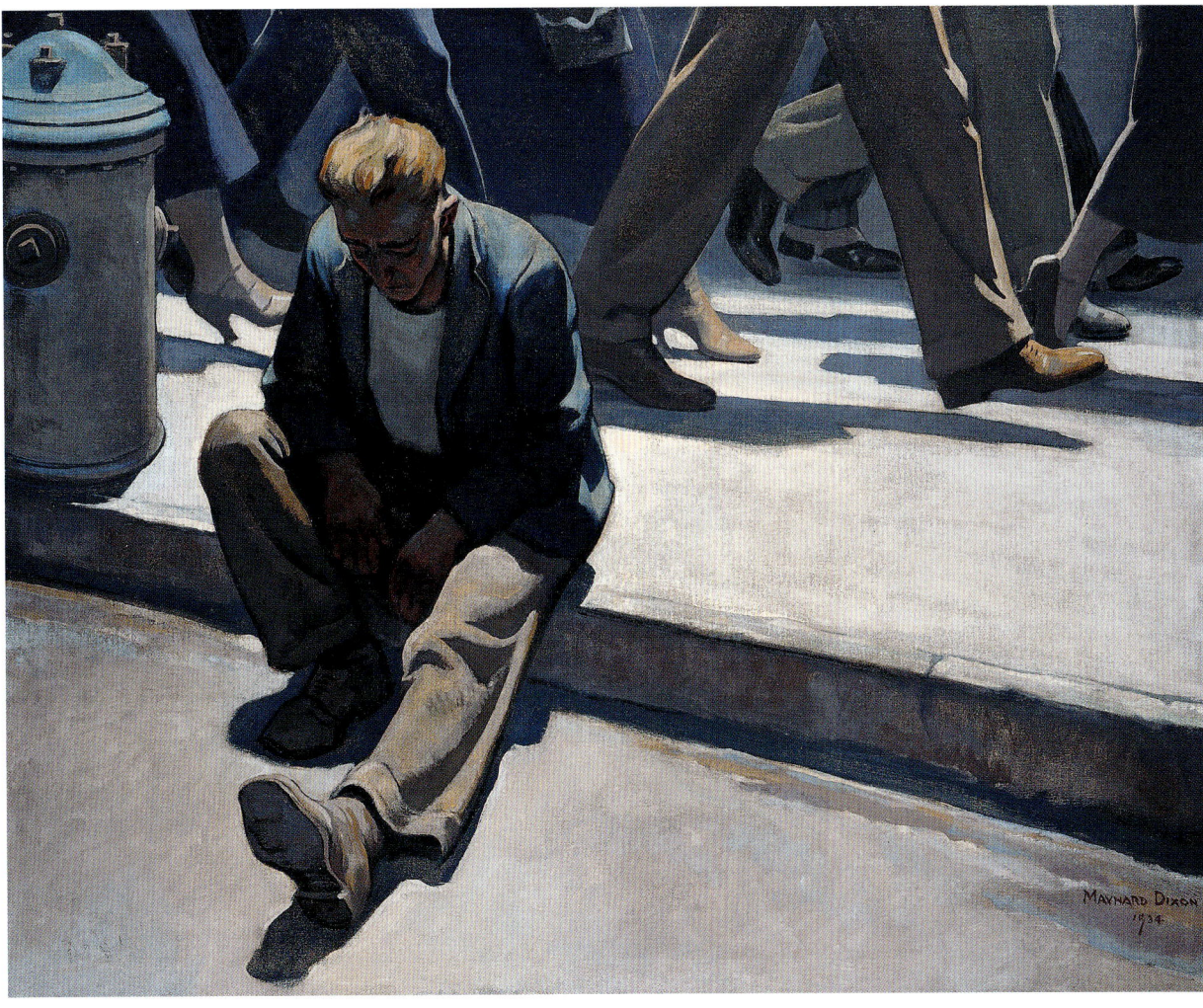

For sharecroppers trapped in a hopeless struggle to hang on, the unit was one man, one mule—a reference to the amount of land that could be cultivated with a one-horse plow. Yet the Jeffersonian ideal of the self-sufficient farmer had already been replaced by agribusiness, featuring absentee landlords who created factories in the fields dependent on migratory labor. Power farming not only displaced tenants from the land, it also ruined the soil. Yet there are many photographs even from the 1930s that convey the fecundity of the land. In 1939 Rothstein made two striking Colorado images. He recorded two FSA beneficiaries, Milton Robinson holding a huge sugar beet on his farm near Greeley and Mr. and Mrs. Andy Bahain on their farm near Kersey. Both present to the viewer their ample produce.[15] The FSA photographers needed to document the problems the agency could help solve, as well as its successes.

The first federal program to benefit the visual arts was the Public Works of Art Project (PWAP), which operated between December 1933 and June 1934. For the PWAP, Ila McAfee Turner took a Colorado theme with her *Mountain Lions* (1933–34). In its strong sense of place, her work is typical of that produced under this program, whose artists collectively depict a broad cultural map of America, while conveying a sense of immediacy linked to the specific location where they were painted. While the artist then lived in New Mexico, she had grown up on a ranch near Gunnison, Colorado, and her handsome canvas blends the impressive landscape of the Black Canyon with typical creatures of the region. Her beautiful pair of normally solitary big cats is together as a result of the mating season; they will soon return to their respective territories. The artist described the landscape

Ila McAfee Turner
Mountain Lions, 1933–4
Oil on canvas, 36½ x 42
Smithsonian American Art Museum, transfer from the U.S. Department of Labor (1964.1.80)

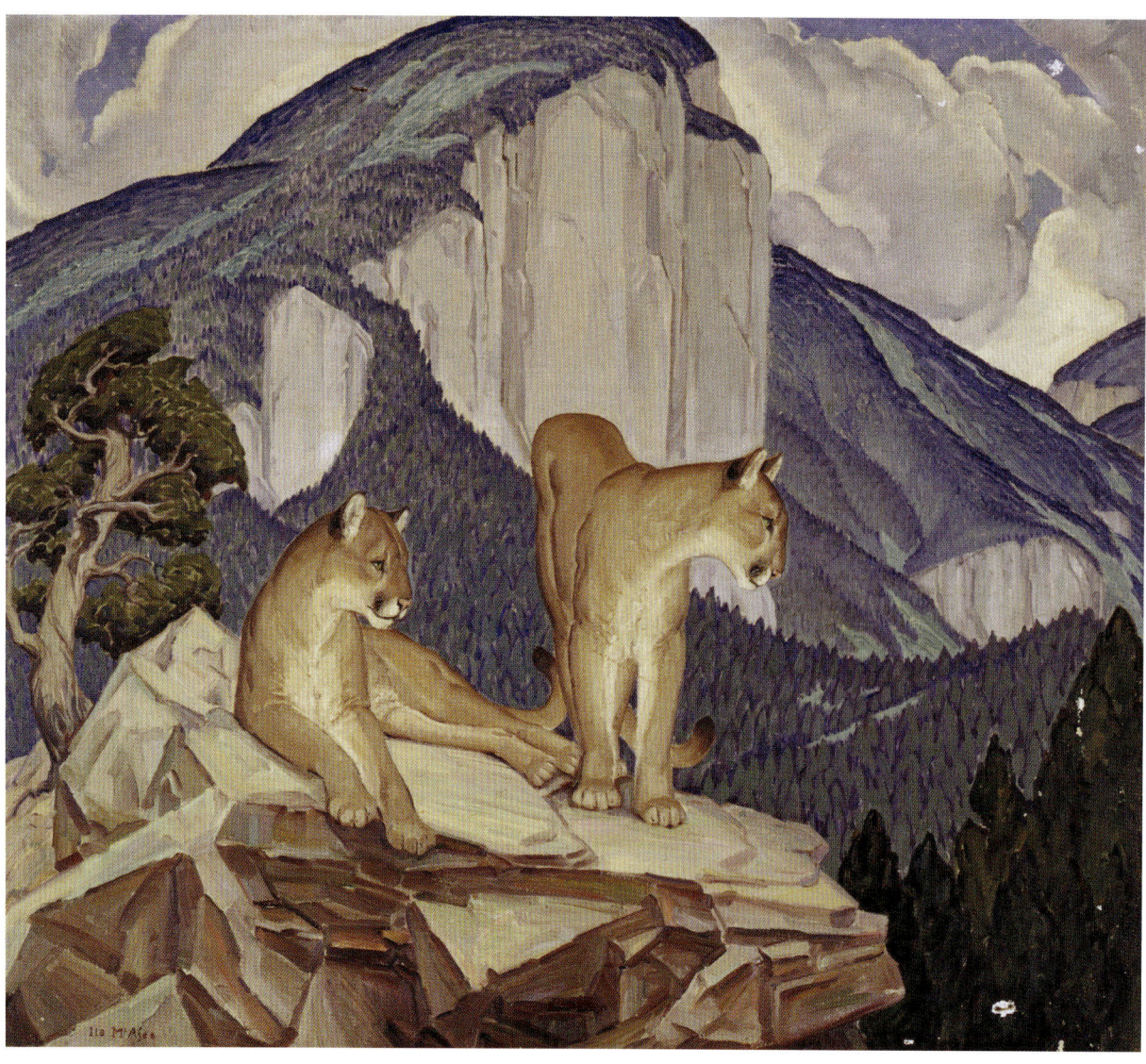

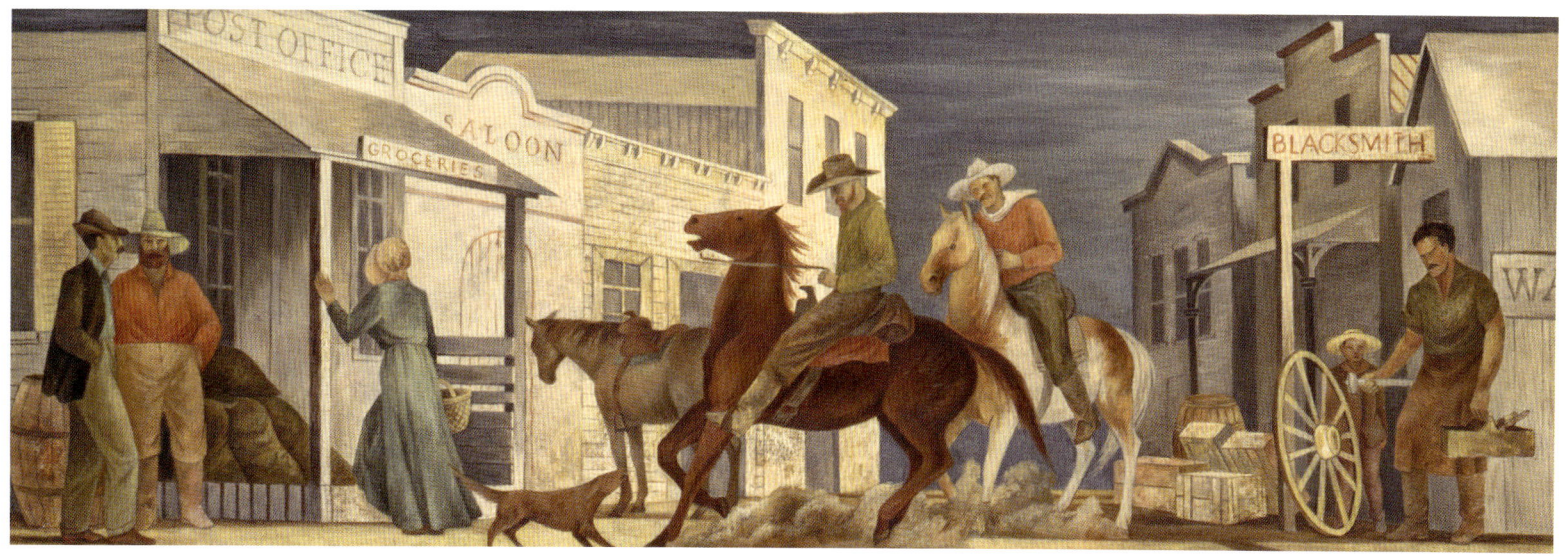

Jenne Magafan, *Western Town* (study for the Helper, Utah, Post Office mural), completed 1941. Oil on fiberboard, 25½ x 43¼. Smithsonian American Art Museum, transfer from the Internal Revenue Service through the General Services Administration (1962.8.44)

15 See Stephen J. Leonard, *Trials and Triumphs: A Colorado Portrait of the Great Depression with FSA Photographs* (Niwot, CO: University Press of Colorado, 1993).

16 Turner quoted in Ann Prentice Wagner, *1934: A New Deal for Artists* (Washington, DC: Smithsonian American Art Museum, in association with London: D. Giles Limited, 2009), 142.

17 For more on the Magafans, see Steve Frangos, "The Twinned Muses: Ethel and Jenne Magafan," *Journal of Hellenic Diaspora* 31, no. 2 (2005): 59–94. See also Patricia Trenton, ed., *Independent Spirits: Women Painters of the American West, 1890–1945* (Los Angeles: Autry Museum of Western Heritage, in association with Berkeley: University of California Press, 1995) and Phil Kovinick and Marian Yoshiki-Kovinick, *An Encyclopedia of Women Artists of the American West* (Austin: University of Texas Press, 1998). Most artists entered multiple competitions. For instance, between 1937 and 1944, Denver artist Louise Emerson Ronnebeck entered sixteen mural competitions and won two of them.

setting she had chosen: "way up there, in thin clean air, far away from anywhere, up on the beautiful western slope, high in the rugged Rocky Mountains."[16] The artist always maintained a strong connection to Colorado, and it must have been gratifying when she received the opportunity to execute *The Wealth of the West* for the Gunnison post office in 1940.

Mural programs were another significant area of support for artists, who were glad of the income and the professional exposure they provided. Compared to the FSA photographers who were tasked to document difficult conditions, these artists produced works that tended to be more upbeat, which is not surprising given their installation in highly public venues requiring local approval. Competition was keen, but gender-blind judging meant that women received an unprecedented number of commissions. Not all post office murals were chosen through a competition, and for smaller jobs, artists were often selected from entries to the more ambitious ones and expected to adapt their designs for a different community.

The new opportunities for women artists are exemplified by Colorado twins Ethel and Jenne Magafan. Both had studied with Frank Mechau, as did Jenne's future husband, Edward Chavez, and the trio learned the trade by assisting Mechau on his WPA murals. Later, the sisters were remarkably successful, winning commissions in Nebraska, Arkansas, Oklahoma, Colorado, Texas, Utah, and Washington, D.C.[17]

Western Town (1941) by Jenne Magafan was installed in Helper, Utah, as a result of the 48 States Competition of 1939, which placed a mural in a new rural post office in every state. Shown here in a study, it conveys the visual character of a typical small early frontier community. The artist took a local historical theme that would be eminently recognizable to Helper's current residents, which was typical of many of these New Deal murals. Two men stop to visit at the left, while a woman in a bonnet and long dress carrying a basket enters the post office and grocery store. A saloon is next door, with a horse waiting patiently outside. Two men on horseback gallop into town, kicking up clouds of dust as they come to a stop in front of a barking dog. Across the street is a blacksmith, who prepares to fix a wagon wheel, watched by a young boy.

The West abounded in landscapes of enterprise, and mining was its transformative industry. The historical importance of mining to the region is memorialized in state nicknames: the Silver State (Nevada), the Copper State (Arizona), the Gem State (Idaho), and the Treasure State (Montana). Landscapes of extraction created an aesthetic of the sublime (albeit one created by human intervention) that competed with the spectacular natural geology of the West in scale and color.

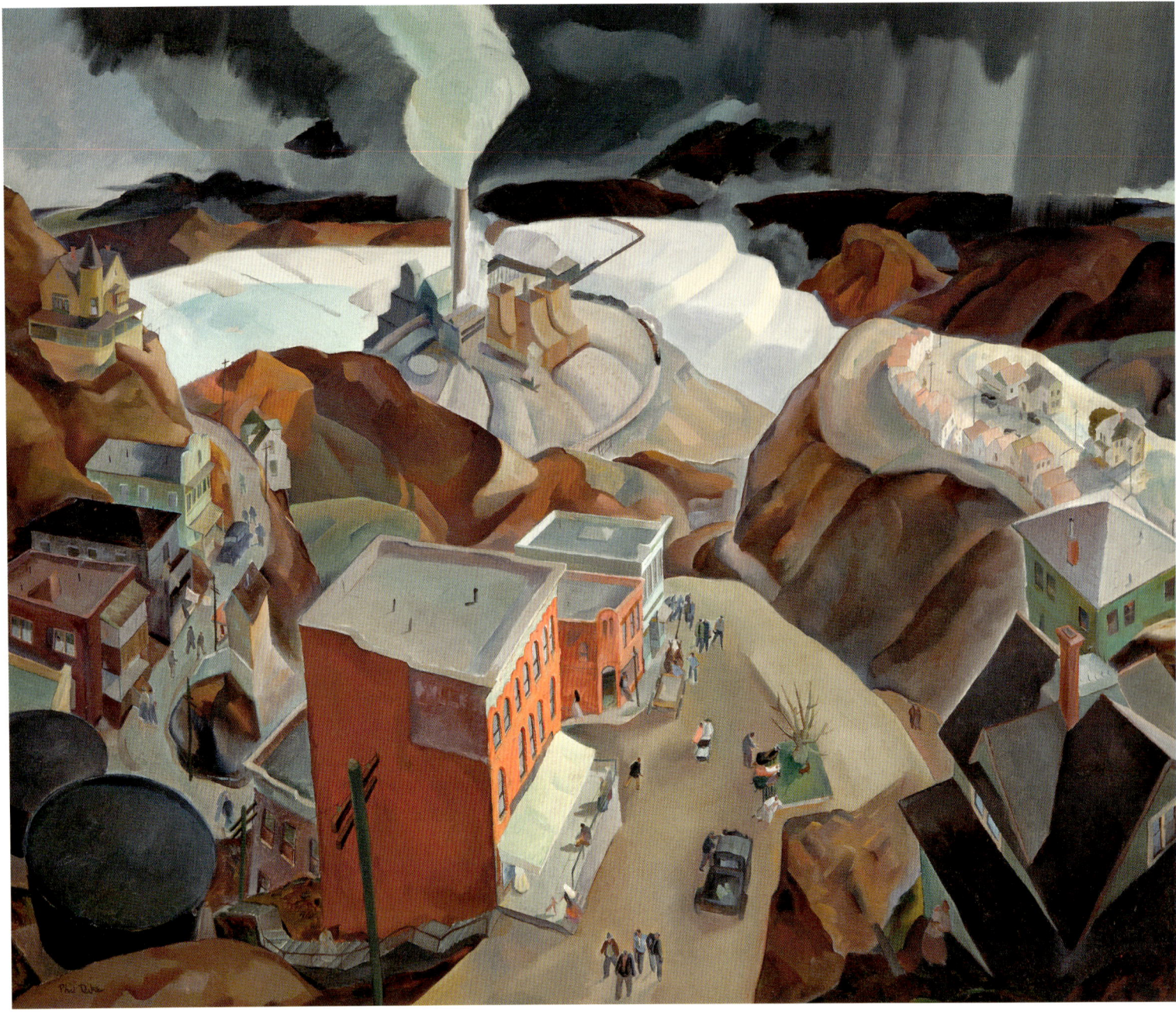

In *Copper*, a powerful panoramic composition, California artist Philip Latimer Dike captured the essence of an Arizona mining town emblematic of such communities throughout the West. Dike traveled through the state about 1931, and his canvas combines the open-pit and underground operations of two different regions. North of Phoenix was the mountain mining community of Jerome; to the east was the open-pit Globe/Miami region. Of his muscular scene of a town cobbled up the mountain, with the extraction and processing operations in the background, he observed:

> Man tackling the vastness of that country, digging and living amid cliffs—crag-riddled mountains—so tremendous in scale as to scare the sense of reality into one. Man-made forms and nature's giant ones with the contrasted elements of thunder-storms and sunsets, setting the stage for a humble but excited painter. The depression also left its impression on the stark pageant as mines closed and towns seemed to shrink under the sun.[18]

Philip Latimer Dike
Copper, 1936
Oil on canvas, 38 13/16 x 46 1/4
Collection of Phoenix Art Museum, Museum purchase with funds provided by Western Art Associates. Photo by Ken Howie

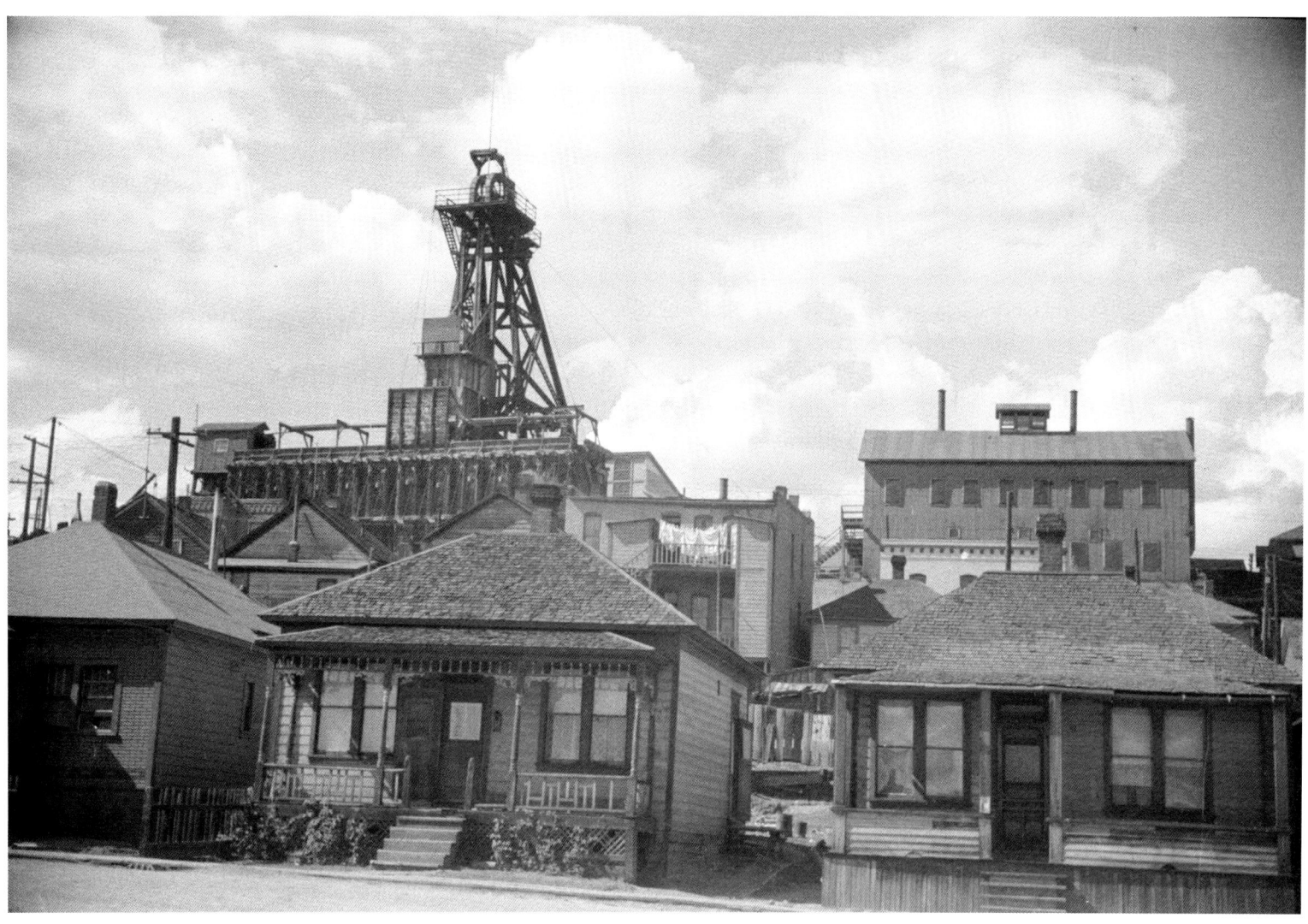

Arthur Rothstein
Houses with mine hoists in backyard, Butte, Montana, Summer 1939
Black & white nitrate negative, 35 mm. Library of Congress, Prints & Photographs Division, FSA/OWI Collection
[LC-USF33-003113-M2]

18 Phil Dike, "Phil Dike: He Captures the Scale of the West," *American Artist* (November 1940): 19.

19 Margaret Bourke-White, *Portrait of Myself* (New York: Simon and Schuster, 1963), 142, quoting *Life* editors.

For the FSA, in 1939, Arthur Rothstein photographed the homes of copper miners and the ubiquitous head frames that marked underground mine shafts in Butte, Montana. In towns like Butte, devoted to a single industry, mining operations were omnipresent, with the town's landscape gradually shifting to accommodate the expanding pit. In Rothstein's image, mine hoists are adjacent to the backyards of the small cottages in which the miners and their families live. Mundane details like laundry hung on the line convey a scrim of domesticity drawn across this dirty and dangerous profession.

Artists celebrated the great public works projects of the decade, and dams were emblematic of the efforts of the Department of the Interior to modernize and tame a vast region. The Fort Peck, Grand Coulee, and Hoover dams remain stunning artifacts of these triumphant engineering feats. Dams, with linked objectives of flood control, irrigation, hydroelectric power, recreation, and job creation, remain among the striking building efforts of the New Deal era. These immense projects represented the ideal of accomplishing a large social good that was at the heart of federal programs. Their scale made them powerful governmental symbols in the midst of the Great Depression, and they were recorded by many artists.

Construction on the Fort Peck Dam began in 1933 and was completed in 1940. Margaret Bourke-White visited there in 1936, and her famous image of the spillway, located several miles from the great earthen dam, then the largest in the world, was published on the cover of the first issue of *Life* magazine on November 23, 1936, accompanied by an extensive photo-essay on "Franklin Roosevelt's Wild West" that was "a human document of American frontier life."[19]

On this same trip, Bourke-White also visited the Grand Coulee Dam on the Columbia River in Washington, which opened in 1942. A watercolor by Z. Vanessa Helder, *Coulee Dam, Looking West*, is one of a series of twenty-two she made between 1939 and 1941. The Bureau of Reclamation gave her full access to the site, and she made pictures of the construction process and the community nearby where workers lived.

In 1941, the Bonneville Power Administration commissioned folksinger Woody Guthrie to compose a series of ballads to accompany a documentary (never made) whose purpose was to gain support for federal regulation of the hydroelectric power produced by these dams. In "Roll On Columbia" he lauded the power that was "turning our darkness to dawn," declaring that the dam that inspired Helder was the "mightiest thing ever built by a man." In another song, the river and the federal government worked together for the good of the nation:

> Uncle Sam took up the challenge in the year of 'thirty-three
> For the farmer and the factory and all of you and me,
> He said "Roll along Columbia, you can ramble to the sea,
> But river, while you're rambling, you can do some work for me."[20]

20 See http://www.woodyguthrie.org/Lyrics/Roll_On_Columbia.htm and http://www.woodyguthrie.org/Lyrics/Grand_Coulee_Dam.htm. Last accessed 3/5/13.

FACING: Margaret Bourke-White, *Fort Peck Dam, Montana*, 1936. Gelatin silver print, 13 x 10½. The Metropolitan Museum of Art, Ford Motor Company Collection, gift of Ford Motor Company and John C. Waddell 1987 (1987.1100.25). ©Getty Images

BELOW: Z. Vanessa Helder, *Coulee Dam, Looking West*, about 1939–41. Watercolor on paper, 18 x 21⅞. Northwest Museum of Arts & Culture / Eastern Washington State Historical Society, Spokane, Washington, purchased from the artist 1954 (2585.3)

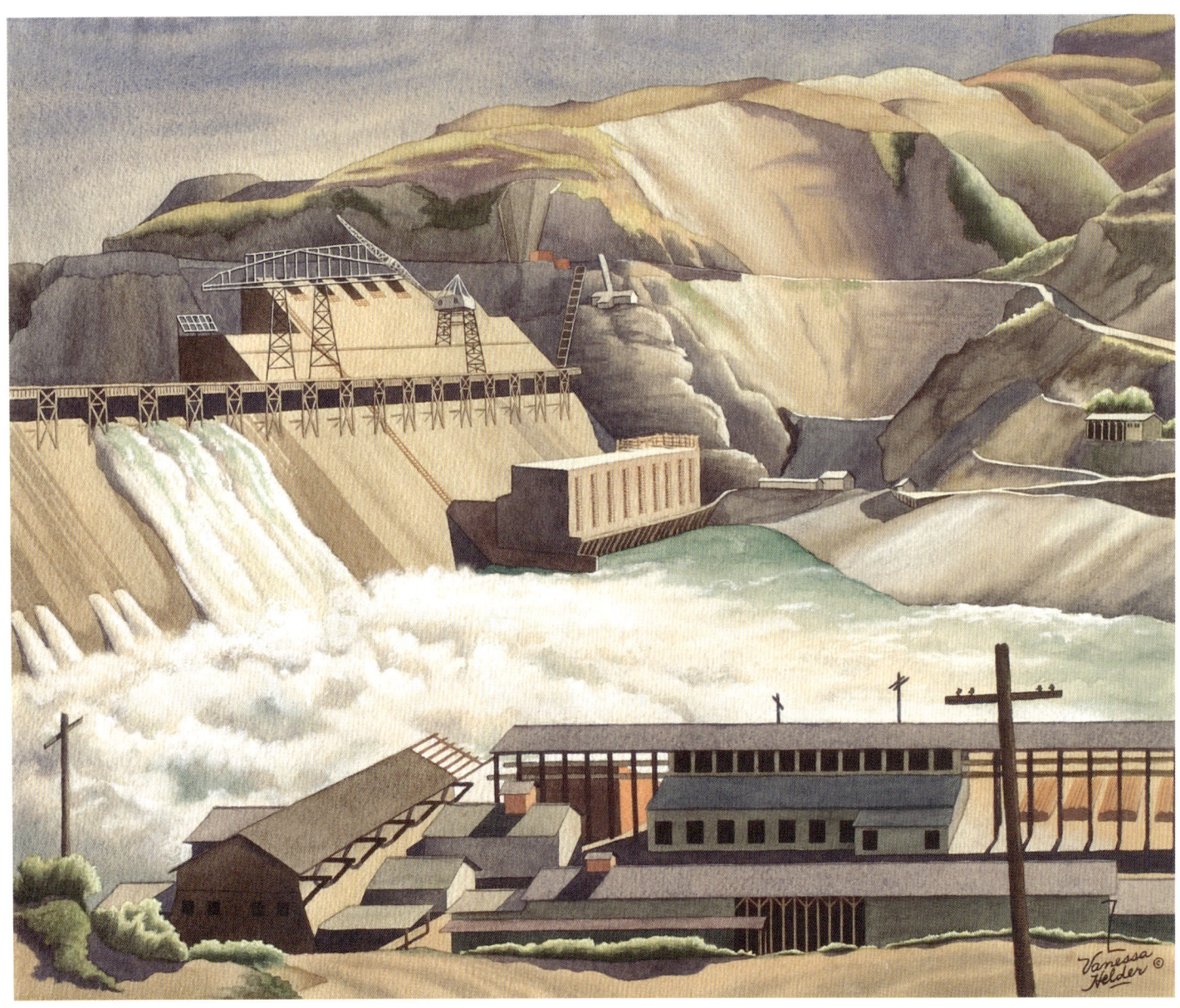

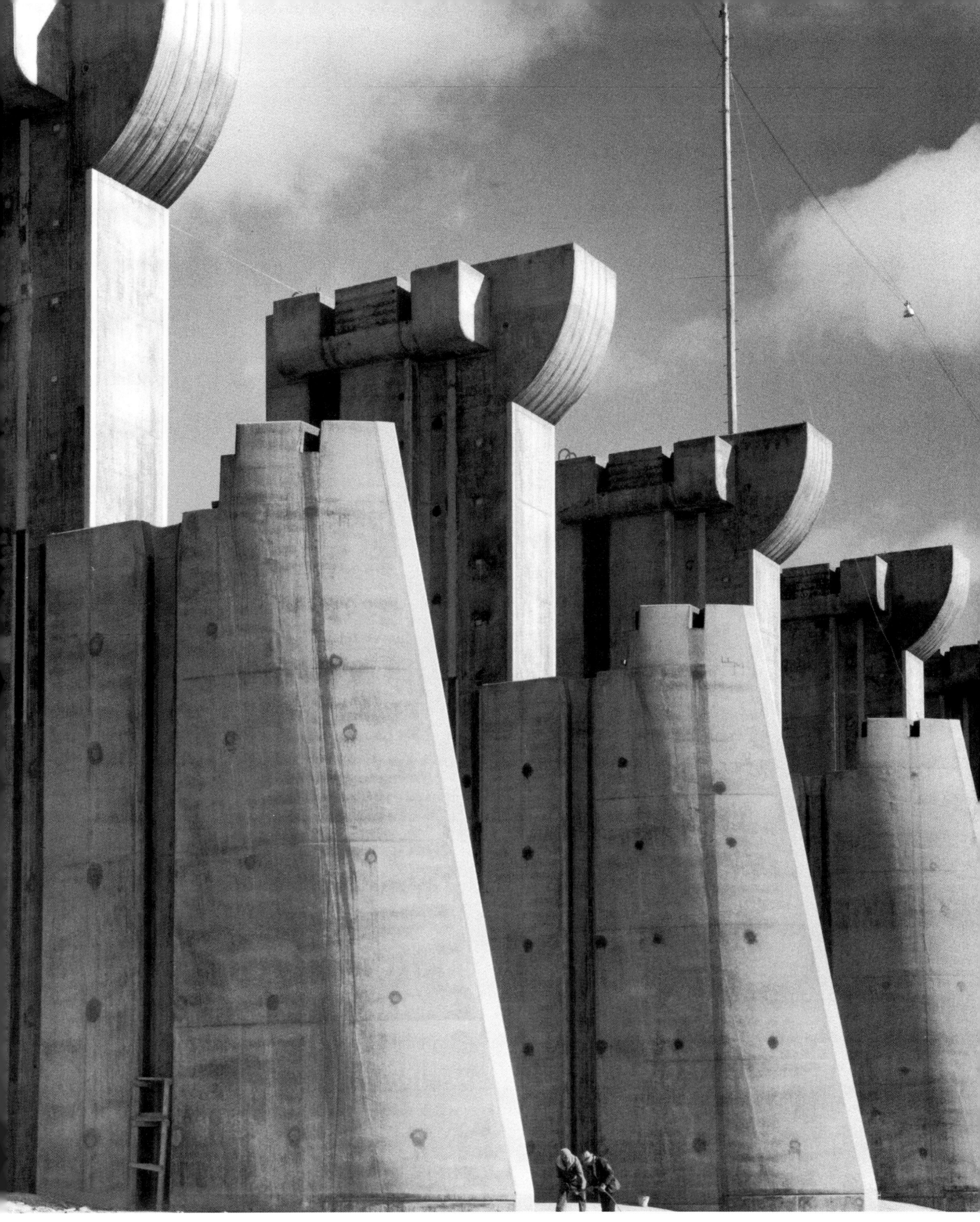

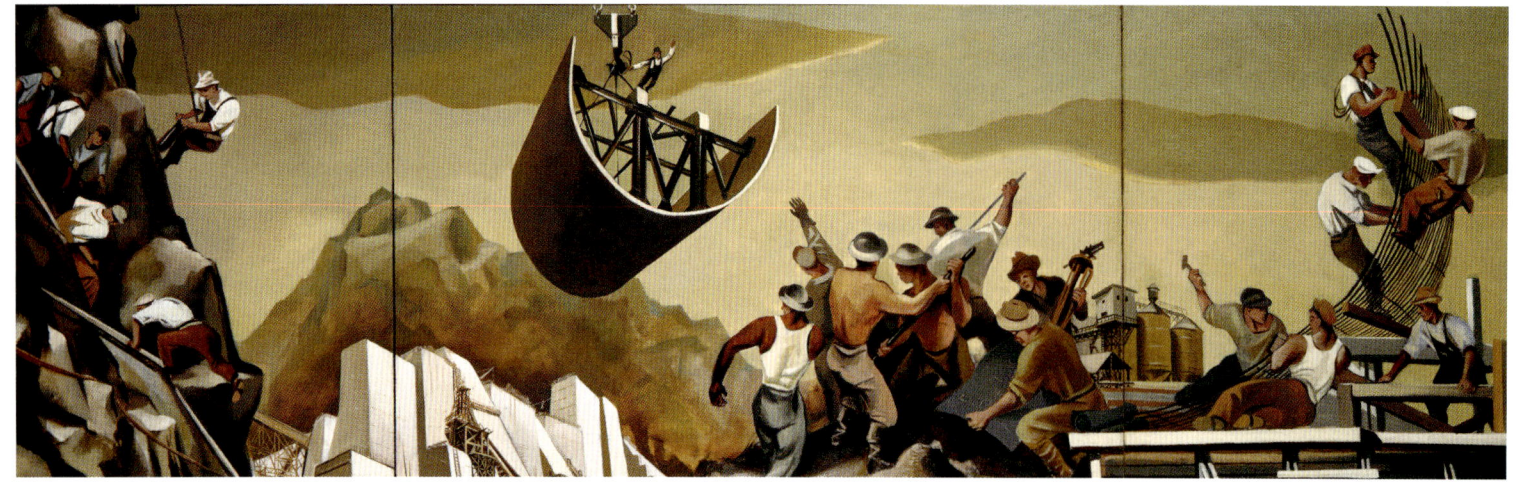

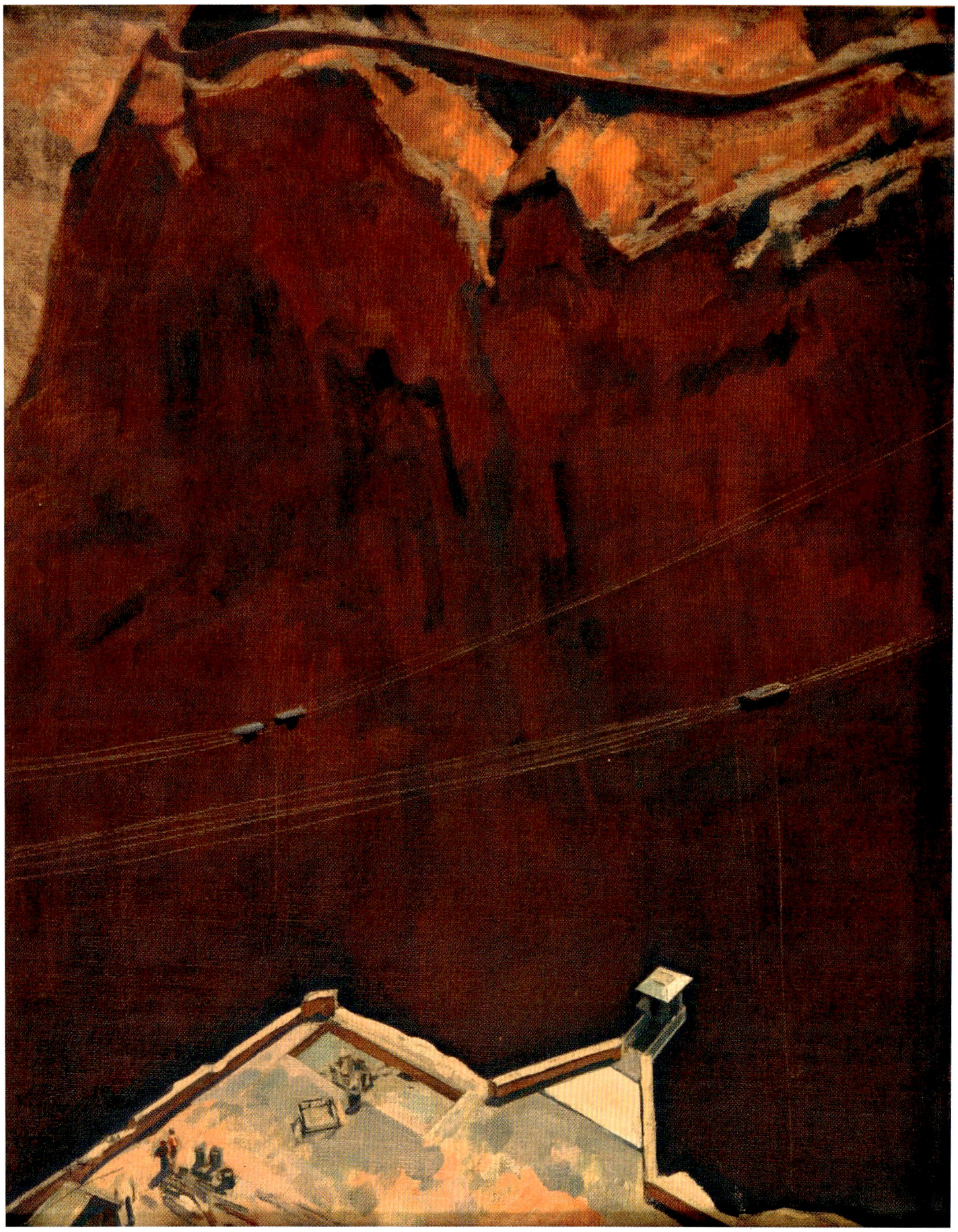

William Gropper
Construction of the Dam
(study for the Department of the Interior mural), 1938
27¼ x 87¼
Smithsonian American Art Museum, transfer from the United States Department of the Interior, National Park Service (1965.18.11A-C)

Maynard Dixon
Boulder Dam, 1934
Oil on canvas, 19 x 15
Special Collections, University of Nevada, Reno Libraries

FACING: Charles Sheeler
Conversation—Sky and Earth, 1940.
Oil on canvas, 27 15/16 x 22 15/16.
Amon Carter Museum of American Art, Fort Worth, Texas, 2009.7

[78]

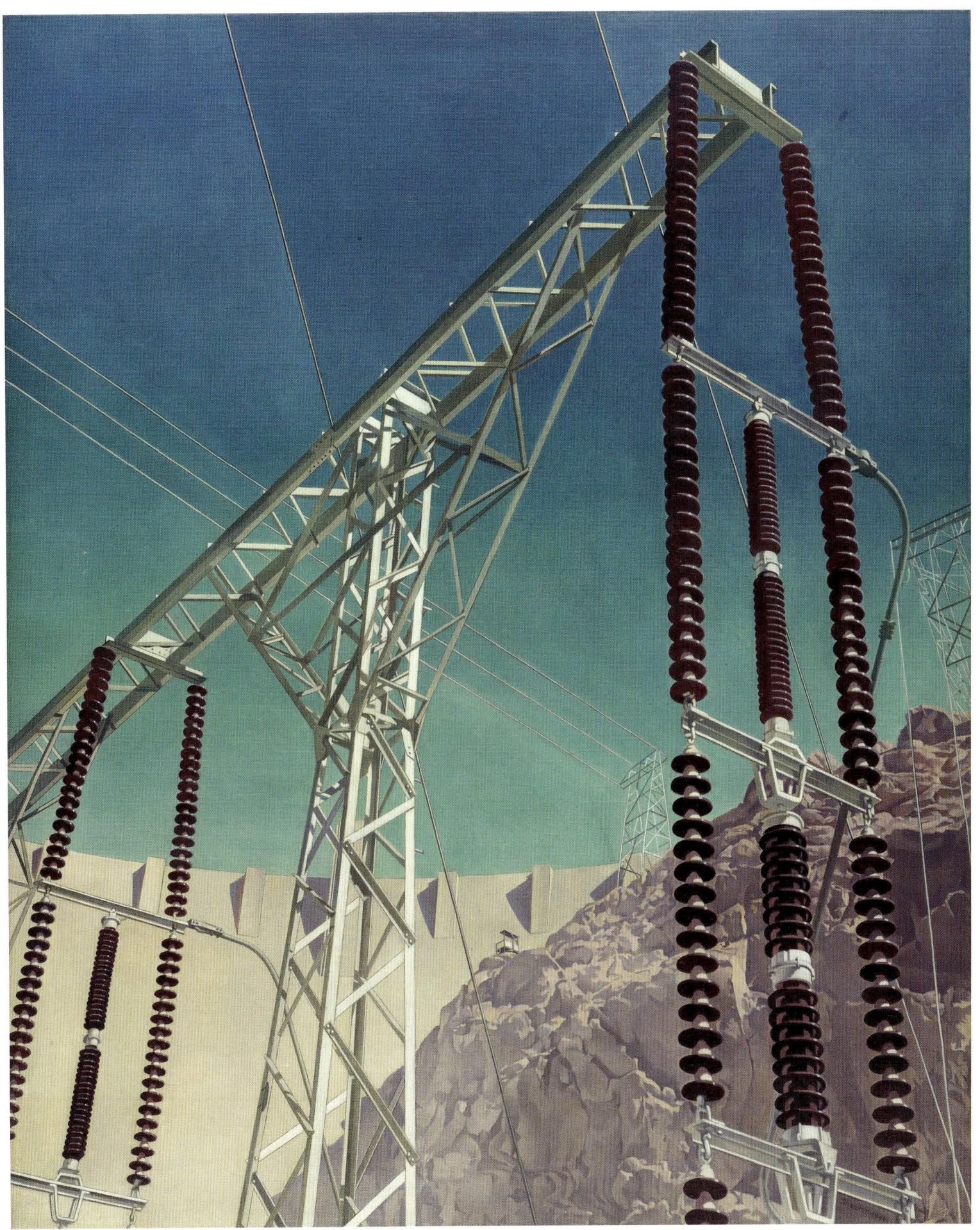

Most impressive of all was the Hoover Dam, which was to serve a constituency of seventeen western states. Authorized in 1928, construction began in 1931 to build what would be the largest dam in the world when it was dedicated in 1935. At 726 feet in height, the sublime scale of one of the Bureau of Reclamation's most massive projects aligned with the breathtaking landscape of the Colorado River. Artists were hired to record all phases of construction.

Commissioned by the Department of the Interior for its new headquarters in Washington, D.C., *Construction of the Dam* (1938–9) by William Gropper measures 10 x 30 feet. Using sketches he made at the Hoover and Grand Coulee dams in 1937 while traveling on a Guggenheim Fellowship, the artist created a composition full of the drama of masculine labor, with each of its three panels representing a specific task.

In April 1934, the PWAP sent Maynard Dixon to Nevada to paint scenes of the Hoover Dam construction, which had been underway for three years.[21] He spent six weeks there and produced twenty-four paintings. Because he felt that "the painting of the mechanical and engineering end of it had been taken care of by other people," he concentrated on the dramatic theme of "Man versus Rock."[22] Most of his canvases picture the rugged landscape, while his figural canvases record exhausted workers at the end of their shift and the high scalers performing dangerous work on scanty unstable boards suspended by a web of seemingly inadequate ropes five hundred feet above the Colorado River. In only one work, *Boulder Dam*,[23] is any of the actual edifice visible. Dixon took a sharply elevated view, with only a small portion of the structure jutting out at the bottom of the canvas. The wire system that transported materials criss-crosses the canyon in delicate threads that contrast with the rugged, sun-heated red rock in the background.

In 1939, *Fortune*, the nation's leading business journal, commissioned Charles Sheeler to do a series of paintings on the theme of power. The only one based in the West was *Conversation—Sky and Earth*, inspired by the Hoover Dam. The artist also photographed the transmission and intake towers, the spillway, and scenes of the surrounding landscape and river. The dynamic composition, with the transmission towers angled across the foreground and poking into an eerily blue-green sky, creates a dramatic painting.[24]

America's entry into World War II in December 1941 ended both the Depression and the New Deal Art programs, the last of which were officially shut down in 1943. By the time the war was over, the art world was recentered in New York, with abstract expressionism supplanting Regionalism and modernism. The remarkable era of the WPA had come to a close. The nation had been the recipient of a considerable body of art by a remarkable cross-section of American artists, all for a relatively small investment. Not until the establishment of the National Endowment for the Arts in 1965 would the federal government again become a significant patron of the arts on a national scale.

21 For more on Dixon's Depression-era work, see Linda Jones Gibbs, *Escape to Reality: The Western World of Maynard Dixon* (Provo, UT: Brigham Young University Museum of Art, 2000) and Donald J. Hagerty, *Desert Dreams: The Art and Life of Maynard Dixon* (Salt Lake City: Gibbs Smith Publisher, 1998).

22 Dixon quoted in Wesley M. Burnside, *Maynard Dixon, Artist of the West* (Provo, UT: Brigham Young University Press, 1974), 108.

23 From 1933 to 1947, Hoover Dam was known as Boulder Dam.

24 See Theodore E. Stebbins Jr., and Norman Keyes Jr., *Charles Sheeler: The Photographs* (Boston: Museum of Fine Arts and Little, Brown, 1987); Carol Troyen and Erica E. Hirshler, *Charles Sheeler: Paintings and Drawings* (Boston: Museum of Fine Arts and Little, Brown, 1987); and Karen Lucic, *Charles Sheeler and the Cult of the Machine* (Cambridge: Harvard University Press, 1991).